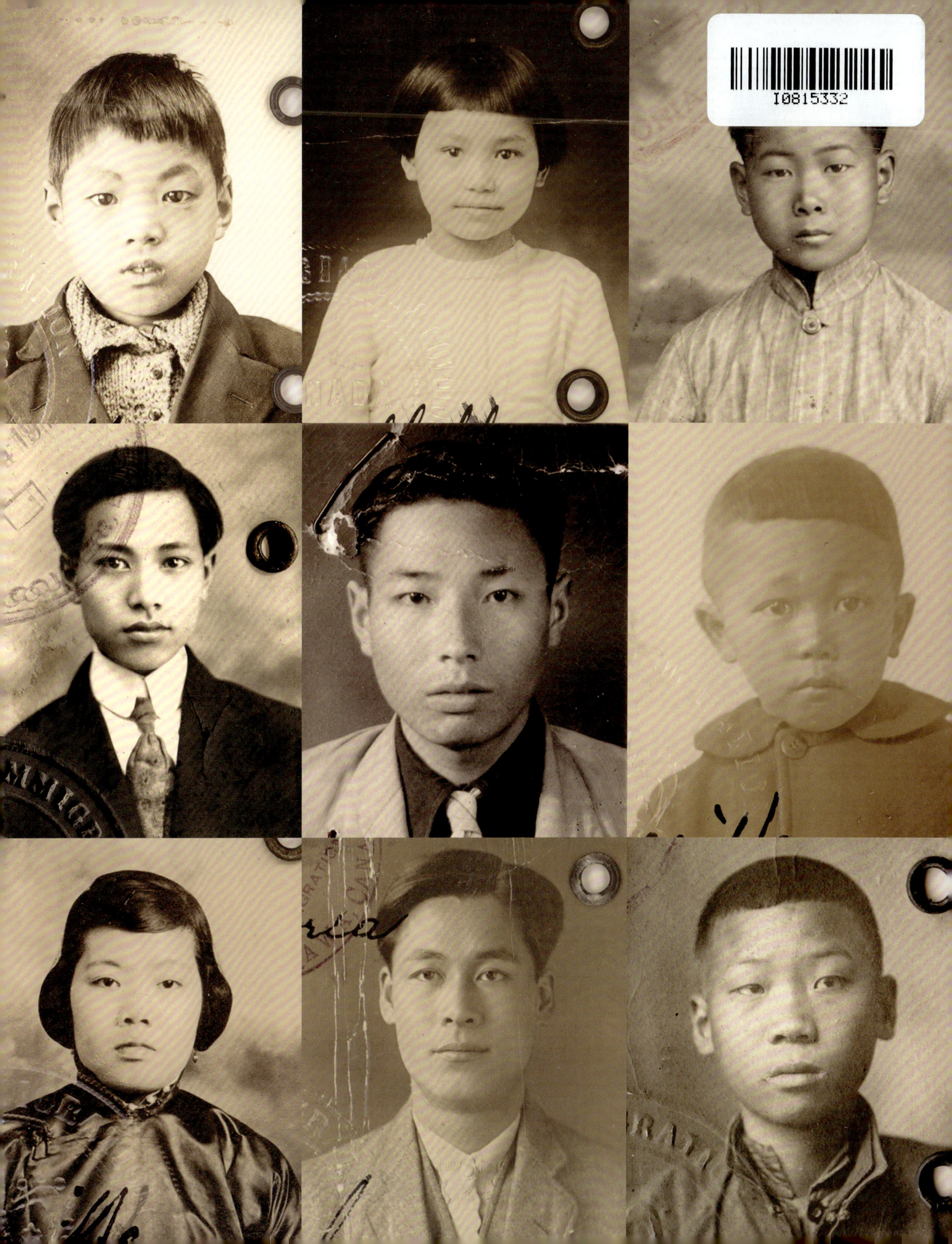

I0815332

The faces featured in this book help us honour those who lived through the Chinese exclusion years.

Cover

CHEUNG Tong

Back Cover

(from left to right, top to bottom)

Annie KEE (Irene LEE), LING Frank, Dan CHAN, MAH Bing, QUAN Yuen Yen, Charlie FOO, LAM Yen Jack (Andrew LAM), CHEW Ying Bull, YEE Sing, MAH Ho Shong, Chen SING, WONG Yong Fong

Endpaper (Front)

(from left to right, top to bottom)

JONG Yue Ot (Art), CHOY Loy Dai, LEE Ping On, CHONG Ham Way, KWAN Gladys, JER Tin Yee (George DEER),

JUE Yit Nock, CHOW Rohda (Rose), LIM Loy Tay (Mary), YEE Chung Yin (Harry), JIM Hong, LEE Wa Kie (Albert),

HUY Hong Duck (Hoy), LEE Suey Shing (Charlie), GEN Ver (JIN Wah Yee), Mrs. CHOW Sun (Annie), LEE Ket, CHONG Kee Chong

THE PAPER TRAIL

to the 1923 Chinese Exclusion Act

In memory of
QUAN Moy and TAI Hing Gom
and others who were like you.
Know that your suffering
was not all in vain.

Image: C.I.28, WONG Hing (Nelson, B.C

THE PAPER TRAIL

to the 1923 Chinese Exclusion Act

CATHERINE CLEMENT

Author: Catherine Clement

Contributors: Naomi Louie,
Andrew Sandfort-Marchese, Victoria So

Published in Canada by Plumleaf Press Inc. This is a first edition.

25 26 27 28 29 6 5 4 3 2 1

Library and Archives Canada Cataloguing in Publication

Title: The paper trail : to the 1923 Chinese Exclusion Act / Catherine Clement.
Other titles: To the 1923 Chinese Exclusion Act
Names: Clement, Catherine, 1959- author
Identifiers: Canadiana 20240527356 | ISBN 9781069093516 (hardcover)
Subjects: LCSH: Canada. Chinese Exclusion Act. | LCSH: Chinese—Canada—History—20th century. | LCSH: Chinese—Legal status, laws, etc.—Canada—History—20th century. | LCSH: Labor policy—Canada—History—20th century. | LCSH: Canada—Race relations. | LCSH: Canada—Emigration and immigration—History—20th century. | CSH: Chinese Canadians—History—20th century. | CSH: Chinese Canadians—Legal status, laws, etc.—History—20th century.
Classification: LCC FC106.C5 C54 2025 | DDC 325.71089/951—dc23

Publisher Cataloging-in-Publication Data (U.S.)

Names: Clement, Catherine, 1959-, author.
Title: The paper trail to the 1923 Chinese Exclusion Act / Catherine Clement.
Description: Oakville, Ontario : Plumleaf Press, 2025. | Summary: "Explores the dark and racist--and largely forgotten--chapter in Canadian history, when the law, in effect from 1923 to 1947, restricted Chinese immigration to Canada and required all Chinese in Canada to register with the government"--Provided by publisher.
Identifiers: ISBN 978-1-06909-351-6 (hardcover)
Subjects: LCSH: Canada – History – 20th century. | Chinese – Canada – History – 20th century. | Chinese – Legal status, laws, etc. – Canada – History – 20th century. | Canada – Race relations – History – 20th century. | Canada – Emigration and immigration – History – 20th century. | BISAC: HISTORY / Post-Confederation (1867-) |HISTORY / Canada / Provincial, Territorial & Local / General. | BIOGRAPHY & AUTOBIOGRAPHY / Historical.
Classification: LCC F1035.C626 2025 | DDC 971.06 – dc23

Designed by: Andrea Maru
Cover Design: Rebecca Bender
Layout conception: Andrea Maru, Rebecca Bender, Karen Gold

Cover photo: C.I.5, CHEUNG Tong, Montreal

Plumleaf Press Inc.
100 Bronte Road, Unit 9,
Oakville, ON, L6L 6L5
www.plumleafpress.com

Printed in China

CONTENTS

Image: C.I.45, SOON “Edith” Young Lum (Vancouver, B.C.

IN THE ANNALS OF CANADIAN migration history, Chinese hold a unique distinction. Two experiences separate them from all other early migrant communities: exclusion and excessive documentation.

Oceans of ink, reams of paper, and armies of bureaucrats were once devoted to the surveillance and control of Chinese in Canada. An ever-expanding and dizzying array of Chinese immigration forms and colour-coded and numbered certificates (all referred to as C.I.s) were created in an effort to monitor, contain, discourage, intimidate, and ultimately exclude this one community.

This fanatical documentation reached its apex with the passing of the federal 1923 Chinese Immigration Act (known as the Chinese Exclusion Act). This unprecedented and draconian law would lock the Chinese community in a vice grip of repression and isolation for almost a quarter century.

This is the story of the Chinese community's darkest and, for some, most despairing period in Canada. This is the story of the human experience of exclusion. It is told through the voluminous paper trail it left behind.

INTRODUCTION

It is ironic that paper – a Chinese invention – should be at the heart of the story of Canada's 1923 Chinese Exclusion Act. Today, the voluminous paper trail spawned by that exclusion bears witness to this tragic but mostly forgotten period in Canadian history.

I first saw the paper trail of the 1923 Chinese Exclusion Act (known formally as the Chinese Immigration Act, 1923) when I volunteered to interview aging Chinese Canadian Second World War veterans. By then, these men were all in their late 80s and early 90s, and I would begin my interviews by posing a simple question: "Where were you born?" The reply was always some Canadian city or small town.

At the end of those interviews, veterans would often haul out a box of old photos and papers. It was then that I first noticed these small, beige identification cards, measuring about 18 cm by 12 cm and bearing a photograph of the veteran as a child. The card was labelled C.I.45.

I was drawn to the photograph first. However, after spending a minute studying the image, my eyes would skim over the rest of the card. Along the top, in capital letters, were emblazoned the words **DEPARTMENT OF IMMIGRATION AND COLONIZATION**. The date of issue was usually sometime in 1924. And at the very bottom of the card was a surprising statement: "This certificate does not establish legal status in Canada."

Every C.I.45 I saw made me pause. Was I reading that line correctly? If these aging men were born in Canada and served their country by risking their lives in the Second World War, then why did they own an immigration card bearing that clause? And why were most of these cards issued in 1924?

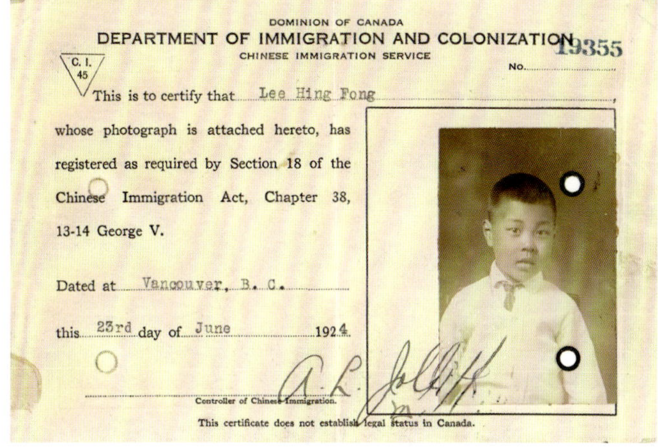

DOMINION OF CANADA
DEPARTMENT OF IMMIGRATION AND COLONIZATION
CHINESE IMMIGRATION SERVICE
No. 19355
C. I. 45
This is to certify that Lee Hing Fong
whose photograph is attached hereto, has registered as required by Section 18 of the Chinese Immigration Act, Chapter 38, 13-14 George V.
Dated at Vancouver, B. C.
this 23rd day of June 1924.
Controller of Chinese Immigration.
This certificate does not establish legal status in Canada.

This certificate does not establish legal status in Canada.

I didn't find the answers to those questions back then. However, my journey to uncover the long and tortuous paper trail left by the 1923 Chinese Exclusion Act had begun.

Catherine Clement, Creator & Curator
The Paper Trail to the 1923 Chinese Exclusion Act: A 100th-anniversary exhibition and archive

◀ Ronald LEE (aka LEE Hing Fong), c. 1944
Image: Ronald H. F. LEE Family

Image: C.I.5, MA Chong Yew (Vancouver, B.C.

CHAPTER 1

DISCOVERING THE PAPER TRAIL

A DIZZYING ARRAY OF PAPER

In 2019, I was wrapping up a major 10-year project called *Chinatown Through a Wide Lens: The Hidden Photographs of Yucho Chow*. Most of the photographs I discovered had been crowdsourced from private family collections. Once the exhibition was over and the accompanying book had been sent to the printers, I had time to consider what I wanted to work on next.

It occurred to me that the 100th anniversary of Canada's 1923 Chinese Exclusion Act was just a few years away. Almost all the individuals who were directly affected by the exclusion legislation – or the Chinese head taxes that preceded it – were no longer alive. However, many had left to their families precious, one-of-a-kind identity documents, called C.I. certificates, that today serve as the last piece of visual evidence from this unprecedented period in Canadian history.

I realized these fragile pieces of paper could unlock for us the story of the individuals who carried the burden of these certificates. We also could learn about the unique struggles of an early immigrant community from these documents, and we could rediscover a largely forgotten chapter in Canadian history.

Sadly, there were only a smattering of these C.I. certificates available in public archives. Of the thousands upon thousands of C.I.s that had been issued, most had been lost, destroyed, or thrown out – either mistakenly or on purpose – once Chinese were granted full Canadian citizenship in 1947. The vast majority of surviving personal C.I. certificates were squirrelled away in boxes, family albums, and drawers – much the way the war veterans themselves had kept them.

To commemorate the 100th anniversary, my first goal was to seek out and scan as many of these surviving certificates as I could from families across Canada. Along with the scans, I would gather whatever stories could be recalled about the original C.I. owner and then create a first-of-its-kind digital archive. My second goal was to take those crowdsourced identity documents and curate a centennial exhibition that would honour the memory of these individuals.

DOMINION OF CANADA
DEPARTMENT OF IMMIGRATION AND COLONIZATION
CHINESE IMMIGRATION SERVICE

C.I. 45

No. 48988

This is to certify that Wong, Paul White Court, Alta., whose photograph is attached hereto, has registered as required by Section 18 of the Chinese Immigration Act, Chapter 38, 13-14 George V.

Dated at Ottawa, Ontario.

this 30th day of June 1924

Controller of Chinese Immigration.

This certificate does not establish legal status in Canada.

The Exclusion Act was a monumental chapter in the origin story of Chinese in Canada. Yet, as I began to reach out to families across Canada, I was astonished by how little Chinese Canadians knew about the Act or the impact it had during the quarter century it was the law.

For something that was initially labelled the "Cruelty Act" by the Chinese community, I was surprised to learn the Act was not talked about or remembered, even among those whose lives were directly affected. I discovered that an intergenerational silence had descended upon the Chinese community soon after the Exclusion Act was repealed in 1947 – two years after the end of the Second World War. Following this traumatic period, I heard how Chinese in Canada longed to get on with their lives, wanting to close a door on this episode, and how they tried to blend in after decades of being singled out and targeted by governments. The result was that within one generation, the tragic experience of these humiliating years was forgotten.

I began to recognize that this centennial commemoration project would be a rare opportunity not only to locate these surviving C.I. certificates but also to recover the forgotten stories from this period. How did this pernicious legislation affect real people, real lives? What did it do to the community? I wanted to understand the experience of exclusion.

Uncovering the stories for this commemorative exhibition absorbed hundreds of hours of original research, mostly involving paper. My team and I scoured the pages of old Chinese and English newspapers, sifted through clan society archives, examined personal correspondence, delved into coroners' reports and court proceedings, and waded through reams of newly released government records.

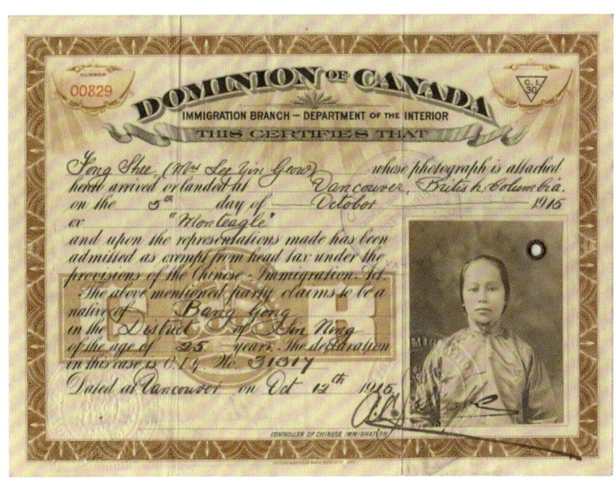
00829

DOMINION OF CANADA

IMMIGRATION BRANCH – DEPARTMENT OF THE INTERIOR

C.I. 30

THIS CERTIFIES THAT

Fong Shee, (Mrs Lee Yin Geow) whose photograph is attached hereto arrived or landed at Vancouver, British Columbia. on the 5th day of October 1915 ex "Monteagle" and upon the representations made has been admitted as exempt from head tax under the provisions of the Chinese Immigration Act. The above mentioned party claims to be a native of Bang Gong in the District of Hin Ning of the age of 25 years. The declaration in this case is C.I.G. No. 31317

Dated at Vancouver on Oct 12th 1915.

CONTROLLER OF CHINESE IMMIGRATION

"The Exclusion Act was a monumental chapter in the origin story of Chinese in Canada. Yet, as I began to reach out to families across Canada, I was astonished by how little Chinese Canadians knew about the Act or the impact it had during the quarter century it was the law."

C.I. 28

12087

DOMINION OF CANADA

IMMIGRATION BRANCH – DEPARTMENT OF THE INTERIOR.

OTTAWA December 23rd 1924

THIS CERTIFIES THAT

Wong Hing of Freemason House, Nelson, B.C. whose photograph is hereto attached claims to be Wong Hing who arrived at Victoria on the – day of May 1883 who was registered at Ottawa under No. at under No. and to whom C.I. No. was issued. It is claimed that C.I. certificate was lost or destroyed and while this certificate is not an admission that the party to whom it is issued was ever legally admitted into Canada, it may, unless cancelled upon presentation, be used when registering out under C.I.9.

CHIEF CONTROLLER OF CHINESE IMMIGRATION

OTTAWA Aug 20th 1924

Chow Sang (Fong Gar Chow) of 841 Cotton St W Moose Jaw Sask whose photograph is hereto attached claims to be Chou Song who arrived at Victoria on the 17th day of May 1899 who was registered at Ottawa under No. 29856 at Victoria under No. 16403 and to whom C.I. No. 24870 was issued. This certificate is given in exchange for C.I. above mentioned and while it is not an admission, that the party to whom it is issued, was ever legally admitted into Canada, it may, unless cancelled upon presentation, be used, when registering out under C.I.9.

CHIEF CONTROLLER OF CHINESE IMMIGRATION

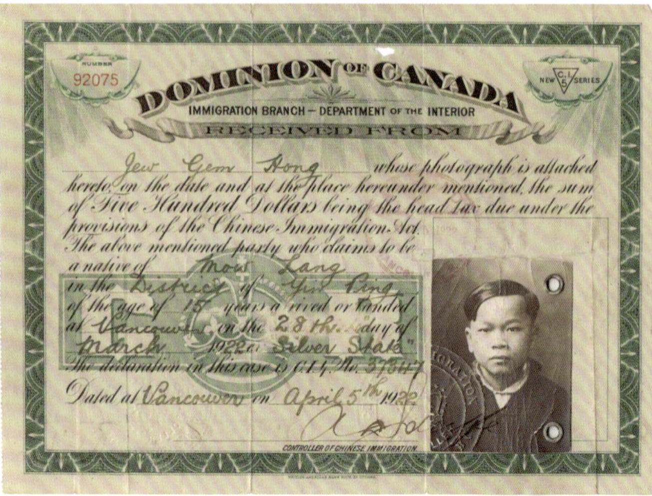

NUMBER 92075

NEW C.I. 5 SERIES

DOMINION OF CANADA

IMMIGRATION BRANCH – DEPARTMENT OF THE INTERIOR

RECEIVED FROM

Jew Gem Hong whose photograph is attached hereto on the date and at the place hereunder mentioned, the sum of Five Hundred Dollars being the head tax due under the provisions of the Chinese Immigration Act. The above mentioned party who claims to be a native of Mow Lang in the District of Yin Ping of the age of 15 years arrived or landed at Vancouver on the 28th day of March 1922 on "Silver State" The declaration in this case is C.I.4. No. 37347

Dated at Vancouver on April 5th 1922

CONTROLLER OF CHINESE IMMIGRATION

We also tapped the memories of hundreds of families across Canada and gleaned what we could from the bits and pieces of stories passed down through the generations. We worked with Library and Archives Canada to release thousands of C.I.44 registration forms that had been created by the Exclusion Act but held for 100 years under privacy legislation.

I found myself brought to tears many times while doing the research and writing for the exhibition. The same was true for the small group of University of British Columbia students who worked with me on the various stories.

The end result was a 100th-anniversary exhibition that took an unflinching look at the exclusion years and their impact.

The Paper Trail to the 1923 Chinese Exclusion Act opened July 1, 2023, at the Chinese Canadian Museum in Vancouver. In the exhibition, spread over four galleries, we revealed the haunting stories of loss and despair as well as powerful examples of courage, perseverance, and resilience. We spoke openly of the tragedy and the triumph that resulted from the Exclusion Act. We felt we owed it to the generations that went before us to be brutally honest.

As well, our aim was to reflect the period in which each individual story took place. Where possible, we incorporated the words and terms used by the Chinese community in Canada during the dark years of exclusion. Our goal was to offer an honest examination of how the law was viewed by the community it affected. And we could not think of a more powerful way nor a more respectful remembrance than sharing the language the community adopted, even when those words may have appeared adversarial in 2023.

Much of this book is based on what appeared in the exhibition. Some of the material is new and includes stories and information we discovered once the show was opened. Some stories that appeared in the exhibition have been omitted in the book, simply due to space.

It is my hope that sharing the experience of exclusion through the stories we have salvaged will reconnect the reader both to the humanity of the individuals that exclusion touched and to the inhumanity of governments that singled out a community that sacrificed so much only to be repaid with a bigotry that has few parallels in our past.

May the stories we recovered serve as a memorial to those who suffered and a solace to those who remain and who seek to remember.

Image: C.I.45, Sue Wai "Mabel" KO (Victoria, B.C.) ▶

Image: C.I.5, YONG Jack Sang (Vancouver, B.C.

CHAPTER 2

THE ARRIVAL OF THE CRUELTY ACT

Victoria Daily Times

VICTORIA, B. C., SATURDAY, NOVEMBER 11, 1922

MUST BAR ORIENTAL COMPLETELY TO SAVE B. C. FOR WHITE RACE

Hon. William Sloan Announces Policy When Legislature Receives Resolution Asking Dominion Government to Amend Immigration Act to Bring About "Total Exclusion"; Foreign Population With Lower Standard of Living Threatens Our Economic Life Here, He Says.

Total exclusion of Chinese, Japanese, Hindus and all other Asiatics, was the wish of Hon. William Sloan, Minister of Mines, in the Legislature Friday afternoon.

In an emphatic way he made it clear that total exclusion is the only way of solving the problem.

In his position as one of the Ministers of the Crown, Mr. Sloan's declaration was accepted by the House as the approved and adopted policy of the British Columbia Government.

THE SLOW SQUEEZE TO EXCLUSION

While the 1923 Act was the pinnacle of Chinese exclusion in Canada, it was not the first attempt to target and shut out this one community.

Wanting to ensure Canada would be a "white" nation, the federal government introduced the first series of exclusionary measures against Chinese in 1885 just as the transcontinental railroad was nearing completion. The initial head tax of $50 – an entry fee levied only on Chinese – was intended to thwart migration. And, for the thousands of Chinese labourers who were already in Canada and who had built the most difficult sections of the railroad through British Columbia, the tax was designed to discourage them from staying and bringing over their families. The tax's astronomical increases over the years – from $50 to $100 and then $500 by 1903 – were attempts to make the tax "more effective."

After the First World War, exclusion expanded. By 1919, both "skilled" and "unskilled" Chinese labourers were denied entry at ports in British Columbia, supported by the rationale that exclusion would ensure jobs for returning white soldiers. That move was followed by a lowering of the age at which a Chinese child would be admitted to Canada. By 1922, only children 13 years of age or under were eligible to join their parents and only to obtain an education.

Chinese also lived in the crosshairs of provincial and municipal governments, who targeted the community and expanded exclusion at the local level. From housing to voting rights to running a business, Chinese were repeatedly singled out and denied equal treatment and opportunities.

Around 1922, frustrated that Chinese continued to arrive on Canada's shores, politicians and bureaucrats, led by British Columbia, successfully argued that the only solution left was the total exclusion of new Chinese migrants. The idea for Canada's Chinese Exclusion Act was born.

"For the thousands of Chinese labourers who were already in Canada and who had built the most difficult sections of the railroad ... the tax was designed to discourage them from staying and bringing over their families."

◀ In the fall of 1922, British Columbia politicians advocated for the exclusion of all "Asiatics." Half a year later, only Chinese were singled out for a complete ban.

CANADA

The Right Land for the Right Man:

Canadian
National
Railways
– The Right Way! –

Full details
obtainable
from our
local agent
or upon
application
direct to –

LONDON
17-19 Cockspur St.
& 44-46 Leadenhall St.

LIVERPOOL
Cunard Bldg.

GLASGOW
75 Union Street

Local Agents:
SERCOMBE & HAYES,
9, South Street, DORCHESTER.

DUDLEY, SPENCER & Co. LONDON.

▲ Editorial cartoons highlighted the government's fear that there were too many Chinese in Canada and that more would come without exclusionary laws in place.
Image: J. W. BENGOUGH, Grip, Toronto, 12 September 1885

◀ At the same time as the Chinese Exclusion Act was becoming law, marketing posters like these were being created in Canada and sent to Europe. The aim was to entice white Europeans to make Canada their new home.
Image: Glenbow Library and Archives

Chinese Immigrants to Canada to be Registered And Finger Prints Taken

Hon. Charles Stewart, Minister of Immigration, Gives Features of Bill Which He Will Bring Down in Ottawa House Next Week

OTTAWA, Feb. 21.—(Canadian Press)—Chinese immigrants to be registered and their finger-prints taken to secure identification—these, announced Hon. Charles Stewart, minister of immigration, in the house today, were features of a bill respecting Chinese immigration which he expected to bring down next week. At the time, the house was considering an immigration bill by A. W. Neill (Independent, Comox Alberni), and the question of Oriental immigration was raised.

Mr. Neill said his bill provided that no immigrants should enter Canada without the permission of the minister o[illegible] ing obtained. [illegible] provisions to [illegible] ed to visit Ca[illegible] on business or [illegible]

Similar legislation, Mr. Neill said, had been adopted in New Zealand, and it had been found that this did not conflict with the rights of other sections of the empire.

One of the problems in the solution of which the bill would assist, argued Mr. Neill, was that of Hindoo immigration. He warned the house tha[illegible] ... to prevent the influx of large num-[illegible]

> "In the spring of 1923, as the federal government finalized the legislation and tried to close every loophole that would allow Chinese into Canada, the community pushed back."

Chinese from Coast to Coast Meet to Protest Against Bill

New Immigration Regulations Exclude Families of Merchants, Tourists, Clergymen, Scientists and Teachers—Cannot Change Their Occupation After Their Arrival.

What is undoubtedly the most important meeting affecting the affairs of the Chinese in Canada was held last night in Victoria Hall, when over 1,000 Chinese assembled in a mass meeting of protest against the proposed changes in the Chinese immigration act as embodied in Bill 45, which came up for its first reading in the dominion house on March 2, 1923.

[illegible]

... seemed thoroughly conversant with the law, there were formerly, and are at present six classes which are exempt; diplomats and government officials, students, tourists, clergymen and scientists, merchants and their families, including only minor children and teachers.

In the new list the families of merchants have been omitted, as also tourists, clergymen and scientists, and teachers. The regulations gov-[illegible]

THE FIGHT AGAINST EXCLUSION

The proposed Chinese Immigration Act, 1923 had provisions that were deeply troubling to the Chinese community. First and foremost, it significantly expanded who would be excluded from entry into Canada going forward; and, at the same time, it more narrowly defined the categories of merchants and students. In the spring of 1923, as the federal government finalized the legislation and tried to close every loophole that would allow Chinese into Canada, the community pushed back. Letters to the editor were written and published in major English newspapers. The Chinese Consul joined the protest against the bill. Community strategy meetings were held, including a large one in Victoria, B.C., in early May 1923 that attracted 1,000 Chinese delegates from across the country. To bring so many people together was no small feat at a time when travel was expensive, and it could take several days to cross the country as only trains were available for distance travel.

CHINESE LOBBY IN THE SENATE

Voluminous Petition Circulated Against Immigration Bill.

Intimated That Measure May Give Offense to Peking Government.

By T. M. FRASER.

OTTAWA, May 16.—The Chinese lobby is vigorously carrying on its efforts to have the Senate amend the Chinese Immigration Bill, and seven or eight members of the race decorate the Senate galleries daily during the discussion of the bill. Each member of the upper chamber has received a copy of a voluminous petition on behalf of the Chinese Association of Canada, prepared by their solicitor, William Proudfoot. It is a document of eighteen foolscap pages and is so voluminous that the majority of the recipients discarded it without perusal.

By mid-May 1923, in what would be a last-ditch effort to halt the more draconian aspects of the bill, a delegation of Chinese travelled to Ottawa, where the legislation was under final review by the Senate. What happened at the Senate was described by *The Province* newspaper. The May 16, 1923, article read: "Each member of the upper chamber has received a copy of a voluminous petition on behalf of the Chinese Association of Canada ... It is a document of eighteen foolscap pages and is so voluminous that the majority of the recipients discarded it without perusal."

One might imagine the indignity of that moment: the contempt with which their concerns were dismissed; the manner in which their report was discarded without being read. It must have been a soul-crushing experience for those Chinese delegates who had travelled so far to make this final plea. They left knowing they had lost.

◀ In the 1920s, fingerprinting was reserved for criminals. The proposal to fingerprint Chinese in Canada caused outrage and led to accusations that all Chinese were being treated as if they were criminals.

THE CRUELTY ACT

The federal government chose a symbolic day to enact the Chinese Exclusion Act: Canada's birthday, July 1, 1923.

The law was only 15 pages long, but the words were life-changing for tens of thousands of Chinese, both in Canada and in China. The Chinese community described the new law as cruel, harsh, and humiliating.

The Act contained two key directives:

1.

the barring of practically all new migrants from China; and

2.

the requirement that, within the year, every Chinese person in Canada, whether born here or abroad, must register. Failure to register by the June 30, 1924, deadline would result in a $500 fine, imprisonment, or deportation.

Technically, the Act still allowed a very limited number of Chinese merchants (but not their families), diplomats, and students into Canada. However, narrower definitions of who was considered a merchant and more onerous restrictions on students meant the door to Canada was sealed shut.

Exclusion would last for almost a quarter century.

13-14 GEORGE V.

CHAP. 38.

An Act respecting Chinese Immigration.

[*Assented to 30th June, 1923.*]

HIS Majesty, by and with the advice and consent of the Senate and House of Commons of Canada, enacts as follows:— R.S. c. 95; 1908, c. 14; 1917, c. 7; 1921, c. 21.

SHORT TITLE.

1. This Act may be cited as *The Chinese Immigration Act, 1923.* Short title.

INTERPRETATION.

2. In this Act and in any order, proclamation or regulation made thereunder, unless the context otherwise requires, Definitions.

(*a*) "Minister" means the Minister of Immigration and Colonization, or the member of His Majesty's Privy Council of Canada charged with the administration of this Act for the time being; "Minister".

(*b*) "Chief Controller" means the chief officer charged, under the direction of the Minister, with the duty of carrying the provisions of this Act into effect and having authority over officers of Immigration and others appointed for the purpose or charged with the duty of assisting in carrying out the provisions of this Act; "Chief Controller".

(*c*) "Controller" means the Immigration or other officer at any seaport or frontier port of entry duly appointed as such and charged with the duty of assisting in carrying the provisions of this Act into effect; "Controller".

(*d*) "Officer" means any person appointed under this Act for any of the purposes of this Act, whether within or outside of Canada, and any person who is an officer within the meaning of section two, paragraph (*b*) of *The Immigration Act;* 1910. c. 27.

(*e*) "Chinese Immigrant" means any person of Chinese origin or descent entering Canada for the purpose of "Chinese Immigrant".

301

残酷法案

"The Cruelty Act"

Page from Senate document; *An Act respecting Chinese Immigration. Assented to 30th June, 1923*
Image: Library and Archives Canada

NOTICE

As required by Section 18 of The Chinese Immigration Act, Chapter 38, 13-14 George V, every person of Chinese origin or descent in Canada, irrespective of allegiance or citizenship, is required to register within one year from the 30th day of June, 1923, with one of the registrars in the list below.

Chinese living at a distance from a registrar may, if they so desire, register with the Postmaster of their district.

Registration forms will be available at each place of registration, and each person applying for registration should produce his landing certificate (C.I. 5, C.I. 28, C.I. 30 or C.I. 36) and must produce three untouched and unmounted copies of his photograph measuring 1¼ inches from the top of head to point of chin, without head covering, full front view showing both ears.

Section 34 of The Chinese Immigration Act, 1923, provides that where any person of Chinese origin or descent fails to register as required by Section 18 referred to above, he shall be liable to a fine not exceeding five hundred dollars, or to imprisonment for a period not exceeding twelve months, or to both.

CHAS. STEWART,
Acting Minister of Immigration and Colonization.

為通告事照得本部頒行華僑移民例
第十八章三十八款凡屬中國人民居留坎
拿大者無論籍民與否均須於一年之內
一律填冊由一九二三年六月三十日起至一九
二四年六月三十日止
一凡居留邊隅之處如無主簿可為填寫者
請向該管內之郵政局長代填便妥
一填冊之格式可向各填冊處取給
一凡到局填冊時須要攜帶其本人入坎
時由本政府發給之照抑別項執照並須
備原照軟相片三張自頭頂至頷下量一寸
四分之一免冠正面兩耳露現為合格自此
通告發出後如有中國之移民不遵上述
第十八章之令於限期內填冊者即犯違
令之罪便依照一九二三年所定華人移民
例第三十四條處罰其罰款不克過五百
元禁監不克過二十個月或禁監罰款
兩者併施特此佈聞各宜遵守
西曆一九二三年七月十四日
署移民部大臣布阻核民佈告

REGISTRARS

ALBERTA

Place	Registrar
Aklavik	The Member of the Royal Canadian Mounted Police in charge
Athabasca	The Member of the Royal Canadian Mounted Police in charge
Banff	The Member of the Royal Canadian Mounted Police in charge
Big Bend	The Member of the Royal Canadian Mounted Police in charge
Blairmore	The Member of the Royal Canadian Mounted Police in charge
Brule	The Member of the Royal Canadian Mounted Police in charge
Calgary	Dominion Immigration Agent
Canmore	The Member of the Royal Canadian Mounted Police in charge
Cardston	Canadian Customs Officer
Coutts	Canadian Immigration Officer in charge
Drumheller	The Member of the Royal Canadian Mounted Police in charge
Edmonton	Dominion Immigration Agent
Exshaw	The Member of the Royal Canadian Mounted Police in charge
Fort Fitzgerald	The Member of the Royal Canadian Mounted Police in charge
Fort Norman	The Member of the Royal Canadian Mounted Police in charge
Fort Resolution	The Member of the Royal Canadian Mounted Police in charge
Fort Simpson	The Member of the Royal Canadian Mounted Police in charge
Fort Smith	The Member of the Royal Canadian Mounted Police in charge
Gleichen	The Member of the Royal Canadian Mounted Police in charge
Grouard	The Member of the Royal Canadian Mounted Police in charge
Jasper	The Member of the Royal Canadian Mounted Police in charge
Lethbridge	The Member of the Royal Canadian Mounted Police in charge
Macleod	The Member of the Royal Canadian Mounted Police in charge
Medicine Hat	The Member of the Royal Canadian Mounted Police in charge
Morley	The Member of the Royal Canadian Mounted Police in charge
Nordegg	The Member of the Royal Canadian Mounted Police in charge
Peace River	The Member of the Royal Canadian Mounted Police in charge
Pinhorn	Canadian Customs Officer
Stand Off	The Member of the Royal Canadian Mounted Police in charge
Tree River	The Member of the Royal Canadian Mounted Police in charge
Twin Lakes	Canadian Customs Officer
Waterton Park	The Member of the Royal Canadian Mounted Police in charge

BRITISH COLUMBIA

Place	Registrar
Aldergrove	Canadian Customs Officer
Alert Bay	The Member of the Royal Canadian Mounted Police in charge
Anyox	Canadian Customs Officer
Bridesville	Canadian Customs Officer
Britannia Beach	Canadian Customs Officer
Carson	Canadian Customs Officer
Cascade	Canadian Customs Officer
Chemainus	Canadian Immigration Inspector
Cranbrook	The Member of the Royal Canadian Mounted Police in charge
Creston	The Member of the Royal Canadian Mounted Police in charge
Cumberland	The Member of the Royal Canadian Mounted Police in charge
Douglas	Canadian Customs Officer
Fernie	The Member of the Royal Canadian Mounted Police in charge
Field	The Member of the Royal Canadian Mounted Police in charge
Grand Forks	Canadian Immigration Inspector
Huntingdon	Canadian Immigration Inspector
Kingsgate	Canadian Immigration Inspector in charge
Ladner	Canadian Customs Officer
Ladysmith	Canadian Customs Officer
Michel	The Member of the Royal Canadian Mounted Police in charge
Midway	Canadian Customs Officer
Myncaster	Canadian Customs Officer
Nanaimo	Canadian Collector of Customs
Newgate	Canadian Immigration Inspector
New Westminster	Canadian Collector of Customs
Ocean Falls	Canadian Customs Officer
Osoyoos	Canadian Customs Officer
Pacific Highway	Canadian Immigration Inspector in charge
Paterson	Canadian Customs Officer
Penticton	The Member of the Royal Canadian Mounted Police in charge
Port Alberni	Canadian Customs Officer
Port Simpson	Canadian Customs Officer
Powell River	Canadian Immigration Inspector
Prince George	The Member of the Royal Canadian Mounted Police in charge
Prince Rupert	Dominion Immigration Agent
Radium Hot Springs	The Member of the Royal Canadian Mounted Police in charge
Roosville	Canadian Customs Officer
Rykerts	Canadian Customs Officer
Sidney	Canadian Immigration Officer
Similkameen	Canadian Customs Officer
Steveston	Canadian Customs Officer
Stewart	Canadian Customs Officer
Telkwa	The Member of the Royal Canadian Mounted Police in charge
Union Bay	Canadian Immigration Inspector
Vancouver	The Commissioner of Immigration
Vernon	The Member of the Royal Canadian Mounted Police in charge
Victoria	Dominion Immigration Agent
Waneta	Canadian Customs Officer
White Rock	Canadian Immigration Inspector in charge

MANITOBA

Place	Registrar
Bannerman	Canadian Immigration Inspector
Boissevain	Canadian Customs Officer
Brandon	The Member of the Royal Canadian Mounted Police in charge
Cartwright	Canadian Customs Officer
Crystal City	Canadian Customs Officer
Dauphin	The Member of the Royal Canadian Mounted Police in charge
Deloraine	Canadian Customs Officer
Emerson	Canadian Immigration Inspector in charge
Gretna	Canadian Immigration Inspector
Gypsumville	The Member of the Royal Canadian Mounted Police in charge
Haskett	Canadian Customs Officer
Hodgson	The Member of the Royal Canadian Mounted Police in charge
Killarney	Canadian Customs Officer
Lac du Bonnet	The Member of the Royal Canadian Mounted Police in charge
Morden	Canadian Customs Officer
Norway House	The Member of the Royal Canadian Police Mounted in charge
Port Nelson	The Member of the Royal Canadian Mounted Police in charge
Shoal Lake	The Member of the Royal Canadian Mounted Police in charge
Snowflake	Canadian Immigration Inspector
Sprague	Canadian Immigration Inspector
The Pas	The Member of the Royal Canadian Mounted Police in charge
Waskada	The Member of the Royal Canadian Mounted Police in charge
Winnipeg	Commissioner of Immigration

NEW BRUNSWICK

Place	Registrar
Andover	Canadian Customs Officer
Aroostook Jct.	Canadian Immigration Inspector
Campbellton	Canadian Customs Officer
Centreville	Canadian Customs Officer
Chatham	Canadian Customs Officer
Clair	Canadian Customs Officer
Connor	Canadian Customs Officer
Debec Jct.	Canadian Immigration Inspector
Edmundston	Canadian Immigration Inspector
Grand Falls	Canadian Customs Officer
McAdam Jct.	Canadian Immigration Inspector in charge
Milltown	Canadian Immigration Inspector
North Head	Canadian Customs Officer
North Lake	Canadian Customs Officer
Richmond Corner	Canadian Immigration Inspector
St. Andrews	Canadian Immigration Inspector
St. John	Dominion Immigration Agent
St. Leonard	Canadian Immigration Inspector
St. Stephen	Canadian Immigration Inspector in charge
Wilson's Beach	Canadian Customs Officer

NOVA SCOTIA

Place	Registrar
Halifax	Dominion Immigration Agent
Louisburg	Canadian Customs Officer
North Sydney	Dominion Immigration Agent
Sydney	Dominion Immigration Agent
Yarmouth	Canadian Immigration Inspector

ONTARIO

Place	Registrar
Amherstburg	Canadian Customs Officer
Aultsville	Canadian Customs Officer
Brantford	Canadian Customs Officer
Bridgeburg	Canadian Immigration Inspector in charge
Brockville	Canadian Immigration Inspector
Bruce Mines	Canadian Customs Officer
Chatham	Canadian Customs Officer
Cobourg	Canadian Immigration Inspector
Collingwood	Canadian Customs Officer
Cornwall	Canadian Immigration Inspector
Corunna	Canadian Customs Officer
Courtright	Canadian Customs Officer
Crystal Beach	Canadian Immigration Inspector in charge
Cutler	Canadian Customs Officer
Depot Harbour	Canadian Customs Officer
Erieau	Canadian Customs Officer
Erie Beach	Canadian Immigration Inspector
Fort Erie	Canadian Immigration Inspector in charge
Fort Frances	Canadian Immigration Inspector in charge
Fort William	Canadian Immigration Inspector
Gananoque	Canadian Customs Officer
Goderich	Canadian Customs Officer
Haileybury	The Member of the Royal Canadian Mounted Police in charge
Hamilton	Dominion Immigration Agent
Kenora	The Member of the Royal Canadian Mounted Police in charge
Kingston	Canadian Immigration Inspector
Kingsville	Canadian Customs Officer
London	Dominion Immigration Agent
Maitland	Canadian Customs Officer
Midland	Canadian Customs Officer
Morrisburg	Canadian Customs Officer
Niagara Falls	Canadian Immigration Inspector in charge
Niagara-on-the-Lake	Canadian Immigration Inspector in charge

ONTARIO.—*continued.*

Place	Registrar
Ohswekew	The Member of the Royal Canadian Mounted Police in charge
Ottawa	The Chief Controller of Chinese Immigration
Owen Sound	Canadian Customs Officer
Parry Sound	Canadian Customs Officer
Pigeon River	Canadian Customs Officer
Point Edward	Canadian Immigration Inspector
Port Arthur	Canadian Immigration Inspector
Port Burwell	Canadian Customs Officer
Port Colborne	Canadian Customs Officer
Port Dover	Canadian Customs Officer
Port Lambton	Canadian Customs Officer
Port Stanley	Canadian Customs Officer
Prescott	Canadian Immigration Inspector in charge
Queenston	Canadian Immigration Inspector
Rainy River	Canadian Immigration Inspector
Rockport	Canadian Customs Officer
Sarnia	Canadian Immigration Inspector in charge
Sault Ste. Marie	Canadian Immigration Inspector in charge
Sombra	Canadian Customs Officer
Thessalon	Canadian Customs Officer
Toronto	Dominion Immigration Agent
Trenton	Canadian Customs Officer
Wallaceburg	Canadian Customs Officer
Walpole Island	Canadian Customs Officer
Windsor	Canadian Immigration Inspector in charge
Wolfe Island	Canadian Customs Officer

QUEBEC

Place	Registrar
Beebe Jct.	Canadian Immigration Inspector in charge
Coaticook	Canadian Immigration Inspector in charge
Comin's Mills	Canadian Immigration Inspector
Dundee	Canadian Customs Officer
Frelighsburg	Canadian Customs Officer
Georgeville	Canadian Customs Officer
Glenelm	Canadian Customs Officer
Hemmingford	Canadian Immigration Inspector
Highwater	Canadian Immigration Inspector in charge
Huntingdon	Canadian Immigration Inspector
Lacolle	Canadian Immigration Inspector in charge
Lennoxville	Canadian Immigration Inspector in charge
Magog	Canadian Customs Officer
Mansonville	Canadian Customs Officer
Megantic	Canadian Immigration Inspector
Montreal	Dominion Immigration Agent
Phillipsburg	Canadian Customs Officer
Quebec	Dominion Immigration Agent
St. Armand	Canadian Immigration Inspector
St. Regis	Canadian Customs Officer
Stanhope	Canadian Immigration Inspector

SASKATCHEWAN

Place	Registrar
Balcarres	The Member of the Royal Canadian Mounted Police in charge
Big Muddy	Canadian Immigration Inspector
Broadview	The Member of the Royal Canadian Mounted Police in charge
Carlyle	The Member of the Royal Canadian Mounted Police in charge
Chesterfield Inlet	The Member of the Royal Canadian Mounted Police in charge
Duck Lake	The Member of the Royal Canadian Mounted Police in charge
East Poplar River	Canadian Customs Officer
Estevan	Canadian Customs Officer
Fort Qu'Appelle	The Member of the Royal Canadian Mounted Police in charge
Herschel	The Member of the Royal Canadian Mounted Police in charge
Humboldt	The Member of the Royal Canadian Mounted Police in charge
Kamsack	The Member of the Royal Canadian Mounted Police in charge
Lloydminster	Dominion Immigration Agent
Maple Creek	The Member of the Royal Canadian Mounted Police in charge
Marienthal	Canadian Customs Officer
Meadow Lake	The Member of the Royal Canadian Mounted Police in charge
Melville	The Member of the Royal Canadian Mounted Police in charge
Moose Jaw	The Member of the Royal Canadian Mounted Police in charge
North Battleford	Dominion Immigration Agent
North Gate	Canadian Customs Officer
North Portal	Canadian Immigration Inspector in charge
Onion Lake	The Member of the Royal Canadian Mounted Police in charge
Prince Albert	The Member of the Royal Canadian Mounted Police in charge
Punnichy	The Member of the Royal Canadian Mounted Police in charge
Regina	The Member of the Royal Canadian Mounted Police in charge
Saskatoon	The Member of the Royal Canadian Mounted Police in charge
Shaunavon	The Member of the Royal Canadian Mounted Police in charge
Swift Current	The Member of the Royal Canadian Mounted Police in charge
West Poplar River	Canadian Customs Officer
Weyburn	The Member of the Royal Canadian Mounted Police in charge
Willow Creek	Canadian Customs Officer
Yorkton	The Member of the Royal Canadian Mounted Police in charge

YUKON TERRITORY

Place	Registrar
Dawson	The Member of the Royal Canadian Mounted Police in charge
White Horse	The Member of the Royal Canadian Mounted Police in charge

THE FIGHT AGAINST REGISTRATION

The federal government chose a symbolic day to enact the Chinese Exclusion Act: Canada's birthday, July 1, 1923. After July 1, 1923, the community turned its attention to its next big concern: the requirement that all Chinese be registered by June 30, 1924, or face fines, imprisonment, or possible deportation. The community's fears were likely magnified by headlines such as the one that appeared in the Regina *Leader Post* on August 21, 1923, which read "RCMP to round up Chinese for Registration and Photos."

Registration fuelled additional outrage because it even mandated registration for those Chinese immigrants who had been residents of Canada for many years and had successfully applied to become naturalized British subjects.

However, the most egregious insult was the insistence that even those Chinese who had been born in Canada were obligated to report to immigration officials and register.

The fact that the registration process required an interview with state representatives only added to the panic. Being forced to report to a government office or a police station and answer a barrage of questions reminded many Chinese of the traumatic interrogation experience they faced when they first landed in Canada. Some feared they would be penalized for not recalling events perfectly or for not being consistent with what the government had on file. Those who had slipped into Canada as "paper" sons or daughters panicked at being discovered.

R.C.M.P. TO ROUND UP CHINESE FOR REGISTRATION AND PHOTOS

In order to carry out an Act of Parliament, passed in the dying hours of the last federal session, all members of the Royal Canadian Mounted Police have been appointed to register Chinese residents of the province. As soon as registration forms and complete instructions arrive from Ottawa, the work will be started. Photographs giving side and front views of all Celestials are required in addition to the information, which will tabulate the names, descriptions, occupation, date of entry into Canada, and other data regarding the Chinese. It is anticipated that the registration will start within a week or ten days.

Many Chinese
of parliament h
P. officials for
registration an
anticipated in o
tion. One of th
istration is to
Chinese into Ca
have come int
"underground
have lost their
registered a c
identification of
on file at R.
and the work
migration laws

EXTRA HELP TO COPE WITH HEAVY TASK OF REGISTERING CHINESE

Thousands Believed To Have Been Smuggled Into Canada May Be Subject To Deportation, According To Estimates Made

Two stenographers, two interpreters and an extra inspector have been added to the Immigration staff in Victoria to cope with the registration of Chinese now proceeding and which must be completed before the end of the month. As the rush of registration increases further additions will be made to the staff so that all the Chinese in the city can be registered within the time set by the amendments to the Immigration Act calling for all Chinese, native born or otherwise, to register and bring photographs to be filed with the registration papers.

WAITING QUEUES

There are two queues at the offices with from thirty to thirty-five Chinamen in each line and at some times the line has contained

Image: Newspapers stories from Regina (above) and Victoria (right)

◀ A Canadian government notice informed Chinese immigrants that they were required to be registered by June 30, 1924, or they would face fines of up to $500 (equal to two years of full-time wages for a labourer), imprisonment, or possible deportation.

N CHOP SUEY HOUSE

("Paper" children were those who had been born in China and arrived using false identity documents claiming they were the direct offspring of a Chinese parent already living in Canada.) Meanwhile, men who had entered as "merchants" and were originally exempt from the head tax wondered what would happen should they admit their business had failed. Rumours abounded that they would be deemed "labourers" and fined the head tax fee of $500 or be deported.

> ***"Being forced to report to a government office or a police station and answer a barrage of questions reminded many Chinese of the traumatic interrogation experience they faced when they first landed in Canada."***

Again, the Chinese community fought back. Once more, it sent delegations to Ottawa. Letters to the editor were published in local newspapers that provided cogent arguments for why registration made no sense, particularly the registration of naturalized and Canadian-born Chinese. The patently racist and discriminatory character of the legislation was clear. Some community leaders, such as **David C. LEW**, a legal adviser in Vancouver, even publicly threatened to ignore the law and test the legality of the regulation in courts.

The campaign to overturn registration continued right up to the bitter end. However, by June 1924, Chinese families recognized the lobbying efforts were futile: hundreds registered their Canadian-born children just before the deadline.

Canadian-born Chinese, like these boys gathered in Vancouver, were required to register by June 30, 1924. More than 6,200 children under 18 years old were registered. *Image: City of Vancouver Archives*

> ***"It has been held by the Privy Council that every alien who is naturalized in Canada, becomes a Canadian subject of the King, and and also that his children are not aliens, and by this legislation it is sought to take away the rights and privileges which we are clearly entitled to as affirmed by the highest court in the British empire ..."***
>
> ***"We question the right of the Dominion Parliament to pass such a law and single us out from other races residing in this Province, and to put a contemptuous stigma on our race."***
>
> ***David C. LEW***
> ***Vancouver***

"Chinese Would Test Legality of Registration," *Victoria Daily Times*, June 14, 1924

CHINESE BITTER ON REGULATION CALLING FOR REGISTRATIONS

Heated Propaganda Describes Requirement As An Insult Calling For An Indignity Not Even Inflicted Upon Criminals; Plans Are Advancing For Humiliation Day, July 1; Petition Circulated Also Calls For Reunion of Families With Chinese Merchants In Canada.

Bitterness and hostility towards what they consider to be an affront to their country in the immigration regulations calling for the registration of all Chinese in Canada, whether born in this country or in China before June 30, are being voiced by Chinese in Victoria.

The feeling against the regulations which have been in force a year, has been heightened by publicity in newspapers printed in

A Victoria newspaper subheadline describes "An Indignity Not Even Inflicted Upon Criminals" as bitter propaganda about registration.

A RUSH FOR PHOTOGRAPHS

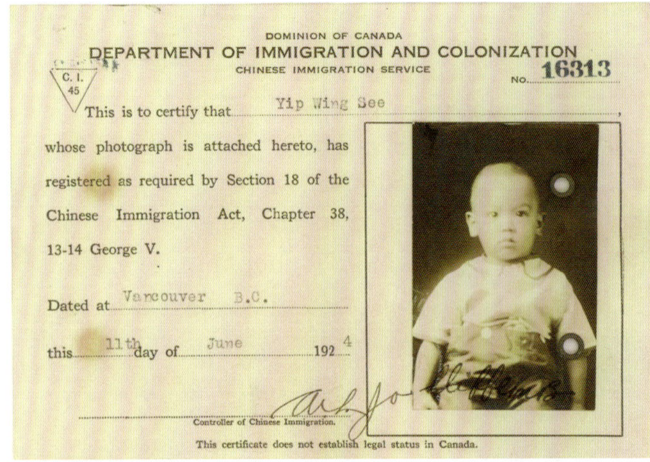
DOMINION OF CANADA
DEPARTMENT OF IMMIGRATION AND COLONIZATION
CHINESE IMMIGRATION SERVICE
C.I. 45
No. 16313
This is to certify that Yip Wing See whose photograph is attached hereto, has registered as required by Section 18 of the Chinese Immigration Act, Chapter 38, 13-14 George V.
Dated at Vancouver B.C. this 11th day of June 1924
Controller of Chinese Immigration.
This certificate does not establish legal status in Canada.

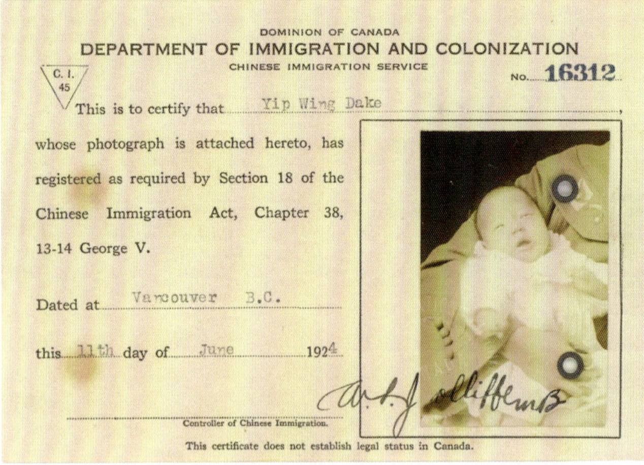
DOMINION OF CANADA
DEPARTMENT OF IMMIGRATION AND COLONIZATION
CHINESE IMMIGRATION SERVICE
C.I. 45
No. 16312
This is to certify that Yip Wing Dake whose photograph is attached hereto, has registered as required by Section 18 of the Chinese Immigration Act, Chapter 38, 13-14 George V.
Dated at Vancouver B.C. this 11th day of June 1924
Controller of Chinese Immigration.
This certificate does not establish legal status in Canada.

The Exclusion Act's mandatory registration required all Chinese to report to a local registrar office by the June 30, 1924, deadline. Registrants needed to have three copies of a recent photograph of themselves. And if they had been born in China, they were required to bring in their C.I. landing certificate.

The need for a recent photograph spawned a booming business for many local photographers. Popular Vancouver photographer Yucho Chow placed ads in *The Chinese Times* newspaper reminding customers of the deadline and the need to get their photos done.

For the relatively few Chinese families living in Canada, the need to submit photographs for all their children could be expensive. Some families used the opportunity to take one family photo and then have the photographer carefully crop out each child's face to produce individual images. The results could be amusing: some identification photographs showed a child held up by the disembodied hands of a parent.

> ***"The need for a recent photograph spawned a booming business for many local photographers. Popular Vancouver photographer Yucho Chow placed ads in* The Chinese Times *newspaper reminding customers of the deadline and the need to get their photos taken."***

In 1924, YIP Kew Sheck and his wife had only two children and were members of the wealthy YIP Sang family of Vancouver. Kew Sheck could afford a family photo as well as the individual images needed by the government. Years later, both his sons, Cecil (seated) and Dick, would enlist in the Army and serve Canada during the Second World War. ▶
Image: Dick and Yvette YIP Archives

註册相
影到六月三拾號

JUNE 30

六月叁拾號以前
晚晚影到十一点
廣東街口對面

周耀初影相館

CHINESE CROWD TO REGISTRATION BOOTH

Long Lines of Orientals Form at Offices In Victoria.

VICTORIA, June 18.—Two stenographers, two interpreters and an extra inspector have been added to the immigration staff in Victoria to cope with the registration of Chinese now proceeding, and which must be completed before the end of the month. As the rush of registration increases further additions will be made to the staff so that all the Chinese in the city can be registered within the time set by the amendments to the Immigration Act calling for all Chinese, native born or otherwise, to register and bring photographs to be filed with the registration papers.

There are two queues at the office with from thirty to thirty-five Chinamen in each line, and at the same time the lines have contained as many as eighty or ninety. Whatever resentment they may hold against the regulations

A REGISTRATION NIGHTMARE

YEE Wai Ben arrived in Canada in February 1921. He was one of at least two dozen "merchants" who arrived on the same ship. As merchants, all were exempt from paying the head tax and were issued a coveted C.I.30.

We don't know why Wai Ben's business plans failed, but by 1924, when the Exclusion Act registration was under way, he was living in Toronto and working as a cook.

27

MERCHANTS

[Section 5, Paragraph (c)]

"Merchant," as used in this Act, shall not include any person who does not devote his undivided attention to mercantile pursuits and who has less than $2,500 invested in a business dealing exclusively in goods grown, produced or manufactured in China or in exporting to China goods grown, produced or manufactured in Canada, and who has not conducted such business for a period of at least three years; any merchant's clerk, or other employee; tailor; mechanic; huckster; peddler or person engaged in taking, drying or otherwise preserving fish for home consumption or exportation, or having any connection whatever with a restaurant, laundry or rooming house.

Section from the Chinese Immigration Act and Regulations 1923 document describing the definition of a merchant

His registration interview must have been a nail-biting experience. He was grilled as to why he was working as a cook and not as a merchant. By the end of that gruelling interview, a note was typed on his C.I.30 announcing that Wai Ben had "ceased to belong to the exempt class" under which he was admitted. He was ordered to pay the $500 head tax retroactively or risk imprisonment and deportation. He managed to pay the fine and remain in Canada.

Wai Ben eventually owned a successful hand laundry business in Toronto. However, even if he had been operating the laundry in 1924, he still would have been fined $500.

Owners of restaurants, laundries, tailoring shops, and rooming houses were not considered "exempt" under the Act. Many of these otherwise enterprising business owners were forced to retroactively pay the head tax during the Exclusion Act registration drive or be forced to leave Canada. It was this fear that drove much of the community's opposition to the mandatory registration.

Wai Ben never told his Canadian-born children what hardships he had endured. It was only decades after he passed away that his secrets were revealed by the paper trail left behind. His family discovered that not only had Wai Ben been fined during the registration drive, but also that he had had a first wife in China, who died during the exclusion years. He never mentioned this loss and never returned to China to visit his first wife's grave.

"This is to certify that YEE WAI BUN whose ph
appears on the face hereof the sum of Five Hundred D
($500.00) he having ceased to belong to the exempt c
under which he was admitted to Canada, thus complyin
with the provisions of Section 27, ss. 1, of the
Chinese Immigration Act, 1923.

Chief Controller of Chinese Immigration.

Dated at Vancouver, B.C. this thirty-first
day of JULY, 1924."

03319

DOMINION OF CANADA

IMMIGRATION BRANCH – DEPARTMENT OF THE INTERIOR

THIS CERTIFIES THAT Yee Wai Bun whose photograph is attached hereto arrived at Vancouver B.C. on the 16 day of February 1921 and upon the representations made was admitted as exempt from head tax under the provisions of the Chinese Immigration Act. The above mentioned party claims to be a native of ... in the District of Hoi Sun of the age of 24 years. The declaration in this case is No 35851

Dated at ... on Feb 21 1921

CONTROLLER OF CHINESE IMMIGRATION

YEE Wai Ben taking a lunch break in his hand laundry shop (c. 1960) ▶
Image: Jean YEE Collection

DISAPPEARING ACTS

No. 02407
DOMINION OF CANADA
IMMIGRATION BRANCH — DEPARTMENT OF THE INTERIOR
C.I. 30
THIS CERTIFIES THAT
Ng Kwong Goon (Ng Kwong Yuen) whose photograph is attached
herein arrived or landed at Vancouver, B.C.
on the 14th day of September 1920
ex Charmer ex "Ixion"
and upon the representations made has been admitted as exempt from head tax under the provisions of the Chinese Immigration Act.
The above mentioned party claims to be a native of Sim Jong
in the district of Sin Ning
of the age of 31 years. The declaration in this case is C.I.9 No. 34555
Dated at Vancouver, B.C. on Sept 23rd 1920

No. 02909
DOMINION OF CANADA
IMMIGRATION BRANCH — DEPARTMENT OF THE INTERIOR
C.I. 30
THIS CERTIFIES THAT
WONG TSUN FUK whose photograph is attached
herein arrived or landed at Vancouver B.C.
on the 22nd day of January 1921
ex S.S. TYNDARIUS
and upon the representations made has been admitted as exempt from head tax under the provisions of the Chinese Immigration Act.
The above mentioned party claims to be a native of Fung Hung
in the district of Hoy Sun
of the age of 25 years. The declaration in this case is C.I.9 No. 35405
Dated at Vancouver on JAN 24 1921

No. 02360
DOMINION OF CANADA
IMMIGRATION BRANCH — DEPARTMENT OF THE INTERIOR
C.I. 30
THIS CERTIFIES THAT
LEE SHU JEE (LI SHIU CHEE) whose photograph is attached
herein arrived or landed at Vancouver, B.C.
on the 16th day of August 1920
ex "Empress of Asia"
and upon the representations made has been admitted as exempt from head tax under the provisions of the Chinese Immigration Act.
The above mentioned party claims to be a native of [illegible]
in the district of Hoy Sun
of the age of [illegible] years. The declaration in this case is C.I.9 No. [illegible]
Dated at Vancouver, B.C. on August 27th 1920

No. 02839
DOMINION OF CANADA
IMMIGRATION BRANCH — DEPARTMENT OF THE INTERIOR
C.I. 30
THIS CERTIFIES THAT
NG SAU YUE whose photograph is attached
herein arrived or landed at Vancouver, B.C.
on the 5th day of January 1921
ex Empress of Russia
and upon the representations made has been admitted as exempt from head tax under the provisions of the Chinese Immigration Act.
The above mentioned party claims to be a native of [illegible]
in the District of [illegible]
of the age of [illegible] years. The declaration in this case is C.I.9 No. [illegible]
Dated at Vancouver, B.C. on January 10th 1921
Controller of Chinese Immigration

It appears that an unknown but small number of Chinese who were in Canada never registered.

Adults like legal adviser **David LEW**, who publicly threatened to boycott registration, cannot be found in the C.I.44 registration records held by the government. And yet, there is significant documentary evidence he was living in Canada at the time.

We also find some evidence of failing to register in the files of a few Chinese merchants whose archives contain C.I. certificates of unrelated men that bear no registration stamps.

In Canada, merchants played outsized roles in the early community. Besides being employers, Chinese merchants also took on the roles of bankers, advocates, investors, employment brokers, and dealmakers.

A number of reasons may account for why some merchants became the custodians of someone else's C.I. certificate. Given their enormous value, the C.I.s may have been offered as collateral for a loan that was provided by the merchant. Or the documents may have simply been held by the merchant for safekeeping and were, somehow, forgotten. In some cases, the C.I. may have been offered to the merchant when the migrant decided to return home to China and therefore no longer needed the paper.

◀ WONG Sou was a Vancouver Chinatown grocer. When he died, his family discovered seven C.I. certificates issued to unknown men who had arrived in Canada under the "merchant" class and, therefore, avoided paying the head tax. All their C.I.30 certificates were discovered in pristine condition and were missing the rectangular Exclusion Act registration stamp (see right) on the back of their certificate (see far right). The lack of that rubber stamp means these men did not register in 1923–24, as mandated by the Exclusion Act. Failure to register risked a fine, imprisonment, or deportation. What happened to these men? Where did they go? *Images: Raymond S.L. WONG Collection*

Interestingly, a number of the men whose C.I.s were kept by a merchant yet bore no registration stamp had arrived in Canada only a few years before the Exclusion Act went into effect. And many owned a C.I. 30, which means they had been admitted under the "exempt" class and did not pay the head tax. (Those exempt from paying the head tax entry fee included merchants, diplomats, teachers, and clergy.)

Why did these men not register given the possible penalties for not doing so ($500 fine, jail, or deportation)? If they had entered as merchants and their businesses had failed, perhaps the fear of being discovered outweighed the risk of punishment. Perhaps they had entered Canada and returned home soon after, discouraged by the hostile environment and the impending legislation. It may be that a few had entered Canada and slipped quietly over the border to the United States – a country with its own Chinese exclusion law. Or in a few cases, the man may simply have died.

We will never know. These men just disappear from the record.

Stamp used to certify registration, as required by Section 18 of the Chinese Immigration Act, 1923

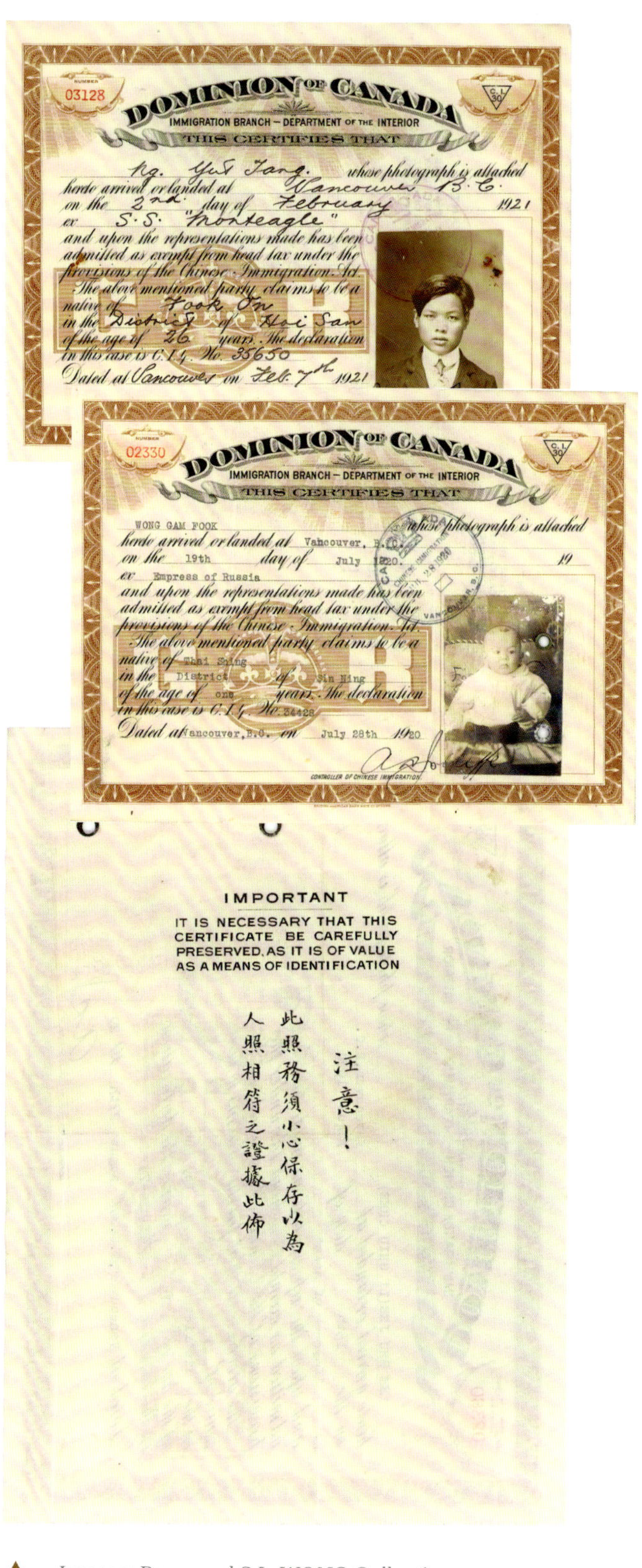

NUMBER 03128

DOMINION OF CANADA

IMMIGRATION BRANCH – DEPARTMENT OF THE INTERIOR

THIS CERTIFIES THAT

C.I. 30

Ng. Yut Tang. whose photograph is attached hereto arrived or landed at Vancouver B.C. on the 2nd day of February 1921 ex S.S. "Monteagle" and upon the representations made has been admitted as exempt from head tax under the provisions of the Chinese Immigration Act. The above mentioned party claims to be a native of Fook On in the District of Hoi San of the age of 26 years. The declaration in this case is C.I.4. No. 35650

Dated at Vancouver on Feb. 7th 1921

NUMBER 02330

DOMINION OF CANADA

IMMIGRATION BRANCH – DEPARTMENT OF THE INTERIOR

THIS CERTIFIES THAT

C.I. 30

WONG GAM FOOK whose photograph is attached hereto arrived or landed at Vancouver, B.C. on the 19th day of July 1920. 19 ex Empress of Russia and upon the representations made has been admitted as exempt from head tax under the provisions of the Chinese Immigration Act. The above mentioned party claims to be a native of Thai Shing in the District of Sin Ning of the age of one years. The declaration in this case is C.I.4. No. 34428

Dated at Vancouver, B.C. on July 28th 1920

CONTROLLER OF CHINESE IMMIGRATION

IMPORTANT

IT IS NECESSARY THAT THIS CERTIFICATE BE CAREFULLY PRESERVED, AS IT IS OF VALUE AS A MEANS OF IDENTIFICATION

注意！

此照務須小心保存以為人照相符之證據此佈

Images: Raymond S.L. WONG Collection

EXCLUSION OF CANADIAN-BORN

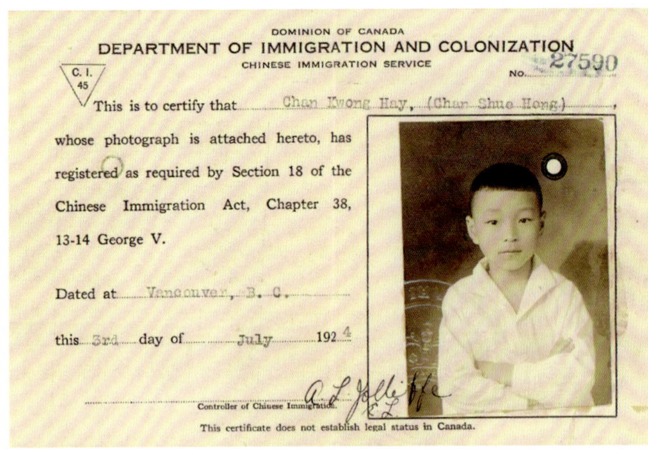

DOMINION OF CANADA
DEPARTMENT OF IMMIGRATION AND COLONIZATION
CHINESE IMMIGRATION SERVICE

C. I. 45 — No. 27590

This is to certify that Chan Kwong Hay, (Chan Shue Hong), whose photograph is attached hereto, has registered as required by Section 18 of the Chinese Immigration Act, Chapter 38, 13-14 George V.

Dated at Vancouver, B. C.

this 3rd day of July 1924

A. L. Jolliffe
Controller of Chinese Immigration.

This certificate does not establish legal status in Canada.

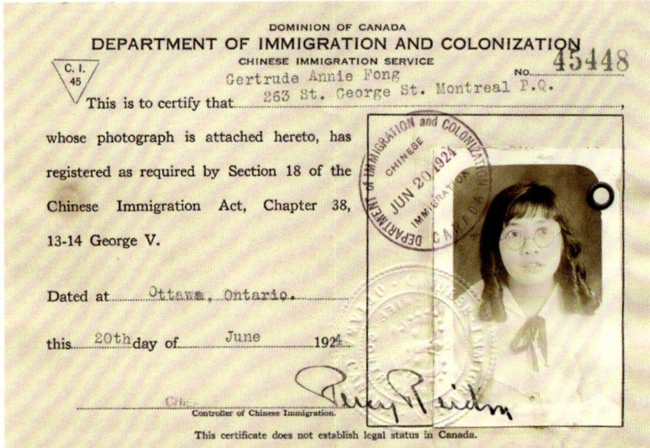

DOMINION OF CANADA
DEPARTMENT OF IMMIGRATION AND COLONIZATION
CHINESE IMMIGRATION SERVICE

C. I. 45 — No. 45448

This is to certify that Gertrude Annie Fong, 263 St. George St. Montreal P.Q., whose photograph is attached hereto, has registered as required by Section 18 of the Chinese Immigration Act, Chapter 38, 13-14 George V.

Dated at Ottawa, Ontario.

this 20th day of June 1924

Controller of Chinese Immigration.

This certificate does not establish legal status in Canada.

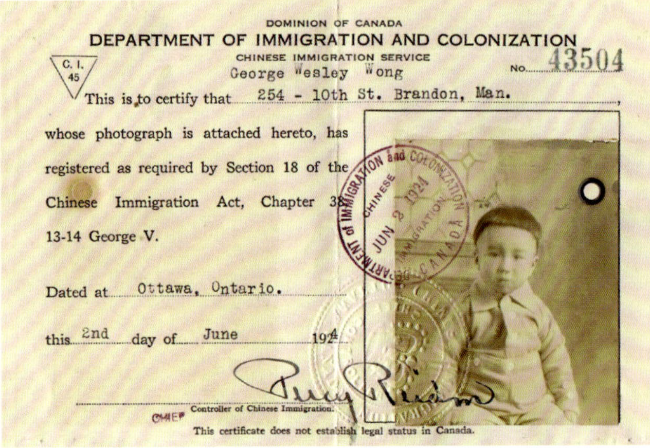

DOMINION OF CANADA
DEPARTMENT OF IMMIGRATION AND COLONIZATION
CHINESE IMMIGRATION SERVICE

C. I. 45 — No. 43504

This is to certify that George Wesley Wong, 254 - 10th St. Brandon, Man., whose photograph is attached hereto, has registered as required by Section 18 of the Chinese Immigration Act, Chapter 38, 13-14 George V.

Dated at Ottawa, Ontario.

this 2nd day of June 1924

CHIEF Controller of Chinese Immigration.

This certificate does not establish legal status in Canada.

The C.I.45 certificate was created in 1923 for the Chinese Exclusion Act registration. It was issued primarily to those who were born on Canadian soil. Since they had been born in Canada, they did not possess a C.I. landing certificate that could be examined and stamped as part of the registration process. Thus, a new C.I. was needed to verify registration.

This small, beige card – often displaying a child's photo – looked innocent at first. However, prominent across the top were the words DEPARTMENT OF IMMIGRATION AND COLONIZATION and along the bottom was the declaration "This certificate does not establish legal status in Canada."

For decades to come, this "immigration card" and its wording reminded Chinese who were born in Canada that they did not belong. Through the C.I.45, exclusion was symbolically transferred to a new generation.

Again, there is some evidence that not all Canadian-born Chinese were registered, as required. Missing C.I.44 registration forms for some Chinese born in Canada and living here at the time of the registration drive suggest that a small number of families did not register their Canadian-born children.

These parents may have refused to have their children documented simply out of protest. Others may have wanted to avoid the permanent surveillance that registration would have entailed for their Canadian children – a lifetime under the watchful eye of a hostile government.

Image: C.I.45 LING "Frank" Fung (Halifax, N.S.) ▶

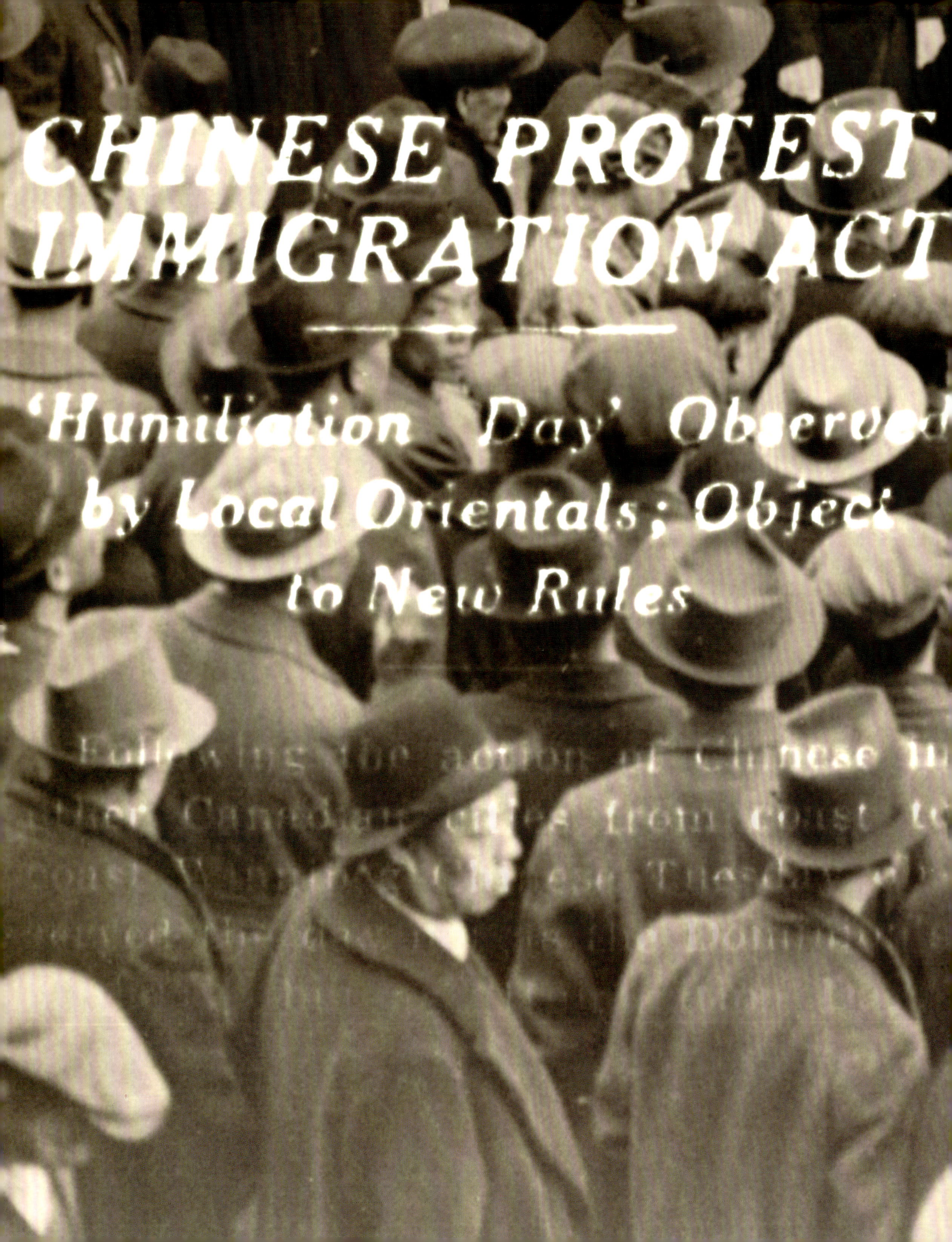

CHINESE PROTEST IMMIGRATION ACT

'Humiliation Day' Observed by Local Orientals; Object to New Rules

HUMILIATION DAY: JULY 1, 1924

As the June 30, 1924, registration deadline loomed, a national protest campaign gained some steam. The call was to have Chinese across Canada mark July 1 as "Humiliation Day" – an occasion to mourn.

Suggestions for mourning included lowering the Canadian flag, placing mourning wreaths in shop windows, wearing special lapel pins, and organizing public meetings.

The way Chinese communities across Canada marked the first "Humiliation Day" was not universal. On July 1, 1924, Victoria, Saskatoon, Winnipeg, and Halifax staged public activities such as parades and open meetings. Even Chinese in Moose Jaw, Saskatchewan, rallied to indicate their opposition to the new law.

On the other hand, Chinese in Montreal and Ottawa decided that although they vehemently opposed the new Act, they did not want to lower the flag and insult "the people of Canada by such a drastic and foolish action on the occasion of Canada's great national celebration" according to a story in Montreal's *Gazette*. In Vancouver, the largest Chinese community in Canada mounted a rather tepid response and decided to await the return of their envoy to Ottawa before taking any further action.

The Border Cities Star

WINDSOR, ONTARIO, SATURDAY, JUNE 14, 1924

Chinese "Humiliation Day" on July 1

Orientals of Canada, Angered by Registration Order, Will Festoon Homes With Wreaths of Mourning While Others Celebrate Dominion's Birthday

VICTORIA, B.C., June 14.—While Canadian flags flutter gaily from the mast-head in commemoration of Canada's birthday, July 1, Chinese flags in the city will fly at half-mast and Chinese homes will be festooned with wreaths of mourning, for, smarting under a deep sense of insult offered them by the recent immigration regulations, the Chinese residents here have designated July 1, as "Humiliation Day."

The offending regulations require that everyone in Canada of Chinese origin, regardless of birthplace, age or sex, must report to the immigration officials before June 30 for registration. They must give the salient facts of their personal history and present the department with photographs of themselves, bought at their own expense.

Fines, imprisonment and deportation are the penalties awaiting non-observance of the regulation. According to the last census 38,000 people are affected by the order.

Humiliation Day will not be confined to Victoria. It will be observed in every city in Canada where Chinese reside. It will not be observed this year alone, but every year hereafter.

Memory of their humiliation, the local Chinese assert, will not be allowed to fade.

A Chinatown street photo is overlaid with a headline from an article in *The Winnipeg Evening Tribune*, published July 2, 1924.

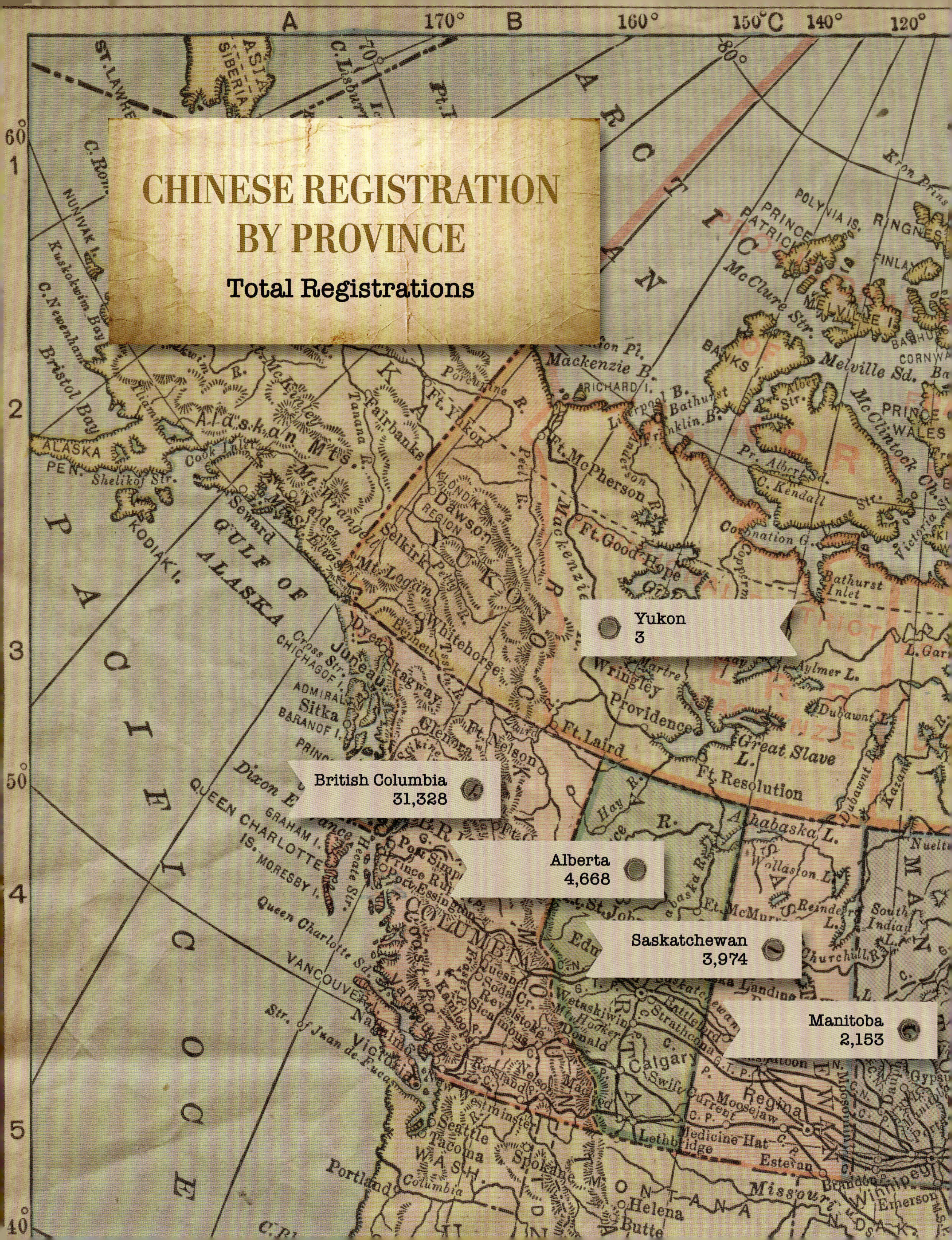
CHINESE REGISTRATION
BY PROVINCE
Total Registrations
Yukon
3
British Columbia
31,328
Alberta
4,668
Saskatchewan
3,974
Manitoba
2,153

DOMINION OF CANADA
AND
NEWFOUNDLAND
Scale of Miles
0 100 200 400 600
Important Towns are shown in Boldface Type.
Quebec
3,762
Ontario
9,395
Prince Edward Isl.
23
New Brunswick
271
Nova Scotia
405
BAFFIN BAY
DAVIS STRAIT
GREENLAND
ICELAND (Den.)
BAFFIN ISLAND
HUDSON BAY
LABRADOR
NEWFOUNDLAND
Hudson Str.
Ungava B.
Gulf of St. Lawrence
St. Johns
Churchill
York Factory
Ft. Severn
James Bay
Port Arthur

THE C.I.44

The nationwide registration of all Chinese resulted in the creation of almost 56,000 new forms with photos and personal information. These registration forms, which were completed and held by the government, were given the designation C.I.44.

Protected by privacy legislation for almost 100 years, Library and Archives Canada released all the C.I.44 records upon the request of *The Paper Trail* 100th-anniversary project and its supporters. These records, although created for the purposes of surveillance and control, today are a gold mine of information and revelations. These documents capture a community as it descended into its darkest period.

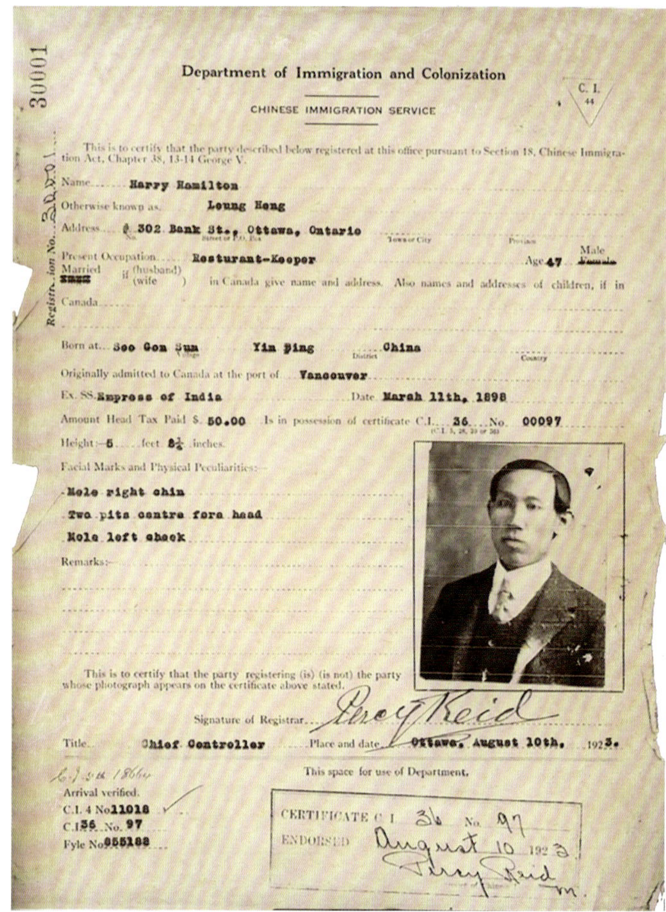

30001

Department of Immigration and Colonization

C. I. 44

CHINESE IMMIGRATION SERVICE

Registration No. 30001

This is to certify that the party described below registered at this office pursuant to Section 18, Chinese Immigration Act, Chapter 38, 13-14 George V.

Name: Harry Hamilton

Otherwise known as: Leung Hong

Address: 302 Bank St., Ottawa, Ontario

Present Occupation: Resturant-Keeper — Age 47 — Male

Married (if husband / wife in Canada give name and address. Also names and addresses of children, if in Canada)

Born at: Soo Gon Sum (Village), Yin Ping (District), China (Country)

Originally admitted to Canada at the port of: Vancouver

Ex. SS. Empress of India — Date: March 11th, 1898

Amount Head Tax Paid $ 50.00 — Is in possession of certificate C.I. 36 (C.I. 5, 28, 30 or 36) No. 00097

Height: 5 feet 8½ inches

Facial Marks and Physical Peculiarities:

- Mole right chin
- Two pits centre fore head
- Mole left cheek

Remarks:

This is to certify that the party registering (is) (is not) the party whose photograph appears on the certificate above stated.

Signature of Registrar: Percy Reid

Title: Chief Controller — Place and date: Ottawa, August 10th, 1923.

This space for use of Department.

Arrival verified.
C.I. 4 No 11018
C.I 36 No. 97
Fyle No 855188

CERTIFICATE C.I. 36 No. 97
ENDORSED August 10 1923
Percy Reid

Despite having the serial number of 30001 on his C.I.44, **Harry HAMILTON** (aka LEUNG Hong) was the first Chinese in Canada to register. He registered in Ottawa on August 10, 1923.

REGISTRATION No. ....

This is to certify that the person, whose photograph appears on the face of this certificate, has registered as required by Section 18, of the Chinese Immigration Act, 1923.

Dated at ....

this ....day of...

Image: C.I.5, WONG Shee/ Mrs. Louie JONG (Edmonton, AB)

In Calgary, **FONG Yui** had been admitted to Canada in 1921 under the exempt merchant class and, therefore, had not paid the $500 head tax. However, at the time of the Exclusion Act registration, Yui admitted he had been working only as a cook since his arrival. He was fined $500 on the spot (the amount of the head tax he should have paid when he first entered). As he only had $50 in his pocket, Yui was jailed until his friends raised the balance.

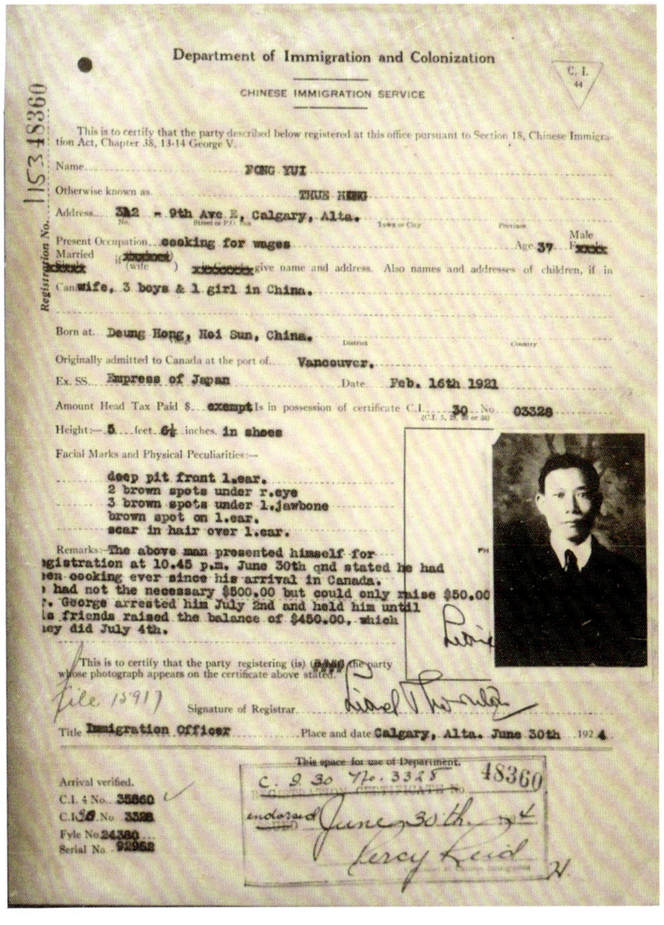

Registration No. 1153 48360

Department of Immigration and Colonization

C. I. 44

CHINESE IMMIGRATION SERVICE

This is to certify that the party described below registered at this office pursuant to Section 18, Chinese Immigration Act, Chapter 38, 13-14 George V.

Name FONG YUI

Otherwise known as THUS HING

Address 3A2 - 9th Ave E, Calgary, Alta.

Present Occupation cooking for wages Age 37 Male

Married if (wife) give name and address. Also names and addresses of children, if in Canada wife, 3 boys & 1 girl in China.

Born at Deung Hong, Hoi Sun, China.

Originally admitted to Canada at the port of Vancouver.

Ex. SS. Empress of Japan Date Feb. 16th 1921

Amount Head Tax Paid $ exempt Is in possession of certificate C.I. 30 No. 03328

Height:— 5 feet 6½ inches. in shoes

Facial Marks and Physical Peculiarities:—

deep pit front l.ear.
2 brown spots under r.eye
3 brown spots under l.jawbone
brown spot on l.ear.
scar in hair over l.ear.

Remarks:—The above man presented himself for registration at 10.45 p.m. June 30th and stated he had been cooking ever since his arrival in Canada. He had not the necessary $500.00 but could only raise $50.00 ... George arrested him July 2nd and held him until his friends raised the balance of $450.00, which they did July 4th.

This is to certify that the party registering (is) the party whose photograph appears on the certificate above stated.

File 15917

Signature of Registrar Lionel Thornley

Title Immigration Officer Place and date Calgary, Alta. June 30th 1924

This space for use of Department.

C. 9 30 No. 3325 48360

endorsed June 30th 24

Percy Reid

Arrival verified.

C.I. 4 No. 35860

C.I. 30 No. 3328

Fyle No. 24380

Serial No. 92962

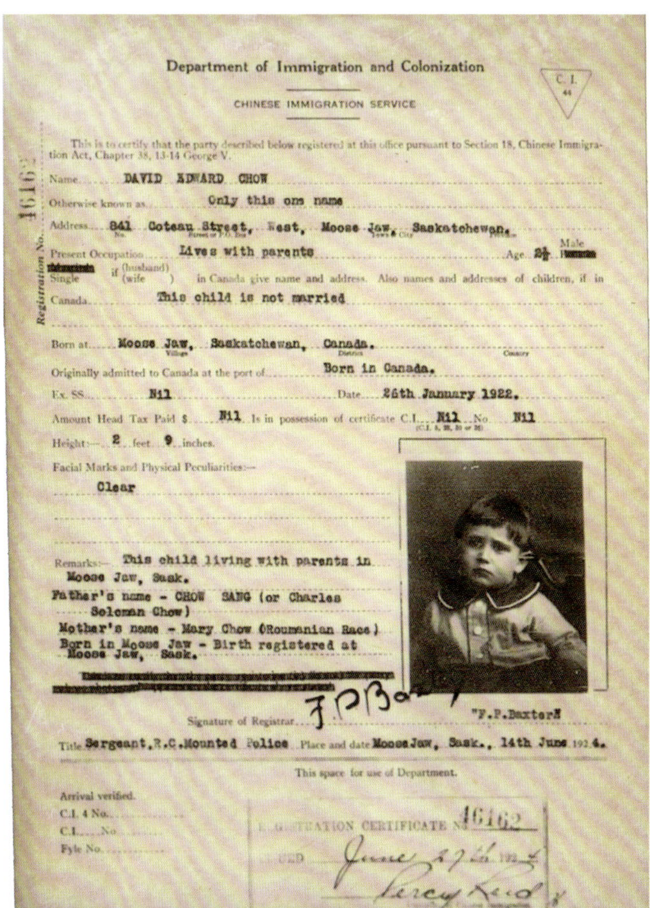

Registration No. 16162

Department of Immigration and Colonization

C. I. 44

CHINESE IMMIGRATION SERVICE

This is to certify that the party described below registered at this office pursuant to Section 18, Chinese Immigration Act, Chapter 38, 13-14 George V.

Name DAVID EDWARD CHOW

Otherwise known as Only this one name

Address 841 Coteau Street, West, Moose Jaw, Saskatchewan.

Present Occupation Lives with parents Age 2½ Male

Single if (husband) (wife) in Canada give name and address. Also names and addresses of children, if in Canada This child is not married

Born at Moose Jaw, Saskatchewan, Canada.

Originally admitted to Canada at the port of Born in Canada.

Ex. SS. Nil Date 26th January 1922.

Amount Head Tax Paid $ Nil Is in possession of certificate C.I. Nil No Nil

Height:— 2 feet 9 inches.

Facial Marks and Physical Peculiarities:—

Clear

Remarks:— This child living with parents in Moose Jaw, Sask.
Father's name - CHOW SANG (or Charles Solomon Chow)
Mother's name - Mary Chow (Roumanian Race)
Born in Moose Jaw - Birth registered at Moose Jaw, Sask.

Signature of Registrar F.P. Baxter "F.P.Baxter"

Title Sergeant, R.C.Mounted Police Place and date Moose Jaw, Sask., 14th June 1924.

This space for use of Department.

Arrival verified.

C.I. 4 No.

C.I. No.

Fyle No.

REGISTRATION CERTIFICATE No 16162

June 27th 1924

Percy Reid

Mixed-race children in Canada were registered under the Act if their father was of Chinese descent. **David E. CHOW** was not mixed race. In fact, he was a completely white child born to a Romanian mother. However, since he had been technically adopted by a Chinese father, **Charlie CHOW** of Moose Jaw, Saskatchewan, David had to be registered.

ONE DOOR LEFT OPEN

With both Canada and the United States instituting Chinese exclusion legislation, Newfoundland remained a far-off beacon of hope for Chinese looking for opportunities in North America. The Dominion of Newfoundland was not yet part of Canada when the 1923 Chinese Exclusion Act became law.

However, the region had its own Chinese head tax of $300, which it imposed in 1906. Like Canada's, the tax was designed to impede migration and resulted in a predominantly male society.

Throughout Canada's exclusion years (1923–1947), Chinese continued to trickle into Newfoundland and Labrador. However, getting there involved an arduous journey. Travelling required a train ride under armed guard through Canada or long, circuitous ocean routes to avoid Canadian ports.

About 380 head tax certificates were issued before the Newfoundland government abolished the tax in 1949 when the region joined Confederation. The majority of those head tax certificates were issued to Chinese landing in Newfoundland during Canada's exclusion period.

Those early Chinese arriving in Newfoundland found themselves in a remote outpost that was subject to harsh weather conditions and a challenging landscape.

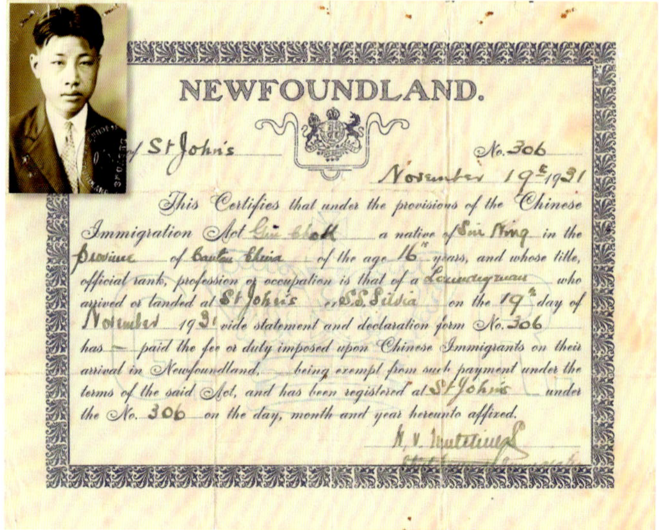

NEWFOUNDLAND.

[illegible] St John's No. 306

November 19th 1931

This Certifies that under the provisions of the Chinese Immigration Act [illegible] a native of [illegible] in the province of Canton China of the age 16 years, and whose title, official rank, profession or occupation is that of a Laundryman who arrived or landed at St John's ex S.S. Silvia on the 19th day of November 1931 vide statement and declaration form No. 306 has — paid the fee or duty imposed upon Chinese Immigrants on their arrival in Newfoundland, — being exempt from such payment under the terms of the said Act, and has been registered at St John's under the No. 306 on the day, month and year hereunto affixed.

[illegible]

Like their counterparts in Canada, work opportunities for Chinese in Newfoundland and Labrador were very limited. The early Chinese arrivals worked in industries such as fishing, mining, and gardening. However, a large number of Chinese migrants initially earned their living in hand laundries. The work was physically demanding and the pay was poor.

By the 1920s, when the laundry market became saturated, some Chinese in Newfoundland turned to operating restaurants and served both Western and Chinese dishes. These eateries became popular gathering spots for white customers and brought the concept of dining out to Newfoundland.

> ***"Newfoundland remained a far-off beacon of hope for Chinese looking for opportunities in North America."***

Members of the Newfoundland Chinese community welcome the Chinese General Consul to St. John's in 1940. ▶
Image: William PING Collection

NEWFOUNDLAND
St Pauls B.
Cow Hd
Granby I.
Bonne Bay
Sandy L.
Bay of Islands
Deer L.
Humber R.
Indian R.
L. Bathurst or Victoria
Mc Gregor L.
Flat B.
George IV L.
Wallace L.
Wilson L.
Bay L.
L. Fitz Gerald
L. Hooker
Jameson L.
Susser L.
Barrasway R.
First R.
Hall B.
Green B.
Indian Vil.
L. Badger
Thwart
F O G O
River of Exploits
Lake Lambert
Gander R.
Indian B.
Trinity B.
Freshwater B.
Bloody B.
Cape Freels
Gambo R.
Clode Sd
Newmans Sd
Goose B.
Smiths Sd
Barrow L.
Forbes L.
Random Sd
S.W. Arm
Bull B.
Sandy Har.
Placentia
Collinet
Holyrood
Trepassey
Penguin Is
THE NICKEL PHOTO PLAYS

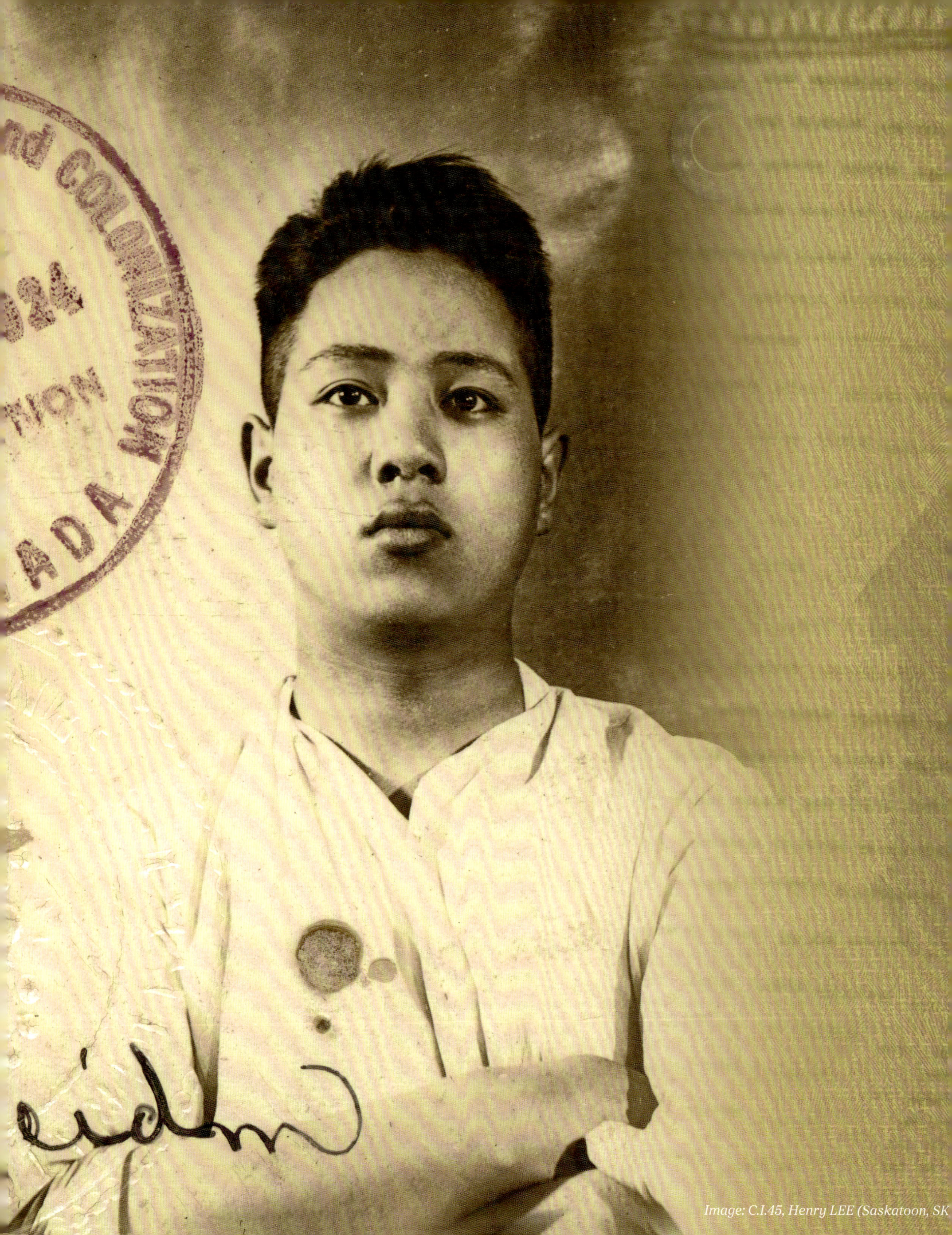

Image: C.I.45, Henry LEE (Saskatoon, SK

CHAPTER 3

THE EXPERIENCE OF EXCLUSION

DOMINION OF CANADA

IMMIGRATION BRANCH - DEPARTMENT OF THE INTERIOR

THE DEFEATED

I. THE DEFEATED

After July 1, 1924, a bleak new reality settled over the Chinese community across Canada. No one knew if or when conditions would change. No one could have predicted the Exclusion Act would remain locked in place for almost a quarter century.

Those intervening years would be miserable: the 1929 stock market crash; the decade-long Great Depression; the Japanese invasion of China; and a second global conflict that resulted in 60 million dead.

During these horrible years, the Chinese population in Canada slowly declined. As well, between 1924 and 1947, when the Act was finally repealed, a government-produced report showed that only 44 Chinese had been granted an exemption and allowed to settle in Canada.

The Exclusion Act was a great success. But what was the human cost? Here are the stories that, 100 years later, give us a glimpse into the "experience" of exclusion.

> ***"Only 44 Chinese had been granted an exemption and allowed to settle in Canada."***

July 1 was marked as "Humiliation Day" — an occasion to mourn.

Image: C.I.44, TAI Hing Gom (Kelowna, B.C.)

RETURNING HOME

Canadian Pacific's *Empress of Japan*
Image: Chung Collection, UBC

The months between the Exclusion Act becoming law (July 1, 1923) and the deadline for the mandatory registration (June 30, 1924) were a time of fear, anger, anxiety, and profound soul-searching. Those 12 months spiralled a number of Chinese men, particularly those who were seasonal and poorly paid labourers, into a deep despondency.

These men had come to Canada alone for the sole purpose of supporting their families back in China. For many, the years of broken dreams, failure, separation, poor working conditions, and poverty had been a heavy burden. Equally hard were the targeting, hatred, and isolation that went hand in hand with the unbridled racism of the time.

However, it was the 1923 Exclusion Act that finally defeated these men and brought them to their knees. Any glimmer of hope they may have held onto gave way to pessimism and fear for the future.

The archives of the Wongs' Benevolent Association in Vancouver house various letters penned by impoverished, elderly Chinese men who announced they were giving up on Canada. The letters are pleas for charity to pay for their passage home. The words offer insight into these men's battles and fears: "I am almost 70 years old [and] still struggling in places where I don't belong ... Many brothers advised me to return to China so that I would not die ... a ghost in a foreign land."

Six months before the registration deadline, goodbye notices started appearing in *The Chinese Times* newspaper. The messages were final words of resignation mixed with gratitude.

Sorrowful goodbye notices posted in *The Chinese Times* in December 1923 ▶

"I have lived overseas for several decades, rootless and drifting ... Now I am almost 70 years old, struggling with sickness, poverty, hunger, and homelessness. My heartfelt thanks to all my relatives and friends for funding my journey back to Canton. I am in a hurry and not able to visit each of you in person to say goodbye. Please let me say a few words in the newspaper to express my gratitude to you all ..."

A Toisanese fool,
MA Jung Yin, bows to you.

Last note from MA Jung Yin

○恭辭旋粵

啓者弟因家事催迫趕於月之廿七號搭詩丕亞俄國皇后船回唐乃蒙致公總堂暨權綜社董事部及各昆仲親朋或飲餞或贈厚贐藉壯行色深銘五中汽笛鳴矣不能一一登門捐別聊誌數言以表謝忱統維亮量

弟鍾基鞠躬

○鳴謝

鄙人萍飄海外數十年屢蒙知交顧愛無奈運途舛滯無能圖報於萬一慚愧實深而今年近古稀疾病頻生窮途潦倒棲食無所又復蒙親朋兄弟堪憐濟我川資回粵銘感五內茲因行色匆匆未能一一踵門拜別謹登數言於報章以申謝悃並恭候

福祉

台山痴人馬重賢鞠躬

○回國鳴謝

啓者鄙人留落英屬四十餘年一籌莫振時思歸國苦無舟資幸逢至友黃禮安照料資本以圖生業獲利歸爲我有鄙人嗜好甚深積聚全無良友見此情形發起慈善之心贈送大金十枚船脚費用兩令歸國得叙天倫之樂鄙人合家子媳孫兒感德靡涯矣愧無以報謹綴數言以鳴謝悃

域埠弟張瓜啓

CHINAMAN WAS TIRED OF LIFE

Body Found in Inlet; Note Is Translated

Identification of the decomposed body found in the ... Inlet today ...

CHINAMAN TAKES LIFE

Ching Chong, aged 24 years, was found dead in the basement of a laundry at 1395 Yonge st. last night with his body hanging from a rope attached to a beam.

CHINAMAN KILLS HIMSELF.

Hamilton, May 25.—Chin Chou, Chinaman, was found this morning hanging in the cellar of 199 York street. It is believed to be a case of suicide.

BODY OF CHINAMAN IS FOUND HANGING BACK OF RESTAURAN

(Special Dispatch to The Herald)

GOLDEN, B. C., Feb. ..—The bod... a Chinaman named Eng Luck wa... discovered yesterday morning hang... in a building to the rear of th... Sunrise restaurant. Deceased ha... the appearance of being strangled a... neck was not broken and his fe...

FROM HOPE TO NO HOPE

We also discovered story after story of Chinese men across the country, who completely lost their footing, fell into despair, and came unmoored in the 12-month period between July 1923 and June 30, 1924.

A few of these men were committed to psychiatric institutions after suddenly displaying erratic behaviour. A number of exhausted souls took their own lives, leaving behind heartbreaking notes that explained they "were tired of life." A few simply vanished off the face of the earth: not even their closest friends knew what had happened to them. Their paper trail was all that remained of their existence in Canada.

We uncovered the stories of these broken men through old newspaper articles and in coroners' records. Sometimes, we stumbled upon their lives while searching for someone else in government files. On occasion, we heard a rumour about a man who gave up, and then we searched for evidence of his life.

We felt it was important to remember that these men existed: to bear witness to their lives, to honour their memory, and to acknowledge their suffering by following their paper trail and sharing their stories 100 years later.

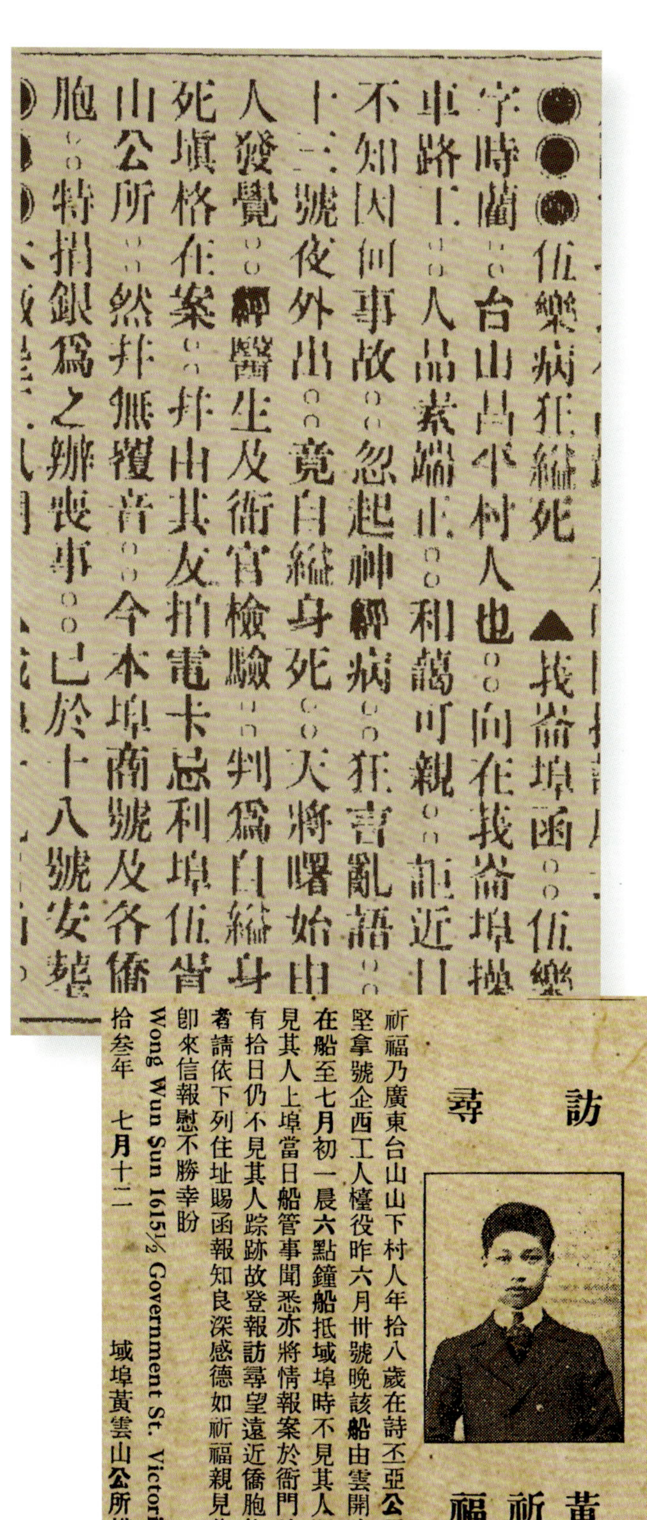

●●● 伍樂病狂縊死 ▲找崙埠函。伍樂字時蘭。台山昌平村人也。向在找崙埠操車路工。人品素端正。和藹可親。詎近日不知因何事故。忽起神經病。狂言亂語。十三號夜外出。竟自縊身死。天將曙始由人發覺。經醫生及衛官檢驗。判爲自縊身死塡格在案。幷由其友拍電卡忌利埠伍胥山公所。然幷無覆音。今本埠商號及各僑胞。特捐銀爲之辦喪事。已於十八號安葬

訪尋

黃祈福

祈福乃廣東台山山下村人年拾八歲在詩丕亞公司輪船麥堅拿號企西工人檯役昨六月卅號晚該船由雲開時其人尚在船至七月初一晨六點鐘船抵域埠時不見其人開工及不見其人上埠當日船管事聞悉亦將情報案於衙門訪尋後計有拾日仍不見其人踪跡故登報訪尋望遠近僑胞能見其人者請依下列住址賜函報知良深感德如祈福親見此廣告祈卽來信報慰不勝幸盼

Wong Wun Sun 1615½ Government St. Victoria, B. C.

拾叁年 七月十二 域埠黃雲山公所謹啟

A few of the many newspaper stories of Chinese men in Canada who committed suicide or went missing during the first year the Exclusion Act came into effect

> *"A number of exhausted souls took their own lives, leaving behind heartbreaking notes that explained they 'were tired of life.'"*

THE BREAKDOWN

The photograph of **TAI Hing Gom** (*c.* 1884–1939), taken in 1924 for his Exclusion Act registration form, speaks volumes. It shows a thin, dejected-looking man in worn-out clothes who appears too broken or ashamed to look at the camera.

We discovered Hing Gom's story when sifting through the C.I.44 registration forms. He had arrived in Canada in 1911 at age 27 and had most likely been selected by his family or village to come to Canada because he was capable and strong. After all, between his steamship fare and head tax, it was expensive to send someone who would not be a reliable breadwinner.

Between 1911 and 1923, Hing Gom worked as a labourer in various towns in British Columbia but mostly lived in the Okanagan Valley.

On July 11, 1923, a few days after the Exclusion Act became law, Hing Gom, now aged 41, suddenly broke down. He was discovered in Victoria, B.C., standing on the CPR dock crying and shouting. In his poor English, he explained he was being called to return to China, but the men who were to join him had disappeared "into the sky."

Apprehended by the police and quickly assessed by a medical team, Hing Gom was deemed to be unsound of mind. He was shipped to Essondale Hospital, a psychiatric institution located east of Vancouver.

Arriving on July 13, 1923, he would be one of several Chinese men admitted in the months leading up to the Exclusion Act registration deadline. All were labourers.

Hing Gom's hospital records described him as "quiet in manner" and "cooperative" but, at times, talkative and excitable. Although he tried to communicate in his imperfect English, hospital staff could barely understand him. Yet the hospital never bothered to seek the help of a translator despite Hing Gom asking for one. As a result, his patient file reveals little about his life before the breakdown.

More than a year after being admitted, Hing Gom was well enough to be assigned some tasks. He was stationed in the hospital's plant nursery and was described as a "very good worker" although childlike at times.

Hing Gom never left Essondale. He would die there of tuberculosis on October 28, 1939, more than 16 years after he first arrived. Due to his tuberculosis, Hing Gom spent his last few days segregated and alone. He was buried in the hospital's cemetery. There was no record of him ever having had a visitor.

A few years earlier, in 1935, about 25 other Chinese patients at Essondale were forcibly deported to China. It was the height of the Great Depression, and governments were tired of footing the bill to house these broken men. For several of these patients, the hospital had no information on where in China they were from.

"It shows a thin, dejected-looking man in worn-out clothes who appears too broken or ashamed to look at the camera."

All communications respecting patients must be addressed to
THE MEDICAL SUPERINTENDENT.

7838

Provincial Mental Hospital

New Westminster, B.C. July 13/23, 192

CANADA

To the Inspector of Municipalities,
Victoria, B.C.:

SIR:

This is to certify that Tai Hing GOM (Name of patient.)

of Victoria, B. C. (Name of town.), in .... Electoral District,

a person lawfully detained as a lunatic, was to-day admitted to the Public Hospital for the Insane.

I have been informed that his next of kin are:—

Cousin - Tai Bing Sing, of 1711 Government Street, Victoria. (Address.)

............, of ....

............, of ....

From information furnished to me by Chong Tai. (Name.)

1711 - Government St. (Address.), he appears to have property as follows:—

Real ....

Personal (including cash) Cash $111.90

Further information as to his affairs may be had from:—

(a.) As above. (Name.) (Address.)

(b.) ....

(c.) ....

I have the honour to be,
Sir,
Your obedient servant,

Medical Superintendent.

500-10-22—8892

Lethbridge Chinese

Gives Away Worldly Goods

Police Forced to Interfere with Oriental's Great Potlatch

Contents of Store Handed Out Freely in Fit of Temporary Insanity

(Special Dispatch to The Herald)

LETHBRIDGE, April 4.—Seized, as it appears, with a sudden fit of insanity, a Chinese who runs a store for the sale of Oriental silk goods here, started giving away his stock to all and sundry who entered store yesterday afternoon. The news spread with quite a number taking advantage of the opportunity ... ing into the store and ... with bales of silk ... other ...

TODAY IN THE LEGISLATURE

Resources Resolution Saturday

Premier Greenfield Will Bring In Motion at Afternoon Session of House

Proposal to ...

A FIT OF TEMPORARY INSANITY

On April 4, 1924, **LONG Woe** (*c.* 1884–unknown) of Lethbridge, Alberta, had a "fit of temporary insanity." He threw open the doors of his silk goods store and invited anyone passing by to grab whatever they wanted. Pandemonium ensued as crowds stormed the store hauling away bolts of silk fabric and other goods. The police were called to halt the looting, and Woe was carted off to the station. Their initial assessment was that the middle-aged Chinese man was having a reaction to some kind of drug and alcohol mixture.

Woe had spent the previous 10 years working on a farm outside of Medicine Hat, Alberta. In the spring of 1923, he decided to open a small store on Fifth Street in Lethbridge. He called his business "Oriental Silk Goods" and began offering an array of fine silk items (fabric, clothing, parasols, etc.) all imported from China.

It is not clear why Woe made the leap from farming to store owner in 1923. Perhaps he believed that by opening a store that imported goods, he would qualify for the status of a "merchant." Moving up to that class of Chinese immigrant would normally have meant his wife could join him in Canada without having to pay the hefty $500 head tax. Woe would have been acutely aware that the impending Exclusion Act would soon foreclose any possibility of family reunification.

Whatever his motivation, Woe's timing was off. Just as he opened his store and paid for a brief advertising campaign in the local newspaper, the door on Chinese immigration slammed tightly shut. And, by April 1924, the lobbying campaign intended to stop the mandatory Exclusion Act registration was looking like a lost cause. Rumours were circulating that even merchants would no longer be able to bring their families to Canada.

We don't know what led the 40-year-old Woe to suddenly snap, but he had no previous history of mental illness.

It was Woe's C.I.44 Exclusion Act registration form that allowed us to learn what happened to this broken man after the great giveaway at his store. He was shipped to the Provincial Mental Hospital in Ponoka, Alberta. Woe remained a patient there for almost two years and was released in February 1925. He never returned to his silk goods store. Instead, the 1931 census shows him living back in Medicine Hat and working, once again, on a farm.

> *"Woe remained a patient there for almost two years and was released in February 1925."*

A COMPLETE LOSS OF HOPE

On July 15, 1924 – two weeks after the registration period closed – **QUON Moy**, 54, took his life.

Moy (*c.* 1870–1924) arrived in Canada in 1896, a young man with big dreams. But for years, he only eked out a living as a cook in Vancouver. Like thousands of other married Chinese "bachelors," he lived a spartan life in a cramped rooming house with other men. His meagre wages vanished quickly as he struggled to repay the debt for his head tax and passage while sending what he could to his family in China.

It took Moy almost 20 years to pay off his debt and save enough to afford a brief visit back to his village in Hoiping. He returned to Canada less than a year later and never saw his homeland again.

When the 1923 Exclusion Act was passed, Moy was then in his mid-50s. His health was failing. He was out of work. A Chinatown shopkeeper noticed he was increasingly despondent.

Despite Moy's growing sense of despair, in February 1924, he dutifully complied with Section 18 of the Exclusion Act and registered himself. The requirement to bring in three copies of a recent photo would have used up what little money Moy had. The image attached to his C.I.44 registration form (shown above) reveals a smartly dressed yet sombre-looking older man.

Five months later, on the night of July 15, 1924, Moy donned his watch and stuffed his C.I.28 certificate into his jacket pocket. Under the cover of darkness, he walked to the foot of Shanghai Alley in Vancouver's Chinatown, put a rope around his neck, and dropped himself from the railing of the Georgia Street viaduct.

Moy's body was discovered the next morning. After a coroner's inquest, he was buried in a simple grave in Mountain View Cemetery. He rests there today, an ocean away from his ancestors: separated in death as he was in life.

We will never know how much the Chinese Exclusion Act added to Moy's sense of defeat and hopelessness. He would be one of several Chinese "bachelor" men who, in 1924, would take their own lives.

"Death by strangulation" was the verdict given by the coroner's jury in the case of Quoy Moy, who was found hanging to a stair railing of Shanghai alley Wednesday morning. Quon Moy had been out of work for some time, and had talked of taking his life, as he was too old to work, and in failing health.

"It took Moy almost 20 years to pay off his debt and save enough to afford a brief visit back to his village in Hoiping."

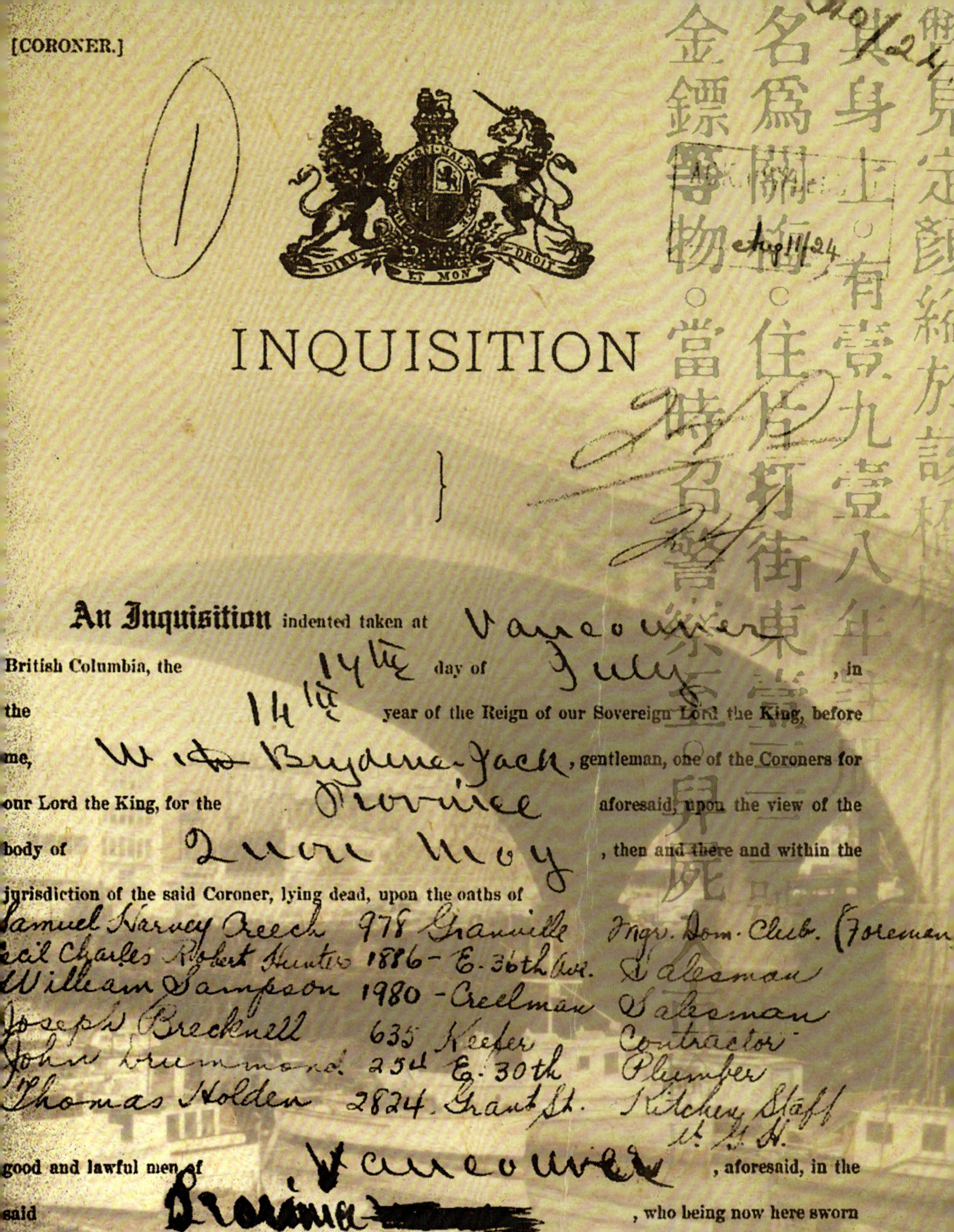

[CORONER.]

INQUISITION

An Inquisition indented taken at Vancouver British Columbia, the 14th day of July, in the 14th year of the Reign of our Sovereign Lord the King, before me, W. H. Brydone-Jack, gentleman, one of the Coroners for our Lord the King, for the Province aforesaid, upon the view of the body of Quon Moy, then and there and within the jurisdiction of the said Coroner, lying dead, upon the oaths of

Samuel Harvey Creech 978 Granville Mgr. Dom. Club. (Foreman
Cecil Charles Robert Hunter 1886 - E. 36th Ave. Salesman
William Sampson 1980 - Creelman Salesman
Joseph Brecknell 635 Keefer Contractor
John Drummond 25 E. 30th Plumber
Thomas Holden 2824 Grant St. Kitchen Staff V. G. H.

good and lawful men of Vancouver, aforesaid, in the said Province, who being now here sworn

金鏢等物。當時召警察至。見屍

Aug 11/24

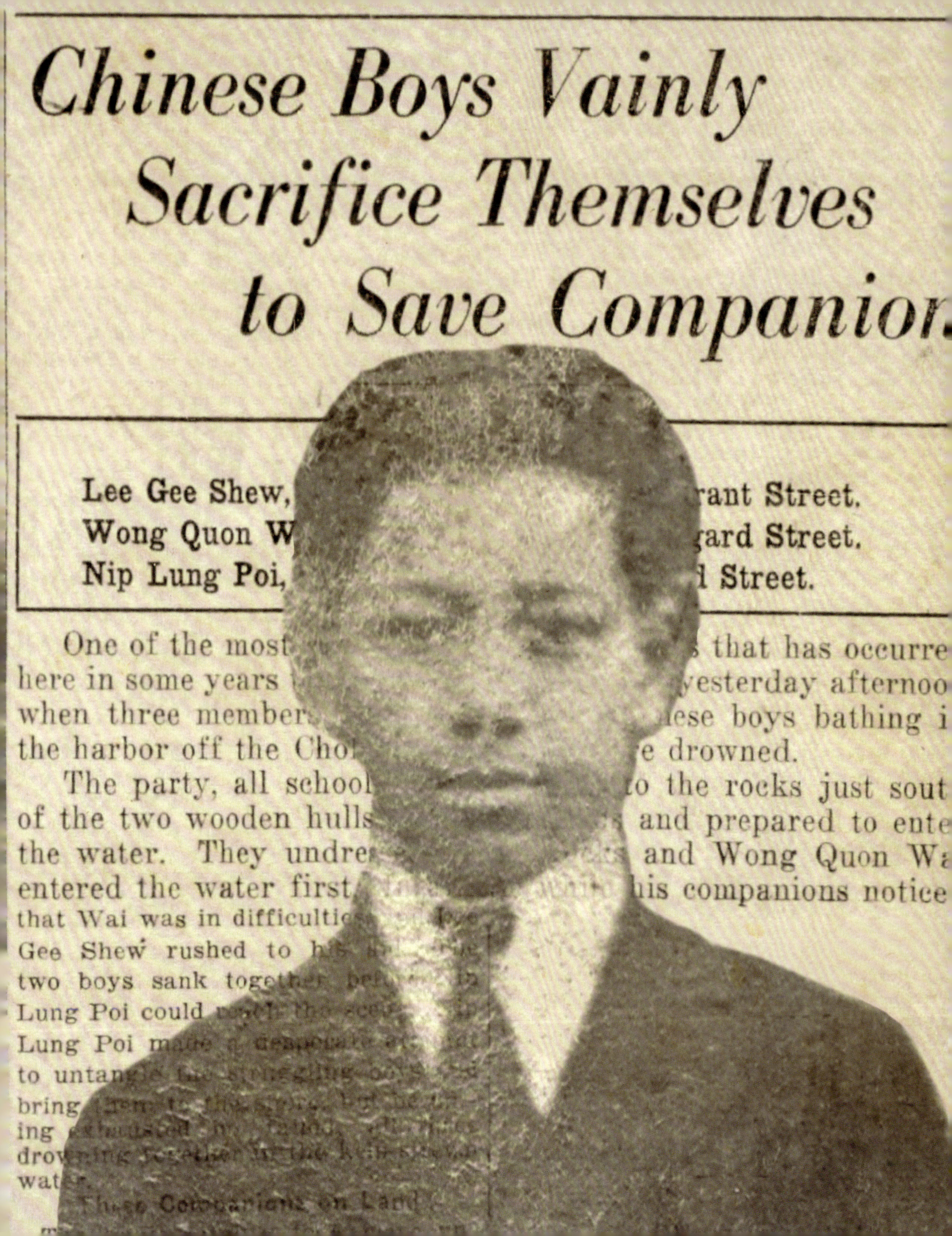

Chinese Boys Vainly Sacrifice Themselves to Save Companion

Lee Gee Shew, ... rant Street.
Wong Quon W... gard Street.
Nip Lung Poi, ... d Street.

One of the most ... that has occurre... here in some years ... yesterday afternoo... when three member... nese boys bathing i... the harbor off the Cho... e drowned.

The party, all school... to the rocks just sout... of the two wooden hulls ... and prepared to ente... the water. They undre... and Wong Quon Wa... entered the water first ... his companions notice... that Wai was in difficulties ... Gee Shew rushed to his ... two boys sank together bef... Lung Poi could reach the ... Lung Poi made a desperate ... to untangle the struggling ... bring ... ing exhausted ... drowning together in the ... water.

These Companions on Land

LIVING WITH A SECRET

Imagine having a secret that has you looking over your shoulder for the rest of your life.

In June 1922, the year before the Exclusion Act went into effect, a drowning accident in Victoria, B.C.'s inner harbour claimed the life of a 16-year-old boy named **NIP Lung Poi**, along with two of his Chinese friends. The loss stunned the community. Newspaper articles lauded the heroic efforts of the Canadian-born Lung Poi, who had died trying to rescue his friends.

Magically, just three months later, NIP Lung Poi would reappear: alive and well and applying for a C.I.9 travel permit to China. His face was different, but his name, date, and location of birth were the same. The name that had been associated with the drowning tragedy now belonged to another young man – a mystery man – who had assumed the identity of the Canadian-born teenager. NIP Lung Poi was now the name of a "paper son."

At the time, there were a few thousand "paper sons" and even some "paper daughters" who were born in China but living in Canada under false identities that had been purchased. The most sought-after identities were those of Canadian-born Chinese children who had died. Such an identity provided an extra measure of assurance since the owner would, technically, have more rights than those paper sons who were identified as foreign-born. It is not known how much was paid for Lung Poi's coveted Canadian identity.

While paper sons felt safe within the Chinese community, the penalty for being discovered by the government was expulsion. We can only imagine what the fictitious Lung Poi was feeling when he reported to the authorities to be questioned and registered for the Exclusion Act. His C.I.44 registration form, dated February 1924, noted he did not produce his Canadian birth certificate. Somehow, this paper son passed the inquisition and was issued a C.I.45 card with his photo and bearing the NIP surname.

If the real NIP Lung Poi met his tragic end in drowning, a different tragedy awaited the paper NIP Lung Poi. After years spent working as a cook in wealthy private homes in Victoria, in 1945 he was committed to the Essondale Hospital, a mental health facility near Vancouver. Records indicate he was admitted to the institution after exhibiting paranoid behaviour. Perhaps that is not surprising. The years spent shadowed by a dead boy's identity, the life of deception, and the daily prospect of discovery and deportation had engendered in him a deep fear and paranoia.

Unfortunately, the paper Lung Poi died in 1950, a decade before the government offered amnesty to those Chinese who had entered the country as paper sons. It was only in death that this second Lung Poi could finally shed his disguise and reveal his secret. On his stone grave marker is inscribed, for all time, his real name: **TSANG Sung Tsim** 曾嵩占.

◀ The real NIP Lung Poi (left) shown here in a school photo and the paper NIP Lung Poi (above) as pictured on his 1922 C.I.9 travel certificate
Image: Original NIP Lung Poi (Ontario Multicultural Society)

THE PAIN OF GUILT

LEW King (1884–unknown) was one of the successful Chinese men who made a fortune in Canada. But because of a single tragic accident, his life unravelled.

Arriving in 1911, King opened a successful jewellery store in Vancouver and became one of the wealthiest Chinese in the city. He purchased a house in a posh neighbourhood, married a Canadian-born Chinese woman, and owned a rare luxury item: a car.

On November 15, 1921, King's life changed. While King was driving, a seven-year-old white boy darted in front of his vehicle. King honked and slammed on the brakes, but the car struck the boy. King rushed the child to hospital, but the boy died.

At the inquest that followed, eyewitnesses testified that King was driving slowly and could not have stopped in time. The coroner determined King was not at fault.

Nevertheless, the accident haunted the jeweller. He turned to opium to dull the guilt. Within two years of the accident, he had gambled away his wealth and lost his house. Hoping to recoup his losses, King turned to selling opium.

In September 1923, King sold the drug to an undercover police officer, who promptly arrested him. Despite his impeccable career before the accident, there was zero tolerance for Chinese who ran afoul of the law. At his trial, the judge sentenced King to nine months at the Oakalla Prison Farm followed by immediate deportation. When the verdict was read in court, King and his wife clung to each other, weeping. King was deported to China on July 31, 1924.

Approximately 75 per cent of all Chinese who were incarcerated during the Exclusion Act registration drive were serving sentences related to drug possession.

"Arriving in 1911, King opened a successful jewellery store in Vancouver and became one of the wealthiest Chinese in the city."

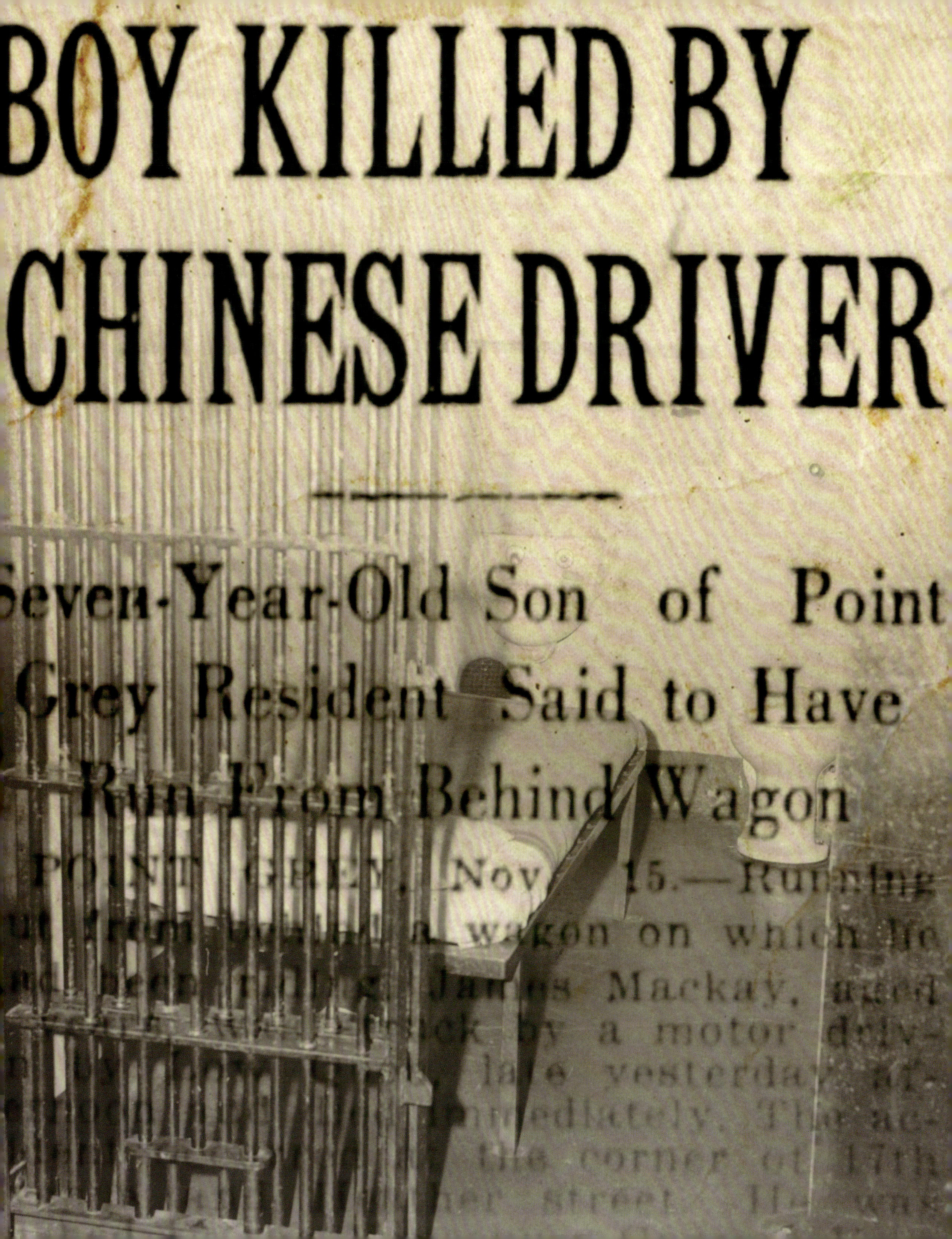

BOY KILLED BY CHINESE DRIVER

Seven-Year-Old Son of Point Grey Resident Said to Have Run From Behind Wagon

POINT GREY, Nov. 15.—Running [illegible] a wagon on which he [illegible] James Mackay, aged [illegible] by a motor deliv- [illegible] late yesterday af- [illegible] immediately. The ac- [illegible] the corner of 17th [illegible] street. He was

274

MISTAKEN IDENTITY?

Identification of individual Chinese had always been a problem for white authorities. Chinese people looked alike to them. It explains why immigration officials recorded not only the height and hair colour of a Chinese person but also their moles and scars. It also explains why Canada's first mass use of photo identification was adopted for Chinese migrants in 1912, just two years after the federal government began taking mugshots of prisoners in the penal system.

HERE'S CHINESE FUGITIVE

LEONG CHUNG

WHO is the object of a police search in Vancouver and other British Columbia points. He is charged with the murder of Constable Ernest Sargent, who died Friday of wounds alleged to have been inflicted by Leong. On his deathbed Sargent identified the Chinese from a picture, picking it out of several which were shown to him. The suspect is believed to be hiding in the city.

On November 5, 1927, at 4:30 a.m., Constable Ernest SARGENT was shot on a dimly lit street in Vancouver. On his deathbed, half delirious and drifting in and out of consciousness, the officer was shown an array of police mugshots of Chinese men. Despite the darkness at the time of the shooting, Sargent pointed to **LUNG Chong** (*c.* 1899 –unknown) as the gunman.

Based on this identification from a dying man – and despite the known challenges of white officials being able to correctly distinguish individual Chinese – police issued a warrant for the 28-year-old Chong, along with a $1,000 reward for his capture. A manhunt ensued, and Chong was arrested days later in Victoria.

Chong had arrived in Canada in 1912 at age 13. He worked as a cook but struggled to make ends meet. He was jailed at least twice, once for breaking and entering.

At the murder trial, Chong maintained his innocence. But it took only 20 minutes of deliberation for the all-white jury to declare him guilty. The judge sentenced Chong to hang in two months' time.

Mere days before Chong's scheduled execution, he was granted a new trial by the B.C. Court of Appeal, which found some of the evidence in the original trial inadmissible, including how police mugshots were used.

In his second trial, after deliberating for three hours, the all-white, all-male jury determined there was not enough evidence to convict Chong. Saved from execution, he walked away a free man.

Chong moved to Calgary. He was arrested again in 1936 for vagrancy.

> ***"It took only 20 minutes of deliberation for the all-white jury to declare him guilty."***

Image: C.I.44, LUNG Chong (Vancouver, B.C.)

CHINESE EXCLUDED

WHEN WILL THIS CRUELTY END?

On July 1, 1923
the Canadian government enacted
the Chinese Immigration Act with
43 cruel sections.

Seemingly a lifetime,
seemingly in no time,
we are now into the tenth year.

We hope all Chinese, from all walks of life
suspend your work or business on July 1
for collective remembrance.

Only together can we remember
and may one day undo
the burning humiliation and shame.

In solidarity,
Chinese Benevolent Association
June 29, 1933

Printed in *The Chinese Times*, June 30, 1933

THE SURVIVORS

II. THE SURVIVORS

In Chinese culture, the plum blossom is recognized for its remarkable ability to bloom and survive the harshest conditions of winter. The flower symbolizes perseverance, strength, and endurance. The plum blossom is the ideal metaphor to describe the vast majority of Chinese in Canada who clung on and endured through the dismal quarter century that was the exclusion period.

For this 100th-anniversary project, we collected from across Canada hundreds of surviving C.I. certificates as well as the biographies of the individuals who once carried the burden of these identity documents. Their stories, shared by their descendants, often arrived like parts of a puzzle with key pieces missing. Yet, collectively, the stories offered us a glimpse into the world between 1923 and 1947.

Fragments of these personal stories exposed the range of human experience during exclusion: tragedy, loss, survival, adaptation, and triumph. And, together, the stories revealed the impact exclusion left on the lives it touched.

All the C.I. certificates and personal stories that we crowdsourced are now available online through the University of British Columbia Library, Rare Books and Special Collections.

For this commemorative book, we could select only a few of these stories. We chose those that best conveyed the salient themes that emerged during our research. The profiles in this section reflect the range of challenges and experiences that beset those Chinese living in different areas of Canada during the long, dark winter of exclusion.

The plum blossom signifies perseverance, strength, and endurance.

"Fragments of these personal stories exposed the range of human experience during exclusion: tragedy, loss, survival, adaptation, and triumph."

Image: C.I.28, QUAN Wing Gow (Vancouver, B.C.)

MAKING INVESTMENTS

As exclusion took hold, the Chinese community felt a sense of urgency to safeguard a culture and a heritage under threat. Specifically, they wanted to ensure that Canadian-born Chinese children were taught Chinese culture, customs, and language (particularly Cantonese).

In 1923, the Wongs' Benevolent Association in Vancouver announced a campaign to expand their building in order to establish a school. In 1925, they officially opened the Mon Keang School on the third floor of their clan building in Vancouver.

By the late 1930s, Mon Keang was one of ten such schools operating in Vancouver offering elementary-level language classes. After the Second World War, it expanded to include language classes at the secondary level.

Over the many decades the school operated, thousands of Canadian-born Chinese children found themselves attending Chinese classes after public school classes and on Saturdays.

Meanwhile, several families sent their Canadian-born children back to China for an education during the early years of exclusion. And that spurred some Chinese in Canada to help fuel a building boom in China in the 1920s.

Successful merchants, such as Vancouver's **YIP Sang**, organized fundraising drives in Canada to support much-needed capital projects in Guangdong province. Sang was a major donor, but he was joined by hundreds of small donors from across the country: owners of cafes, laundries, and grocery stores, and even labourers.

Together, they helped fund the construction of important institutions such as the Taishan/Toisan Middle School, which opened in 1926. It became one of the first secondary schools in China and was renowned for its academic and athletic excellence. Nearly a century later, it still exists.

Image: Wongs' Benevolent Association ▼

A DIFFICULT DECISION

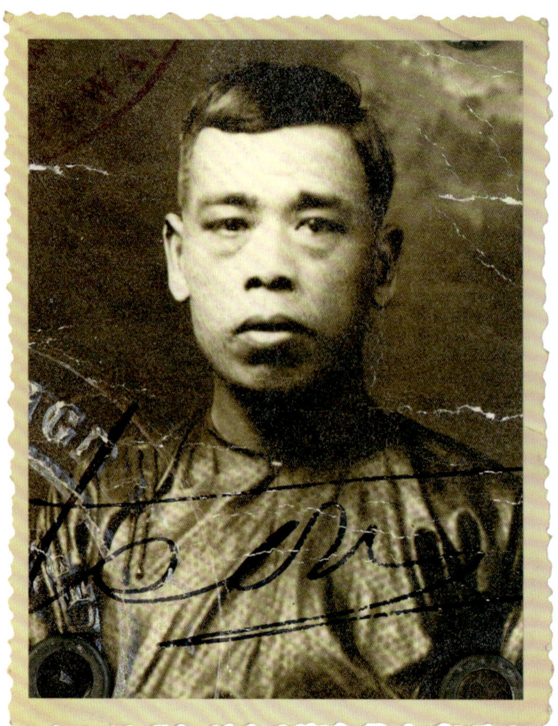

Image: C.I.28, MAH Tin Yick (Salmon Arm, B.C.)

1924 was a tragic year for **MAH Tin Yick** (1866–1949). His young wife, Jean ING, died on January 18, shortly after giving birth to their second child in Salmon Arm, B.C. Her untimely death forced Tin Yick to give up his two Canadian-born children.

Tin Yick ran a hand laundry business and worked long, gruelling hours, seven days a week. It left him with little time or energy to care for his two young daughters: five-year-old Helen and a newborn, Marian Laura. With the Exclusion Act now law, Tin Yick recognized his prospects of finding another Chinese wife were slim to none. There were approximately 1,300 adult Chinese women in all of Canada, and most were married. And, with the Exclusion Act barring all new immigration, there was no chance he could find and bring over a new bride from China to care for his children.

Tin Yick faced a painful choice: sell his daughters for adoption or surrender them to an orphanage. He chose the latter and handed the girls over to the Oriental Home and School in Victoria, run by the Methodist Church. Although this choice meant his children would be far away, it would allow him to continue to be their father and have some role in their lives.

The girls were at the Home by the time the Exclusion Act registration drive took place, and they remained there until they were adults. They were among about 210 Chinese women and children who passed through the Home's doors between its opening in 1886 and its closing in 1942.

During a time when few people owned cars, the distance between Salmon Arm and Victoria must have seemed enormous. Yet Tin Yick did his best to stay in touch with his daughters and remained a part of their lives until his death.

C.I.45 photos of Tin Yick's daughters, Helen (above left) and Marian Laura (right), taken at the orphanage in Victoria, B.C. *Images: UBC Library*

MAH Tin Yick (centre) with daughters Helen (left) and Marian Laura, *c.* 1940s

Image: Janet BRADLEY-WORTHINGTON Collection

LEE Sing Wong, 1935
Image: LEE Sing Wong family

THE SOLE BREADWINNER

LEE Sing Wong's (1893–1987) entrepreneurial spirit kept her going when she suddenly became a widowed mother with six children to feed.

The LEE family had been operating a series of laundries in various small Ontario towns, including Peterborough, Tillsonburg, Chatham, and Windsor. When Sing Wong's husband, LEE Yip, died suddenly in 1939, Sing Wong took over the Windsor laundry. Balancing the heavy, physical work of a hand laundry while caring for her children, the youngest of whom was only three years old, Sing Wong kept the shop afloat while many Chinese men, with fewer familial responsibilities, often struggled with the gruelling labour of laundry businesses.

Besides encountering sexism while running her business, Sing Wong also encountered racism. Her family remembers the time someone left a laundry bag at the front door of their shop, as was the custom. Instead of containing soiled laundry, however, the bag held a dead cat.

Hoping her family would have an easier time elsewhere, Sing Wong moved her children to Vancouver in 1944. She gave up the laundry business and, to feed her family, ran a series of small businesses throughout the next two decades, including the Mocambo Café, F&K Grocery, Domestic Produce, Duchess Confectionary, and Lee's Fish and Chips.

Sing Wong spoke little English and often had little money, but she was determined to support herself and her family. It was that resolve that kept her family together throughout the long hard years of exclusion and beyond.

LEE Sing Wong (centre) with children, 1942. Despite operating a hand laundry and being a single mother, she managed to take the family to Niagara Falls, Ontario, for a vacation.
Image: LEE Sing Wong Family

> ***Besides encountering sexism while running her business, Sing Wong also encountered racism.***

ON THEIR OWN

The death of both parents left nine Chinese Canadian children with no one to care for them.

Mabel CHOW (1900–1940) was the eldest daughter of the popular Vancouver photographer Yucho CHOW. As a child, she had spent many years working in her father's commercial studio. In 1921, Mabel married **NG Dick Jong** (1895–1937) – a man her mother felt was beneath the CHOW family's station in life. Dick was working as a chauffeur. Given there were so few adult Chinese women at the time in Canada, Mabel's mother may have felt that her daughter should have married a man of higher social status.

Despite her mother's strong opposition to the marriage, Mabel did her best to stay connected to the CHOW family. She continued to work for her father and often brought her young children to the photography studio.

The first tragedy struck the NG family in 1937 when Dick died. Two years later, a second misfortune came

when Mabel's health began to fail. It was clear she, too, was going to die. Vancouver's Social Services department made an appearance – always an ominous sign. However, rather than risk having the children split up, a local church minister and his wife intervened to keep the family together. Mabel's oldest daughter, Hazel, was only six months shy of her 18th birthday – an age at which she would be considered an adult. The minister averted the separation by convincing the authorities that the children would be fine once Hazel came of age and became their legal guardian.

On a warm August day in 1940, Mabel quietly slipped away. Her death left behind nine children ranging in age from four to 18. Four months after Mabel's death, another tragedy hit the family: the second oldest child, Beatrice, age 17, also died. The remaining children were now on their own. Some deep yet unknown divisions within the extended family meant the maternal grandparents did not offer any support to the children.

Fortunately, kind-hearted people pitched in to help. One man took the children to Chinatown's gambling dens, introduced them as NG Dick Jong's orphans, and asked for donations. One Chinese bachelor, who worked on a ferry, brought them food from the ship's kitchen. Another man, who was employed in a brothel, rode the streetcar to bring them groceries. Kindnesses like these, from bachelor men who had little themselves, helped the family pull through.

Meanwhile, the older NG children worked together to get by. Since Hazel was home with the younger siblings, she earned extra money by offering daycare services to other families. The older NG children found jobs and contributed their earnings to support the household.

◀ The NG family in 1933 with seven of what would be nine children
Image: Mamie FUNG Collection

The surviving eight NG Children in the early 1940s
Image: Mamie FUNG Collection

The children eventually moved to Chinatown, where they found cheap accommodation – $25 a month for a house that had once been a brothel. It took some time before the former clients of the brothel realized it had closed and the place was now a house full of kids.

While the NG children grew into healthy, productive adults, the pain and humiliation of being abandoned by their extended family remained with them for the rest of their lives.

LOST HALF HIS CHILDREN

For the relatively few Chinese families living in Canada during the exclusion years, having Canadian-born was children was the greatest achievement.

Even before the onset of the 1923 Exclusion Act, Canadian-born Chinese children were rare due to the impact of the exclusion laws. There were scarcely any Chinese women in Canada and few Canadian-born children. Consequently, each child was considered precious: a legacy, a guarantee for the future. Children were so highly valued that the Wongs' Benevolent Association kept a ledger in which they listed every Wong child born in Canada.

At the same time, childhood diseases were rampant. With no vaccines and overcrowded living conditions, it was not uncommon for a family to lose a child.

Simon KO BONG (1880–1957) was a businessman originally based in Victoria, B.C. He and his wife, JEW Fun Shee (*c.* 1885–1938), had brought 10 children into the world. However, their joy of securing such a promising legacy for their family would later be eclipsed by several deaths. Over the exclusion years, the KO BONG family would lose five of their ten children within a span of only seven years. All died of tuberculosis, a disease which is curable today.

Above: C.I. photos of Simon KO BONG and his wife JEW Fun Shee

The portraits of these children can be found on their C.I.45 cards issued as part of the Chinese Exclusion

Next page, top:
1922 family photo showing the KO BONG children. Missing is Garnet, who was not yet born.
Image: KO BONG Family

DOMINION OF CANADA
DEPARTMENT OF IMMIGRATION AND COLONIZATION
CHINESE IMMIGRATION SERVICE
C.I. 45
No. 26890
This is to certify that Mark Go,
whose photograph is attached hereto, has registered as required by Section 18 of the Chinese Immigration Act, Chapter 38, 13-14 George V.
Dated at Vancouver, B.C.
this 20 day of June 1924
Mark Simon June 4/28
Controller of Chinese Immigration.
This certificate does not establish legal status in Canada.

Mark (d. June 2, 1928, age 17)

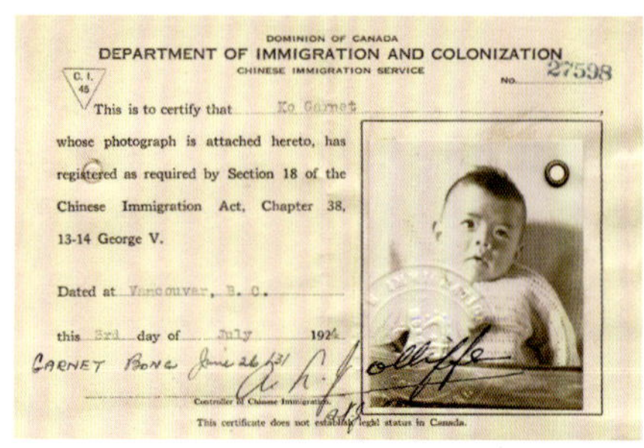

DOMINION OF CANADA
DEPARTMENT OF IMMIGRATION AND COLONIZATION
CHINESE IMMIGRATION SERVICE
C.I. 45
No. 27598
This is to certify that Ko Garnet,
whose photograph is attached hereto, has registered as required by Section 18 of the Chinese Immigration Act, Chapter 38, 13-14 George V.
Dated at Vancouver, B. C.
this 3rd day of July 1924
GARNET BONG June 26/31
Controller of Chinese Immigration.
This certificate does not establish legal status in Canada.

Garnet (d. June 24, 1931, age 7)

Act registration drive. This surveillance document, issued by the Canadian government and hated by Chinese, serves as one of the few pieces of photographic evidence that these children existed.

Simon's wife died in 1938. Despite the great sorrow their father must have felt losing so many children as well as his wife, four of his remaining children decided to enlist and play a part in the Second World War.

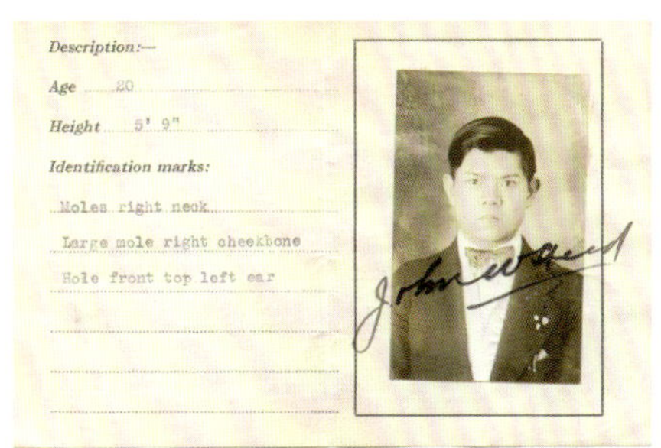

Description:—

Age 20

Height 5' 9"

Identification marks:

Moles right neck

Large mole right cheekbone

Hole front top left ear

Luke (d. May 5, 1932, age 20)

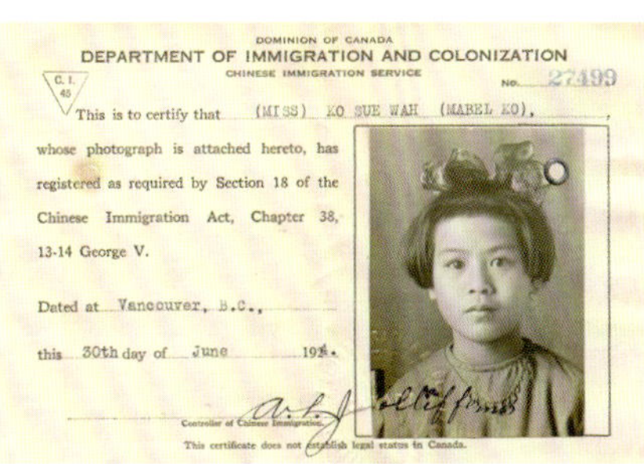

DOMINION OF CANADA

DEPARTMENT OF IMMIGRATION AND COLONIZATION

CHINESE IMMIGRATION SERVICE

C. I. 45

No. 27499

This is to certify that (MISS) KO SUE WAH (MABEL KO), whose photograph is attached hereto, has registered as required by Section 18 of the Chinese Immigration Act, Chapter 38, 13-14 George V.

Dated at Vancouver, B.C., this 30th day of June 1924.

Controller of Chinese Immigration.

This certificate does not establish legal status in Canada.

Mabel (d. January 6, 1935, age 21)

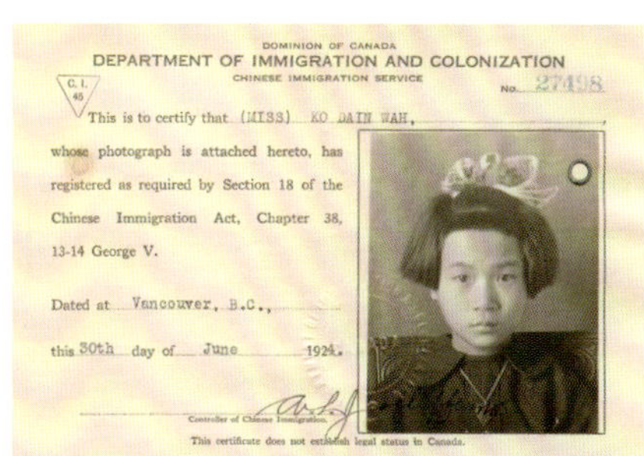

DOMINION OF CANADA

DEPARTMENT OF IMMIGRATION AND COLONIZATION

CHINESE IMMIGRATION SERVICE

C. I. 45

No. 27498

This is to certify that (MISS) KO DAIN WAH, whose photograph is attached hereto, has registered as required by Section 18 of the Chinese Immigration Act, Chapter 38, 13-14 George V.

Dated at Vancouver, B.C., this 30th day of June 1924.

Controller of Chinese Immigration.

This certificate does not establish legal status in Canada.

Ruby (d. June 24, 1935, age 20)

A PAINFUL SALE

The inability to make enough money to support one's family back in China could have devastating consequences for the wives and children in China. During the worst times – in the years of famine caused by floods or drought – many in China starved to death. Driven by poverty and desperation, some families took extreme measures to stay alive. Such was the case for **MAH Hang Foo's** small family.

Foo (1893–1977) came to Canada when he was 20 years old. He worked as a cook for the Canadian Pacific Railway in Edmonton. But due to Foo's low wages and his need to pay back the loans he took for his voyage to Canada and the $500 Chinese head tax, he was not able to save enough money to support his family back home.

To survive the severe hardship in China, Foo's wife sold their only child, a son, without Foo's knowledge. It would have been a terrible blow to Foo and likely led to a sense that he had failed in his duties to his family.

For years, Foo's two sisters in China searched tirelessly to locate Foo's son. They eventually found the child and informed Foo.

Years later, Foo's son and grandson immigrated to San Francisco, and Foo finally had a chance to meet his only child. Although distance had kept them apart, during the later years of his life, Foo's son and grandson visited him annually in Edmonton – a welcome solace to assuage the lost years of separation.

Image left: C.I.5, MAH Hang Foo (Edmonton, AB)

Image below: Library and Archives Canada

SAVED BY INDIGENOUS FRIENDS

YEE Nin Fun (*c.* 1908–1989), also known as **George YEE**, became extremely ill and almost lost his life. It was the time before universal medicare, and doctors cost money. But even if George could have afforded treatment, the white doctors in the small Alberta town where he lived would have refused to treat him simply because he was Chinese.

In 1921, George arrived in Canada alone, at the age of 13. The man assigned to be his travel guardian stole everything the young boy had, including his head tax money, and jumped ship in Japan. The result was that when George finally arrived in Canada, he was held in the detention shed for a month and a half until the immigration officers cleared him to enter.

For several years, George worked in restaurants in Gleichen, Alberta. It was while in Gleichen that he first met local Indigenous people from the Siksika Nation, who lived in the area. It is not clear how or where George became friends with some of their members. But when he became extremely ill and no white doctor would treat him, it was people from the Indigenous community who nursed him back to health. George eventually learned how to speak their language.

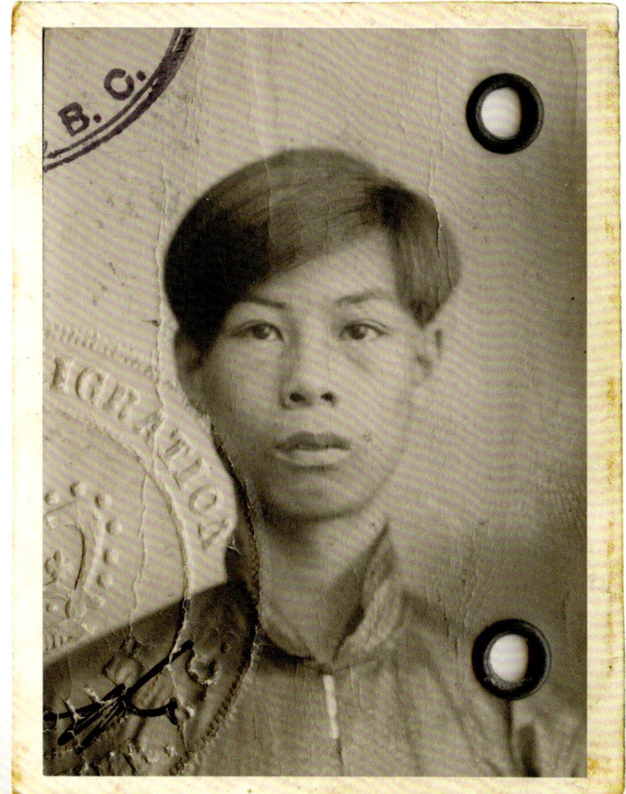

Decades later, George remembered this act of kindness, and he never let anyone in his family ever say a disparaging word against Indigenous people. A unique connection between Chinese immigrants and Indigenous people was repeated often in the survival stories of Chinese Canadians. Perhaps it was the shared experience of racism that so often bound these disparate peoples together.

Image left: C.I.5, YEE Nin Fun (Gleichen, AB)

Image below: Glenbow Library and Archives

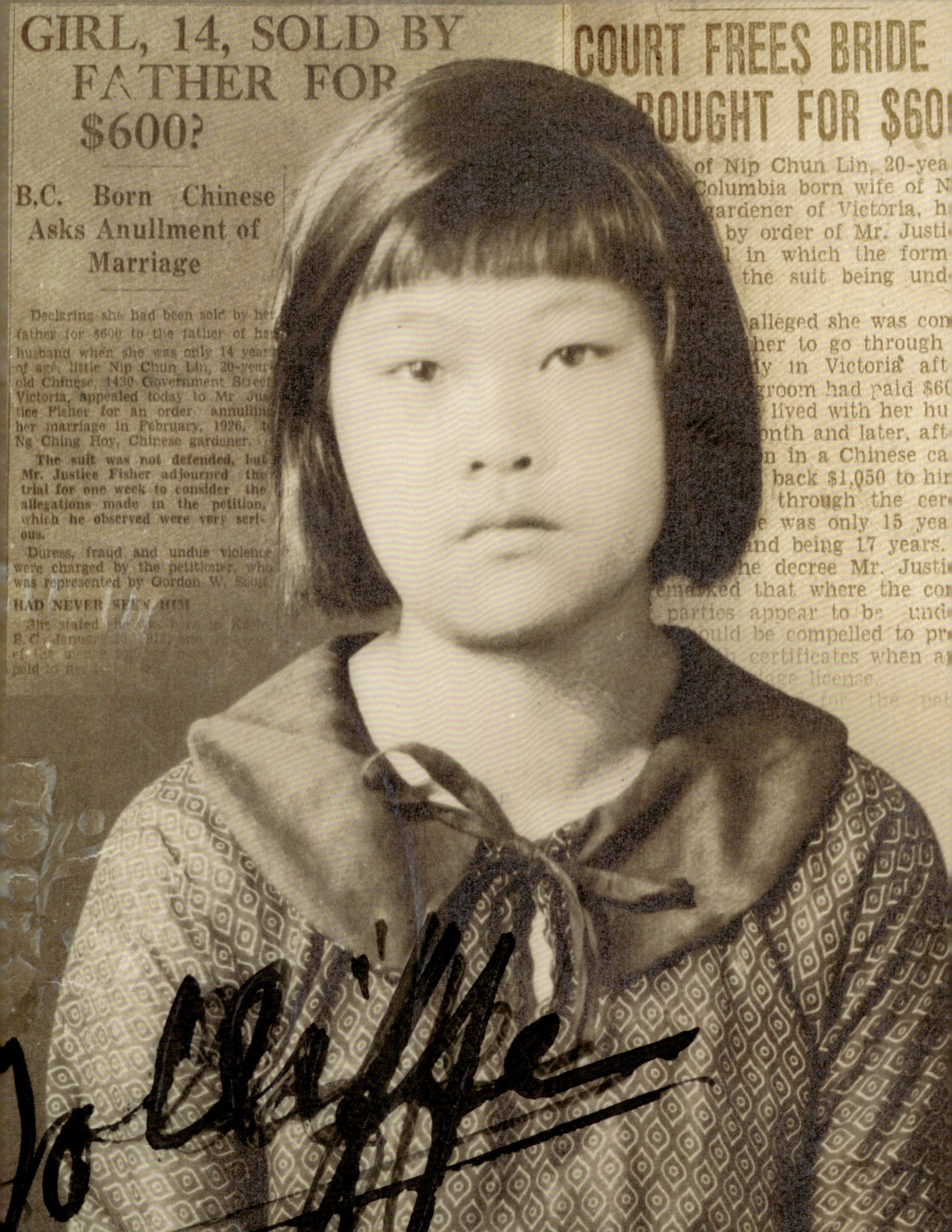

GIRL, 14, SOLD BY FATHER FOR $600?
B.C. Born Chinese Asks Anullment of Marriage
Declaring she had been sold by her father for $600 to the father of her husband when she was only 14 years of age, little Nip Chun Lin, 20-year-old Chinese, 1430 Government Street, Victoria, appealed today to Mr. Justice Fisher for an order annulling her marriage in February, 1926, to Ng Ching Hoy, Chinese gardener.
The suit was not defended, but Mr. Justice Fisher adjourned the trial for one week to consider the allegations made in the petition, which he observed were very serious.
Duress, fraud and undue violence were charged by the petitioner, who was represented by Gordon W. Scott.
HAD NEVER SEEN HIM
COURT FREES BRIDE BOUGHT FOR $600
To Cliffe

REJECTING TRADITION

Years of exclusion created a society where adult Chinese men outnumbered adult women by almost 35 to 1. Caught in the cross-currents of male desperation and competition, there was enormous pressure on some Canadian-born girls and young women to marry men chosen by their fathers. The clash of cultures, of East versus West, resulted in a few of these women publicly rebelling against the decisions over which they had no say.

Irene LEE (1911–1981), known originally as **Annie KEE** or **NIP Chun Lin**, was one such girl whose fight to extract herself from an arranged marriage made newspaper headlines. Irene had been born in Kaslo, B.C., in 1911. She was only 14 when her father committed her to marry a Chinese migrant, NG Ching Hoy, whom she had never met. Irene's father had been offered a $600 dowry by the young man's family. The money was too good to pass up, and her father gave no thought to what his Western-raised daughter might want.

Petrified by the idea of marrying a total stranger, Irene nevertheless felt pressure to go ahead with the wedding. According to the traditions in China, a daughter was expected to obey her father and not question his choices for a husband.

The couple wed in February 1926. Unknown to the clergyman, the bride and groom were too young to legally marry in British Columbia. On their marriage registration form, Irene claimed she was 18 and Ching Hoy was age 21.

Within a month of the nuptials, Irene fled the marriage. She later would accuse Ching Hoy of molestation and undue violence. However, even separated, Ching Hoy continued to harass Irene. He demanded she pay back the dowry, with interest, before he would leave her alone.

Determined to extricate herself from such a brutal man, Irene took work as a waitress. She eventually paid Ching Hoy $1,050 for her freedom, an extraordinary sum of money at the time. Yet the drama was not over.

By 1931, Irene wished to marry a widowed Vancouver businessman. She went to court to annul her first marriage. Irene told the judge how she was forced to marry a stranger. She openly shared how Ching Hoy used violence and intimidation. And she admitted that both parties were underage when they were married. The judge was surprised that Irene, a Canadian-born woman, was forced to marry someone she had never met. The judge quickly annulled her marriage.

Irene would go on to marry LEE Kepment and raise his four children as well as two of her own children. Ching Hoy also would marry again. However, for his second wife, he chose a woman who had been born in China.

"Irene took work as a waitress. She eventually paid Ching Hoy $1,050 for her freedom, an extraordinary sum of money at the time."

Image: C.I.45, Irene LEE (née Annie KEE) (Victoria, B.C.)

THE SERVANT GIRL

There were relatively few Chinese women in Canada, but a number who arrived on these shores were *mui tsai*. While the translation literally means "little sister," these girls – mostly children – were, in fact, indentured servant girls. All had been born to desperately poor families in China who were compelled to sell their young daughters to wealthier families. The practice in China was that the *mui tsai* would leave her birth family and identity behind and become a servant to her new family. The understanding was that, once she reached puberty, the adopting family would arrange a marriage and set the girl free. Her obligations would then be to her new husband.

Many of these girls, having spent their childhood in servitude and as outsiders within a family, were affected by the experience for the rest of their lives. Many would not be given an education. Most would go to their graves never knowing their real name or remembering anything about their biological family. A few would be molested by a member of the wealthy family.

Twesing LING (1899–1962) was a *mui tsai* brought to Canada at the age of 11 by the CHONG family. Today no one knows how old she was when she was purchased.

Twesing would later recall that the father of the CHONG household was kind, but the matriarch was difficult and mistreated her. It affected Twesing's confidence – she was shy all her life – and the trauma undermined her sense of belonging.

When Twesing reached puberty, the CHONG family arranged for her to marry LING How, a widower almost 20 years her senior who ran a produce farm in Nova Scotia. She would bear him seven children, but the marriage was not happy. How was surly and temperamental and showed little interest in his wife or daughters.

Despite all the hardships she endured, Twesing remained a kind, generous soul. She taught herself to read Chinese so that she could cook traditional dishes for her family. As well, every Sunday, she invited the Chinese bachelors working on the farm to join the family for a feast. She also frequently gave away produce to customers in need.

Twesing was intelligent and resourceful. She taught herself to knit by replicating other patterns. She also learned English and rode the bus to attend night school after a day's work.

But the sadness of her life story clung to her. At times, Twesing could be found shedding tears over the things she had lost in life. Despite everything, she developed a strong and loving bond with her daughters. In adversity and through her strength of character, she had forged a family for herself.

"Many of these girls, having spent their childhood in servitude and as outsiders within a family, were affected by the experience for the rest of their lives."

Twesing LING on the family fa
Nova Scotia, and (below) with
of her children
Image: Mary MOHAMMED

IN LOVE WITH A WHITE WOMAN

NUMBER 88549

DOMINION OF CANADA

NEW C.I. 5 SERIES

IMMIGRATION BRANCH – DEPARTMENT OF THE INTERIOR

RECEIVED FROM

Chew Ying Bull (Jew Ying Ball) whose photograph is attached hereto, on the date and at the place hereunder mentioned, the sum of Five Hundred Dollars being the head tax due under the provisions of the Chinese Immigration Act. The above mentioned party who claims to be a native of [illegible] in the District of [illegible] of the age of 17 years arrived or landed at Vancouver on the 3rd day of November 1918 [illegible]. The declaration in this case is C.I. 4 No. [illegible]

Dated at Ottawa on December 7th 1918

[illegible]

CONTROLLER OF CHINESE IMMIGRATION

It was difficult for society to understand or accept a Chinese man in a relationshp with a white woman. But the years of living as a single man in Toronto had taken their toll on **CHEW Ying Bull** (1901–1943), who was also known as **Henry CHU**. In the 1930s, he fell deeply in love with a white woman.

In Toronto, Henry operated a Chinese gift shop – the Oriental Trading Company. To boost sales, he sometimes would peddle items door to door. On one of these visits, he met Ethel NEALON, a white immigrant from South Africa. An unlikely romance blossomed.

When Henry's relatives in China discovered he was dating a white woman, they summoned him to China and forced him into an arranged marriage. Henry and his new wife had a son, but the Exclusion Act meant he could bring neither of them to Canada.

By the time Henry returned to Toronto, Ethel had married too and had given birth to twins. But she soon found herself drawn back to Henry, and they rekindled their affair. Eventually she left her white husband to be with Henry. In the process, Ethel lost custody of her children and gained the scorn of some in the white community who were shocked by her decision to be with a Chinese man and accused her of being a "loose woman."

The couple moved into the apartment above Henry's store. When the gift shop fell on hard times during the Great Depression, Henry closed the store. He moved the shop's contents into the basement of a rooming house he owned and crammed his young family into two rooms in the house. Shortly afterwards, Henry developed liver cancer and passed away. Ethel, now forced to raise three young mixed-race children alone, took over the running of the rooming house.

Despite society's reaction to her first interracial marriage, Ethel later wed Henry's friend, LEW Kung Chee, a Chinese barber, with whom she would have two more children.

Left: Henry CHU in Toronto
Right: Henry and Ethel, with children Mavis (front left) and Dennis, 1942
Image: Mavis GARLAND Collection

IGNORING OPPOSITION

In Montreal, as in many parts of Canada, love between a white man and a Canadian-born Chinese woman was equally scorned before and during the exclusion period.

Ann FONG (1916–2016), a talented painter working in Montreal's printing industry, fell in love with Norman Greig STANLEY, a young white man she had met at work. It was a time when even interracial romance in movies was considered taboo.

Norman was a pilot in training in the Canadian Air Force and needed his commanding officer's permission to get married. Initially, his commander denied Norman permission, warning that "mixed marriages never work." Meanwhile, some of Norman's relatives also vehemently opposed the relationship.

Despite so much opposition, the brave couple got married in 1943, and Ann became known as **Ann STANLEY**. At times, the racism the young couple experienced was so intense that they vowed never to have children "for fear the sins of the parents would be visited on the children." Even their wedding ceremony attracted a crowd of gawkers as mixed-race marriages were so rare.

Fortunately, once the war and then the Exclusion Act ended, societal attitudes softened, and the couple eventually changed their minds about having children. In 1950, Robert was born, followed by Timothy in 1953. Their younger son would go on to become a historian with a focus on anti-racism education.

Ann and Norman remained together for 59 years until Norman's death in 2003.

"In Montreal, as in many parts of Canada, love between a white man and a Canadian-born Chinese woman was equally scorned before and during the exclusion period."

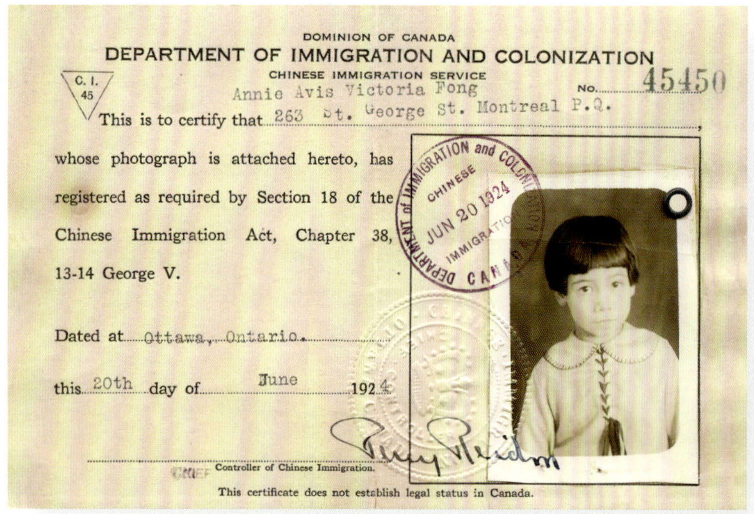

DOMINION OF CANADA
DEPARTMENT OF IMMIGRATION AND COLONIZATION
CHINESE IMMIGRATION SERVICE

C. I. 45 No. 45450

This is to certify that Annie Avis Victoria Fong 263 St. George St. Montreal P.Q.

whose photograph is attached hereto, has registered as required by Section 18 of the Chinese Immigration Act, Chapter 38, 13-14 George V.

Dated at Ottawa, Ontario.

this 20th day of June 1924

Chief Controller of Chinese Immigration.

This certificate does not establish legal status in Canada.

▲ Above: Ann's C.I.45
Right: Official wedding photo with husband Norman STANLEY, 1943 ▶
Images: Timothy STANLEY Collection

FORCED TO CHANGE NATIONALITY

There were relatively few adult Chinese women in Canada due to exclusion. Women who were Canadian-born and married a Chinese immigrant paid a high price for their union: they were forced to forfeit their Canadian status and inherited their husband's nationality. That's how Canadian-born **Jean WONG**, later known as **Jean LUMB** (1919–2002), became a Chinese national.

Born in Nanaimo, B.C., Jean attended a segregated school and grew up acutely aware of all the opportunities from which she was excluded by being Chinese. To escape the overt racism on Canada's west coast, Jean moved to Ontario at the age of 16. There she met and married Doyle LUMB, a Chinese immigrant, in 1939. However, the marriage meant Jean would be excluded from being considered a "Canadian." She was now deemed to be a Chinese national and so lost the few privileges to which her Canadian birth had entitled her.

That experience and others shaped Jean's lifelong commitment to ending anti-Chinese discrimination. After the repeal of the Chinese Exclusion Act in 1947, she fought to remove the continued limitations on family reunification. In 1957, Jean was the only woman in a delegation of Chinese Canadians who went to Ottawa to lobby Prime Minister John Diefenbaker to end the immigration restrictions. She served as the spokesperson, believing that the government would be more inclined to listen to a woman speaking about family reunification. Diefenbaker listened carefully to her argument, and the restrictions were eventually loosened.

Jean also was a staunch advocate for Toronto's Chinatown. In the 1960s, she led the efforts to stop the City of Toronto from further expropriation of the historic neighbourhood. Meanwhile, Jean and her husband ran the Kwong Chow Chop Suey House, a central Chinatown hub, for 26 years.

Jean did regain her Canadian status. In 1957, both she and her husband applied for and were granted Canadian citizenship. For her activism, Jean became the first Chinese Canadian woman to receive the Order of Canada.

"The marriage meant Jean would be excluded from being considered a 'Canadian.' She was now deemed to be a Chinese national and so lost the few privileges to which her Canadian birth had entitled her."

Jean with her husband Doyle standing in front of their first house in Toronto
Images: Jean LUMB Collection

TAI HON KONG BO LTD.
THE CHINESE TIMES
PUBLISHED DAILY EXCEPT SUNDAY, AT
443-445 CARRALL STREET VANCOUVER, B. C.
Volume 23, No. 81 Twelve Six-column Pages $9.75 Per Year
ENTERED AT THE POST OFFICE AT VANCOUVER B AS SECOND CLASS MATTER
Phone Seymour 7072 (SATURDAY,) June 30 1923 P. O. Box 280

大漢公

中華民國拾二年六

夏曆歲次癸亥年五

本社論說

慘哉今日之廣東 (鈞衡)

粵東今日不幸有孫文、亂粵也、尤不幸有孫文之子科、賣粵也、亂粵賣粵、均出於孫氏一家、我粵人何仇於孫氏而孫氏父子。竟舉我粵三千萬同胞之生命財產、犧牲之。蹂躪之、而快快於心乎、讀棄舉斥孫文借債賣產之通電、與夫孫科訓令總商會四善堂籌款文。而不怒髮衝冠罵孫氏父子之無良者、必係凉血動物也、何則、誠以孫文亂粵害粵、孫科又爲之操人勒贓。我粵人屈於暴力淫威之下。無可告訴。宰割由他、魚肉任他、觀近來孫氏父子之所行所爲。無一不橫行蠻理、大昧良心、如縣會聯合會議長程學源、任意羈縶、斷以詆毀孫文之罪、罰款十萬元而始釋放、全省米行勒令報效東米、每日三千石。總商會與九善堂各借款餉五十萬元、廣州市每戶口加捐一月、全市廟宇寺院及各項公產、均編列號數拍賣、極之人力車之苦工、須預繳兩年之餉、方准開操、瞽目老人之栖留我、與及死者寄厝停柩之場、亦次第召變、尤甚者娼妓兵費之征收、倘發交議妥覆核施行、無論如何遙

The Gazette.

MONTREAL OCTOBER 25, 1929

BIGGEST CRASH SINCE 1914 HITS STOCK MARKET

The Edmonton Bullet

JANUARY 31, 1924

WHITE GIRLS IN ORIENTAL CAFES CAUSING FURORE

Mayor Preparing Prevent ive Bylaw on Request of Many Citizens

Mayor Blatchford is preparing a bylaw which will be submitted to council in the near future which, if passed, will prohibit Chinese and Japanese proprietors of restaurants and laundries in the city from employing white female help. Several requests to this effect have been received by the mayor recently from different organizations in the city who contend that any business operated by either a Chinese or Japanese proprietor is not a proper place for white girls to work.

VANCOUVER, TUESDAY, SEPTEMBER 6, 1924

Witnesses Tell of Janet Smith's Fear Of Chinese Servant

Entering Cabinet

Assert that Housemaid Was Object of welcome Attentions On Part of Yout Girl Was Heard Singing On Morning Tragedy.

THE VANCOUVER SU

VANCOUVER, BRITISH COLUMBIA, TUESDAY, MARCH 19, 1935

Miss Hellaby Keeps Smile Under Fire

Hilda Hellaby wears the smile that won't wear off in the face of death threats, accusations of profiteering and assorted grief which is her portion as deaconess in charge of the Chinese relief dining room at 143½ East Pender Street.

Hilda Hellaby

Miss Hellaby's job involves the feeding of 600 destitute Chinese daily Two meals for each. The Anglican Board of Missions, which operates the dining room, gets a grant of 16 cents a day per person for the work.

The Nugget

NORTH BAY FEBRUARY 13, 1925

Clergyman Will Not Marry White Girl to Oriental

Toronto, Feb. 13.—(By Canadian Press—Ministerial objections prevented the marriage of Florence Fisher, aged 20, laundress to Frank Louis, Chinese chef, yesterday, despite all arrangements and the tearful protests of the intended bride. As announced yesterday, the wedding was to have taken place in the evening at a private house and Rev. Bertram Nelles, of Dale Presbyterian Church, had promised to perform the ceremony.

Just before the hour set for the wedding, a note arrived from Mr. Nelles which read: "I have decided to have nothing to do with the matter you and Miss Fisher consulted me about last evening. From a legal point of view, it may be considered right—but morally it is wrong and I refuse absolutely to take any part."

"We are going to find a minister somehow," declared Miss Fisher. "My sister has come up from Buffalo for the wedding and it's going to take place."

HON KONG BO LT
THE CHINESE TIMES
PUBLISHED DAILY EXCEPT SUNDAY AT
CARRALL STREET VANCOUVER
EDNESDAY,) January 8 1935

於廣
老華
四百
蜆灘
、已閱一星期。既無醫藥
昨早爲人破門入視。始發

THE VANCOUVER DAILY PROVINCE

July 8, 1924

Wednesday at 1:30 p.m.

OUTDOOR EFFECTS AND BASEMENT—Water ballast lawn roller, tennis net and posts, garden seats and chairs, lawn marker, mower, hose, wheelbarrow, garden and carpenters' tools, **gentlemen's bicycle**, picnic baskets and many other items, also the contents of Chinaman's bedroom.

mage: City of Vancouver Archives

BACK OF THE BUS

Johnnie SHUEN when he worked as a lumberjack
Image: Norah WONG Collection

> ***"Often the only Chinese person on a worksite, Johnnie was bullied frequently."***

In some towns in Canada, Chinese were barred from public pools, forced to sit at the back of theatres, and relegated to the back of buses.

Johnnie SHUEN (1924–1997) was born in Canada at the start of the exclusion period. Growing up in Vancouver, he remembered having to sit at the back of public buses.

With limited job prospects, Johnnie found work where and when he could and had brief stints as a lumberjack, a coal miner, and a tailor. He eventually became a construction worker.

Often the only Chinese person on a worksite, Johnnie was bullied frequently. But his ability to stand his ground against those who harassed him worked in his favour as he ended up having a long career in the construction industry. Johnnie helped build a number of large, important projects in Western Canada, including the Ironworkers Memorial Second Narrows Bridge, which connects East Vancouver with the North Shore. Johnnie was the only Chinese tradesman on that project, which saw 18 workers die during the construction of that bridge.

Reacting to the racism he experienced over and over again, Johnnie did everything to make life easier for his children, including taking them to second-hand stores to buy spelling books that would help them perfect their English. He constantly reminded his children that "if you speak perfect English without an accent, you won't be bullied as much."

LAST TO BE SERVED

Sometimes racism expressed itself in subtle ways that could still humiliate and sting.

Soo Hoo DANG (1905–1985) was the mother of seven children and helped in her husband's tailor shop in Vancouver's Downtown Eastside. In the neighbourhood was a large, bustling department store called Woodward's, a landmark in the city.

Joe DANG, one of Soo Hoo's sons, remembers: *"There are vivid recollections in my mind as a youngster and still clinging onto Mother's skirt as she tried, in vain, waiting in a shopping crowd for someone to serve her at a counter in Woodward's department store. She was constantly bypassed until there was almost no one left ... Race discrimination was very prevalent and the sight of her vainly trying to attract the attention of clerks as they continued to ignore her was devastating and disheartening. The sadness still lingers in my heart as many of these instances are flashing back the thoughts of the shabby second-class treatments endured by both Mother and Father."*

Above: Soo Hoo (centre) with son Joe DANG (left) and daughter Marion, 1945
Left: Soo Hoo at work
Images: Joe DANG Collection

LOSING EVERYTHING

Chen SING (1860–1941) was one of the early Chinese arrivals in Canada. He landed in 1876, years before the first Chinese head tax. Growing up an orphan in China and living in dire poverty, he was easily lured by the offer of steady work building a railroad in Canada.

By the time Chen arrived in Canada, he owed $800 to the labour contractor who had arranged for his transportation and employment contract. Earning only a dollar a day, it would take years for Chen to pay off that debt.

By 1885, when the western and eastern rail lines met in Revelstoke, Chen was put out of work. Rather than return to China, he settled in the B.C.'s Nicola Valley and eventually bought a ranch near Merritt. He was even fortunate to find a local Chinese woman to marry: Kitty CHIN (1878–1968) of Kamloops.

By 1924, when the Exclusion Act registration was under way, Chen was 63 years old and had six children ranging in age from 16 to a newborn. His Canadian-born children were issued C.I.45 immigration cards.

Although Chen weathered many difficult periods in his life, the decade-long Great Depression of the 1930s proved to be too much. He was forced to sell his ranch and give up on his dream of passing the land down to his children. There was little to no government assistance for Chinese at the time, so Chen relocated to Vancouver, where he lived until his death in 1941.

Like so many others who came to Canada early, Chen paid a high price to be here. He was responsible, he worked hard, and yet the Great Depression stripped him of everything he had built. Sadly, Chen did not live long enough to witness the repeal of the hated Chinese Exclusion Act.

Three of Chen's sons – George, Ernie, and Jim – would volunteer to fight for Canada in the Second World War.

“Although Chen weathered many difficult periods in his life, the decade-long Great Depression of the 1930s proved to be too much.”

◀ Chen SING in Vancouver after he was forced to give up his ranch in Merritt, c. 1940
Image: Chen SING Family

FINDING ENOUGH TO EAT

Image: C.I.5, CHOY Lee (Montreal, PQ)

During the Great Depression of the 1930s, jobs were especially hard to come by for Chinese in Canada. With few government support services available to the Chinese community, unemployment could, and sometimes did, lead to starvation, disease, and death.

Although **CHOY Lee** (1886–1974) had worked in the restaurant industry in Montreal, he had a hard time finding a job and frequently went hungry during the Depression and war years.

He once made a desperate offer to a local restaurant: he would work for free in return for a few meals. The restaurant accepted the deal but soon fired Lee. They felt the starving volunteer ate too much.

Lee learned that even the food he made for himself could be taken away at any moment. Once, while he was cooking himself a beef and daikon stew, the smell wafted over to his neighbour's quarters. The neighbour hated the odour, so he ran into Lee's kitchen and seized the pot. Lee had to chase after the man to try to get his food back.

A married bachelor, Lee had a wife and two children in China but never reunited with them after the Exclusion Act was repealed. Years later, a grandson became the only direct family member to settle in Canada. However, the years of separation had taken their toll: Lee never formed a close relationship with his grandson. It was another family that welcomed Lee into their lives and took care of his burial.

"With few government support services available to the Chinese community, unemployment could, and sometimes did, lead to starvation, disease, and death."

SHARING A PLATE

CHOY Lin (1887–1958), better known as **David Su TOYE**, was a restauranteur who owned the Mount Royal Café in Montreal. He lost most of his money when the stock market crashed in 1929 and the steady flow of diners to his restaurant dried up. However, since he owned the restaurant, he could still feed his family of five children with meals from the cafe's kitchen.

Despite the enormous scarcity during the Depression years, David developed a reputation for generosity. Whenever he could, he would give hungry neighbours a free plate of food from the restaurant so that they wouldn't starve.

Later, during the war years, business at the Mount Royal Café picked up, but it also drew the attention of criminal gangs. Envious of the restaurant's great location and its liquor licence, local mobsters pressured David to hand over the restaurant or face the consequences. He was forced to sell his restaurant at a loss, thus ending the hard-earned fruits of a life's effort. David then retired.

Despite the many struggles he faced, David managed to establish a home in Canada and set his children up for success. He saved whatever money he made from the restaurant and, after retirement, any earnings he made from the stock market to help advance his children's education. He constantly stressed to them the need to learn English first and to speak it the way "it was meant to be spoken." Only afterwards, he noted, should they learn Chinese. Every one of his children went on to graduate from McGill University.

Image: CHOY Lin, c. 1920s, CHOY Lin Family

"Whenever he could, he would give hungry neighbours a free plate of food from the restaurant so that they wouldn't starve."

A NOVEL WAY TO EARN MONEY

Number 71781

DOMINION OF CANADA

IMMIGRATION BRANCH — DEPARTMENT OF THE INTERIOR

NEW C.I. 5 SERIES

RECEIVED FROM

whose photograph is attached hereto, on the date and at the place hereunder mentioned, the sum of Five Hundred Dollars being the head tax due under the provisions of the Chinese Immigration Act. The above mentioned party who claims to be a native of in the District of of the age of years arrived or landed at VICTORIA, B.C. on the day of JUL 5 1912 19 ex The declaration in this case is C.I. 4 No.

Dated at VICTORIA, B.C. on JUL 5 1912 19

CONTROLLER OF CHINESE IMMIGRATION

Tom KONG's (1885–1975) large family made it through the dark years of exclusion and the Great Depression by entertaining audiences with daring feats of agility: his wife and several of their children became acrobats.

Tom had arrived in Canada in 1912 as an educated man and was well versed in Chinese classics, calligraphy, and traditional Chinese traditional medicines. He also could read and write English. One of his earliest known jobs was teaching in a Chinese Catholic mission school near Vancouver's Chinatown.

By 1924, Tom was married with two small children and was making a meagre living operating a restaurant in the small town of Colonsay, Saskatchewan. He also had a family back in China.

It was a chance viewing of the acrobatic troupe from China called "Wing Wing" that changed the family's aspirations and fortunes. After watching a performance of the group in the 1930s, Tom's wife, May, decided to train herself and her children in the art form. The KONG troupe became so good and so popular that they were paid to perform all over western Canada and the United States. During the Second World War, their performances helped sell war bonds. May would eventually train two groups of her children in acrobatics, and the family performed well into the late 1940s.

Meanwhile, Tom continued to do his part to help support what became a family of 13 children. After a few odd jobs, he eventually returned to the restaurant industry in 1944 when he purchased a restaurant in Burnaby, B.C., called Glenburn Fish and Chips. Its menu was a combination of Chinese food, Western dishes, and, of course, fish and chips. Tom did much of the work running the restaurant himself: often he was simultaneously the cook, waiter, and dishwasher. On occasion, when his family was not performing, they would help him in the restaurant. Tom did not retire until 1963 at the age of 78.

"May would eventually train two groups of her children in acrobatics, and the family performed well into the late 1940s."

Various images of different troupes of the KONG acrobatic family ▶
Images: Vincent KONG Collection

THE KONG ACROBATS

IMPORTANT
IT IS NECESSARY THAT
CERTIFICATE BE CAREF
PRESERVED, AS IT IS OF V
AS A MEANS OF IDENTIFIC
此照務須小
人照相符之
NUMBER
90426
IMMIGRATION BRANCH – DEPARTMENT
Fee Mee
hereto
the date and at the place hereun
Hundred Dollars being the
a native of
in the District of
years arrived or landed
30
day of
April
1921
The declaration in this case
Dated at Vancouver
CONTROLLER OF CHINESE IMMIGR
38062
April
1924

C.I. CERTIFICATES

Many C.I. certificates served several purposes. They functioned as identification papers, landing certificates, and, for many Chinese, head tax receipts. The C.I. certificates were highly coveted and valuable, and, on occasion, they were used as a form of collateral. The certificates also were a burden, a constant and shameful reminder of how Chinese were subjected to onerous monitoring.

Before and during the exclusion period, Chinese migrants in Canada would have to produce their papers on demand, so many carried their C.I. certificate with them at all times. Over the years, some certificates became worn, dog-eared, and torn. Missing pieces and held together by tape, the papers are a testament to how much these certificates were referred to in day-to-day activities.

All of these certificates are C.I.5s. This means the individual to whom it was issued was deemed to be a "labourer" and was charged the head tax.

Images: The Paper Trail Collection, UBC Library, Rare Books and Special Collections

A DEGREE MEANS NOTHING

Bill WONG's graduation from UBC Engineering
Image: Wongs' Benevolent Association

The story of **Bill WONG** (1922–2017) underscores the limited opportunities for Chinese during the exclusion years, even for those with an advanced education.

Bill was born in Vancouver, the son of a tailor. He dreamed of a professional career and studied engineering at the University of British Columbia. However, upon graduation, Bill could not find work: no engineering firm or government civil engineering department would hire him, simply because he was Chinese.

Bill decided to work for his father who ran Modernize Tailors in Vancouver's Chinatown – a shop that had opened in 1913. Eventually, Bill and his younger brother Jack, also an engineering graduate, took over the tailor shop and used their skills to make beautiful, handcrafted suits. In the 1940s and 1950s, Modernize Tailors was open seven days a week and employed about 20 people.

As the demand for custom-made suits waned in the 1960s, Bill found a new customer for Modernize Tailors: the film industry. The shop had kept the original patterns for suits from various decades and could make any style from any period. In addition, they had a large inventory of wool fabrics that dated back to the 1940s.

Bill and Modernize Tailors were renowned for their longevity: the shop operated for more than 100 years under the Wong family and, in that time, dressed mayors and movie stars. Bill was still sitting at the sewing machine well into his 90s.

Modernize Tailors became the subject of numerous news stories and documentary films, including a feature film entitled *Tailor Made: Chinatown's Last Tailors*. Bill was usually the one who spoke on behalf of the shop. He never refrained from talking about the doors of professional opportunity that were closed to him simply because he was born Chinese.

In 2014, Bill co-authored with Joanne POON a book called *A Year in China: Bill Wong's Diaries in His Father's Home Village 1936–37*. In 2017, the engineer-turned-tailor passed away in Vancouver. He was 95 years old.

> ***"No engineering firm or government civil engineering department would hire him, simply because he was Chinese."***

Bill WONG (left) and brother Jack in Modernize Tailors
Image: City of Vancouver

Original Modernize Tailors storefront in Vancouver
Image: Bill WONG Collection

A DOOR OPENS ... FINALLY

Meanwhile, the Second World War helped **Benjamin Bun WONG** (1907–1985) land a job normally reserved for white men.

Born in Victoria, Ben grew up in Vancouver. Like so many others, his experience at school was marked by the racism he faced: white children would frequently bully their Chinese and Jewish schoolmates. In response, the Jewish and Chinese students, including Ben, banded together to stave off harassment.

After elementary school, Ben needed to work to support his mother and his younger brother's education. He was never able to attend high school, and so his job opportunities were limited. Ben found work as a bellhop and elevator operator at the Marble Arch Hotel in Vancouver near the CPR station. Sometimes he worked as a bodyguard or in a fish cannery.

However, during the Second World War, young white men were drafted into the Canadian Army, and that left a shortage of workers. The shipyards began to hire Chinese workers as replacements for jobs that had previously been off limits to Asians. Ben was delighted to land a job at the Burrard Dry Dock Shipyard. He worked as a layout man, setting up plans from a blueprint and laying out the metal parts that needed welding.

After the war, this invaluable job experience served Ben well. He stayed on with Burrard Dry Dock Shipyard as it changed hands and changed names over the years. The decent salary helped Ben and his wife, Pearl, raise four children.

Above: Ben WONG with his daughter Carole
Left: Ben WONG, c. 1909
Image: Ben WONG Family Collection

> ***"The shipyards began to hire Chinese workers ... for jobs that had previously been off limits to Asians."***

ONE OF THE FEW

CHAN Chick Foo (1909–1990), later known as **Ernie CHAN**, was one of the few Chinese to be admitted during the exclusion era. According to the government's own records, only 23 Chinese were given exemptions to immigrate between 1924 and the end of 1946, the year before the Exclusion Act was repealed.

CHINESE IMMIGRATION 1906-1949

Year		Number
1906	-	70
1907	-	1,542
1908	-	2,163
1909	-	1,883
1910	-	4,667
1911	-	6,660
1912	-	6,995
1913	-	6,227
1914	-	1,600
1915	-	82
1916	-	313
1917	-	547
1918	-	2,988
1919	-	2,084
1920	-	1,329
1921	-	2,732
1922	-	810
1923	-	811
1924	-	7
1925	-	...
1926	-	...
1927	-	2
1928	-	1
1929	-	1
1930	-	...
1931	-	...
1932	-	1
1933	-	1
1934	-	1
1935	-	...
1936	-	...
1937	-	1
1938	-	...
1939	-	...
1940	-	...
1941	-	...
1942	-	...
1943	-	...
1944	-	...
1945	-	...
1946	-	8
1947	-	21
1948	-	76
1949	-	803
	TOTAL	44,436

Exclusion Years

Immigration Branch (RG 76, Volume 122, File 23635, part 9)

PUBLIC ARCHIVES
ARCHIVES PUBLIQUES
CANADA

Likely Ernie felt driven to prove himself deserving of the rare opportunity he had been granted. In Canada, he became a devoted teacher and was well known for his extensive community involvement.

Growing up in China, Ernie attended an American boarding school. His talents drew the attention of Canadian missionaries, who sponsored him to come to Canada. Ernie arrived here in 1928 and was the only Chinese person allowed to immigrate that year.

Ernie joined his sister in Moose Jaw and worked in a fruit store to earn money. He graduated from the University of Saskatchewan with a degree in mechanical engineering. However, he never found work as an engineer.

Instead, he discovered his calling as a teacher. From 1939 until 1974, Ernie taught high school. Over his long career, he taught everything from drafting and engineering to navigation and surveying. At one point, 15 of the 16 drafting teachers in Saskatchewan were his former students.

In his spare time, Ernie was involved in a variety of community groups, interests, and causes, including the arts. For many years, he could be seen, twice a day, in front of the *Star Phoenix* newspaper offices hand-painting the latest news headlines on the building.

For his service, Ernie received many awards, including being named a Member of the Order of Canada in 1984. Today we are left to wonder if Ernie's enormous dedication to his community was partly driven by a desire to prove himself deserving of the rare opportunity he was granted in 1928.

Image: C.I.30, CHAN Chick Foo (Saskatoon, SK) ▶

FROM LAUNDRY TO NOODLES

LEE Hee Chong (1883–1954), also known as **LEE Fat Sing**, rose from being a laundryman in a small Quebec town to running Wing's Noodles Ltd. in Montreal, a leading producer of Chinese noodles and foods.

LEE Hee Chong in 1914
Background image: Richmond LAM

It wasn't always a smooth road. After Hee Chong landed in Canada in 1903, he moved to Saint-Jean-sur-Richelieu. He worked long, gruelling hours helping to operate a hand laundry, all the while dreaming of running his own business one day.

Hee Chong's big break came when he moved to Montreal and became a partner and a manager of Wing Lung, an import-export trading company. He eventually earned enough to buy a ticket back to China, where he married and had a daughter. Being a co-owner of an import-export business now meant he was a bona fide "merchant" and could bring his family to Canada without having to pay a head tax for their entry. In 1915, his wife and daughter arrived. The Chinese family, a rare sight in Montreal, would eventually have six more children, all boys.

The Second World War hit the Wing Lung business hard when shipments from China were cut off. It was Hee Chong's oldest son, Arthur, who had an idea to keep the family business afloat. He founded Wing Hing Lung, a noodle manufacturing business, which later became known as Wing's Noodles Ltd. The Montreal Chinatown company did well and slowly expanded its product line to include sauces, wraps, and even cookies. Eventually, Wing's became a recognized brand name, helped, in no small part, by the fact that several generations of Canadians who dined at Chinese restaurants would be offered a Wing's fortune cookie at the end of their meal.

Hee Chong died in 1954, not long after the repeal of the Exclusion Act. In 2024, Wing's Noodles was still operated by his descendants.

THE COURAGE TO SUE

Once his produce store in downtown Vancouver became successful, **QUAN Wing Gow** (1891–1969) used the fruits of his labour to support the Chinese Canadian community and his relatives.

Gow established Parkview Produce on Robson Street the same year the Exclusion Act took effect. To be first in line to buy the best produce from market garden wholesalers, he was out of the house by 4:00 a.m. each day. Gow delivered produce right to his customers' front doors and to restaurants. Locals appreciated his chatty nature and gave him the English name "Harry."

Once his business was well established, Gow found ways to support his community. He employed fellow villagers and relatives. He helped newcomers settle in and was active in community organizations. He was regularly featured in *The Chinatown News*. The success of his business also enabled him to raise his entire family in Canada – a wife and six children – a rare feat for a Chinese man.

Gow also had a strong sense of justice and stood up for his extended family. In 1933, one of his cousins, QUAN Wing Fun, died in a produce truck accident. A few years later, in 1937, a brother of Wing Fun, QUAN Shim, also was killed on the job when his produce truck was hit by a speeding vehicle. The teenage driver of the other vehicle was charged with manslaughter. However, after two trials, he was found not guilty.

Outraged over the verdict and concerned that Shim's family in China had lost the income they needed to survive, Gow decided to sue the young driver. It was not common for Chinese in Canada to bring cases against white Canadians. Chinese were barred from becoming lawyers, and it could be difficult and expensive to find a white lawyer willing to take on their cases. But Gow's determination to press the case won his cousin's family a settlement of $1,000.

Harry QUAN, 1931
Image: Walter QUAN Collection

ENT OF IMMIGRATION AND COLONIZATION

CHINESE IMMIGRATION

C. I.
9

rning thereto.

Kong

Where I have resided

ENT OF IMMIGRATION AND COLONIZATION

CHINESE IMMIGRATION BRANCH

No. 44457

NOV 23 1922

To the Controller of Chinese Immigration,

Port of Vancouver

I hereby give notice that I desire to leave Canada with the intention of returning thereto.

My proper name is GIN WING DEN

I first came to Canada in the year 1919 Vancouver - Emp Japan - Feb.

My place of residence in Canada is Vancouver

My present occupation is that of Student

My place of birth was Shang Lee Hung

My present age is 17

DEPARTMENT OF MINES AND RESOURCES

IMMIGRATION BRANCH

28th Oct 1947

Vancouver, B.C.

om I would refer you for correctness

(Signature of Chinese Person.)

Particulars and photograph

this day.

Dated at Vancouver

THE FREQUENT TRAVELLER

Number 89085

DOMINION OF CANADA

IMMIGRATION BRANCH – DEPARTMENT OF THE INTERIOR

C.I. 5 New Series

RECEIVED FROM

Gin Wing Den whose photograph is attached hereto, on the date and at the place hereunder mentioned, the sum of Five Hundred Dollars being the head tax due under the provisions of the Chinese Immigration Act. The above mentioned party who claims to be a native of Shang Lee Hung in the District of Sun Ning of the age of 14 years arrived or landed at Vancouver on the 4th day of February 1919 ex Em Japan The declaration in this case is C.I. 9 No. [illegible]

Dated at Vancouver on Feb 4th 1919

[illegible]

CONTROLLER OF CHINESE IMMIGRATION

During the exclusion years, it was no small feat to go back and forth to China to visit family. Travelling by ship was the only option. The journey was long and expensive. It could include train fare to Vancouver; the cost of the ship ticket; the gifts for family; and the lost wages for the months away from work. As well, Chinese who planned to return to Canada had to obtain a C.I.9 travel permit and provide a recent photo of themselves. These travel permits generally limited the amount of time a Chinese migrant could be away to two years.

Many Chinese men visited China only once or twice between the early 1920s and the late 1940s, when exclusion was repealed. Some did not return at all. However, there were a few men who managed to make three or four trips back. These men were not necessarily wealthy merchants. Many worked as labourers, but they shared a determination to see their families as much as they could.

GIN Wing Den (1905–1971) was one such frequent traveller. Arriving in Canada in 1919, he first worked as a houseboy for a wealthy Vancouver family, where he learned to speak perfect English. Later, he became the chief cook for a steamship line that plied the waters between Vancouver and Alaska.

Only three years after his arrival in Canada, Wing Den took his first trip back to China. The entry stamps on the back of his C.I.5 certificate show that he returned from abroad in the years 1924, 1928, and 1932. Each visit resulted in a child. His visit from 1930 to 1932 yielded two children.

When Wing Den returned to Canada in 1932, he had no idea he would have to wait almost 15 more years to see his family again. Japan's invasion of China, followed by the outbreak of the Second World War, meant most overseas travel was suspended. To compound the prolonged separation, men in Canada faced challenges staying in touch with and sending money home to their families. There were long periods when men in Canada fretted as they did not know what was happening to their loved ones in China.

When the war ended and the Exclusion Act was repealed, Wing Den made a final trip to China in 1948. The visit resulted in yet another child. Ultimately, Wing Den was able to bring his wife and four of his children to Canada. His eldest son was refused entry because he was over the age of 18. Meanwhile, his youngest son would have the distinction of being the only child in the family who was raised by two parents.

◀ Top: Photo of Wing Den's wife and children, taken in China during the family's "separation" years (*c.*1934)
Image: GIN Wing Den Family

◀ Bottom: The C.I.9 travel permits issued to GIN Wing Den for his numerous trips to China between 1922 and 1947
Images: Library and Archives Canada

Image: City of Vancouver Archive

Extra! **The Brantford Expositor** Extra!

WITH WHICH IS INCORPORATED "THE BRANTFORD COURIER"

LISHED 1853 BRANTFORD, MONDAY, DECEMBER 8, 1941

WAR RAGES IN THE PACIFIC

rning, Attacked U. S. Possessions

本埠新

中華會館佈告紀念會館為七一僑恥紀念照得自民國十二年「否一日。加政府頒行華

Japan To Take Nanking'

—Yosuke Matsuoka

lust Control All Chin To Save It from Communism'

ew Bombardment Rakes Shangha

By Associated Press

IENTSIN, Oct. 14.—In an inter today, Yosuke Matsuoka, presi of the South Manchuria Rail Company, disclosed that Japa control of the whole of Chin

The Citizen

Cloudy. Warm ...27; Sets 7.37

Ottawa, Canada, Monday, September 4, 1939.—24 Pages. Price Three Cents.

Temperatures Yesterday Min. 60; Max. 79

R ATHENIA, BOUND FOR CANADA, TORPEDOED; AIN AND FRANCE NOW AT WAR WITH GERMANY

Said To Be Figh

UBC Soccer Star Reported Missing

FO. Quan J. Louie, 24, a winner of the Big Block letter in soccer at UBC, has been reported missing in action overseas, according to word received here by his mother, Mrs. H. J. Louie.

At the time of his enlistment in November, 1942, he was studying commerce at the University.

He graduated as a bombardier with a commission in October, 1943, and went overseas last January. He was lost in a flight near the end of his first tour of operations.

FO. Q. J. Louie

oronto Tongs Sheath Sword Chinese Unite Against Japan

e ancient broadsword of the s is officially sheathed. took an invasion of their home- to make Canadian Chinese ze that all must stand together. e new association, to be known e Chinese Patriotic league, con- of several tongs and associa-

Victoria Daily Times

SEPTEMBER 18, 1943

LAC. Arthur Ernest Jung, Victoria Chinese flier, who gained his wings recently at No. 7 S.F. T.S., Macleod, Alta., attained the highest standing of his class and received the gold identification bracelet. The Yat Ching Jung's, his parents, live at 728 Cormorant Street. His elder brother, Capt.

THE EVENING

OTTAWA NOVEM

OD CANADIANS . . THREE—The recruiter in Winnipeg got the surprise of his life his trio walked in and asked to enlist "for anywhere." Their mother is in China. ave not seen her since outbreak of war.

Lee, restaurant owner of Souris, Man., they are left to right: Alfie, Jimmy and Willie. The three Chinese-Canadians enlisted the same day, when they were "old enough to fight," they explained. And they took it the hard way ... infantry

Case for B.C. Chinese

: I am one of the hundreds of Ca-born Chinese, of military age, and the privilege of fighting and dying nada.

re are a few facts I would like to place before the Canadian public to get their opinion on whether it does or does not constitute British fair play.

First—Although my parents are naturalized British subjects for 35 years and myself born in Vancouver, I am not allowed to vote. The government's reason, I am an alien.

Second—Although I possess registered firearms for hunting, I must surrender them by September 30, 1940. The government's reason, I am an alien.

Third—Canada adopts conscription, therefore I am drafted into the Canadian army. The government's reason, I am a British subject.

(Chinese-Canadians were not accepted when they volunteered for active service).

Although the above are all true facts

LIVING FRUGALLY

Jack LUM, 1960
Image: Jack LUM Family

Kew Shing LUM (*c.* 1880–1961), known as **Jack LUM**, was both industrious and frugal. It was how he survived. He spent his life in Canada living in a small shack, rent-free, on a farmer's land in Ladner, B.C. There was no electricity and no running water. He would collect wood from the riverbank and drinking water from a public tap nearby.

In his early years, Jack raised pigs. To feed those pigs, he would ride to Vancouver with his horse and cart, sleeping most of the way. The horse was so well trained that it had memorized the 27-kilometre route. Once in Vancouver, Jack would make his rounds collecting food scraps from various restaurants to feed his pigs.

In fact, Jack's frugality was so well known it earned him the nickname "Tight-Fisted Lum." But he was also generous and often helped his friends financially. When Jack passed away at the age of 81, his heirs paid tribute to his generosity by forgiving some of the loans still owing to him.

KEEPING THE FAMILY FED

Sometimes to survive, one must improvise. **POON Lin Tsing** (1886–1927) was 26 years old and very pregnant when she made the long and arduous ocean voyage to Canada in 1912. Within two weeks of landing, she gave birth to her first child, a boy named Paul WONG (1912–2004).

Image: C.I.30, POON Lin Tsing (Whitecourt, AB)

The family was constantly on the move, travelling among British Columbia, Alberta, and Saskatchewan, where they owned or operated a series of small-town cafes, grocery stores, and laundries.

Prairie life was tough, and there was little to no support for any Chinese who fell on hard times. Once, when there was no food for Lin Tsing to feed her family, she got desperate: she killed a skunk and fed it to the family for supper. It is not known whether the family knew it was feasting on a very rare dish of meat. Fortunately her butchering skills were good, and she managed to miss the scent glands.

Her eldest son, Paul WONG, would later own and operate two restaurants in Alberta. Neither eatery offered skunk on their menu.

TRYING TO FIT IN

Dan with his catch from ice fishing in Owen Sound, Ontario
Image: Dan LEE Family Collection

LEE Lin Toy (1906–1990), also known as **Dan LEE**, did everything he could to adapt to the culture and lifestyle of the people in his adopted town of Owen Sound, Ontario.

Dan had arrived on his own in Canada when he was only 14 years old. Without speaking a word of English, he sailed the Pacific, took a train to Toronto, and then boarded a bus for the final 200-kilometre trip to Owen Sound, where he met up with his father.

Dan ended up spending years working with his father in the family laundry business. Labouring tirelessly seven days a week, he never took a day off or time for a vacation. Every day counted, and he needed to support not only his immediate family in Owen Sound but also his extended family back in China.

Dan also wanted to fit in with the Owen Sound community. Being Chinese, he felt the full force of being an outsider in small-town Ontario, so he worked hard to fit in. Dan went to school and learned how to speak, read, and write English decades before English Language Development programs existed. He learned to fish, including ice fishing, and to hunt. Dan also befriended local farmers so that he could learn how to make maple syrup. Ultimately, this outsider wanted to be like everyone else: he wanted to belong.

> ***"Being Chinese, he felt the full force of being an outsider in small-town Ontario."***

FEARS OF A PAPER SON

86391

DOMINION OF CANADA

NEW C.I. 5 SERIES

IMMIGRATION BRANCH – DEPARTMENT OF THE INTERIOR

RECEIVED FROM

Loue Loong Chuk whose photograph is attached hereto, on the date and at the place hereunder mentioned, the sum of Five Hundred Dollars being the head tax due under the provisions of the Chinese Immigration Act. The above mentioned party who claims to be a native of in the district of of the age of years arrived or landed at on the day of 1918 The declaration in this case is C.I.4. No.

Dated at Ottawa on September 1918

ASSISTANT CHIEF CONTROLLER OF CHINESE IMMIGRATION

For several decades, **Gin YUEN** (1890–1975) was known as **LOUE Loong Chuk**. It was a name and identity he had purchased – the identity of another man who was ten years younger than him. Coming into Canada under a false identity was not Gin's preferred way to enter the country. However, it was all that was available to him in 1918 when the Canadian government started to restrict Chinese labourers entering at ports in British Columbia.

Gin settled in Carberry, Manitoba, where he opened the Liberty Cafe with his cousin. Later, he bought the C.V.M. Cafe on Main Street, which was right next door.

Gin was well liked and well known in the little town, and customers often saw him smoking a bamboo water pipe by the cash register. Yet Gin carried with him this dark secret about who he really was. According to family lore, one day when Canadian politician Lester B. Pearson made a campaign stop at the C.V.M. Cafe, Gin fled out the back door rather than bask in the attention. He was fearful his identity would be discovered.

Years later, Gin shared that his biggest regret about being a paper son was that he had to wait an additional ten years before he was eligible to receive his Old Age Security Pension benefits.

Liberty Cafe and C.V.M. Cafe
Image: Carberry Plains Archive

Mary WONG (right) in one of her seven fur coats with an unidentitifed woman
Image: Elsie MAH Collection

THE GAMBLERS

Gambling was a popular pastime during the exclusion era. Deeply rooted in Chinese culture, gambling was a way to pass the time; earn a bit of extra cash; and socialize with other community members. A lot of gambling was centred on traditional Chinese games, such as fan-tan and pai gow. And, given the number of Chinese men living without families in Canada, gambling was predominantly a male activity.

WONG Yong Fong (1902–1986), also known as Mary, was a successful businesswoman who, over the years, had become a partner in a number of Edmonton restaurants. In her spare time, Mary was an opera performer. She was also a notorious gambler – something very rare for a woman at that time. A skilful player, during one period she grew so wealthy from her gambling and business successes that she owned seven fur coats. Mary also was generous to a fault, lending money to people in need and seldom being paid back. But however lucky she was in business, her reputation as a gambler meant that Mary made few women friends.

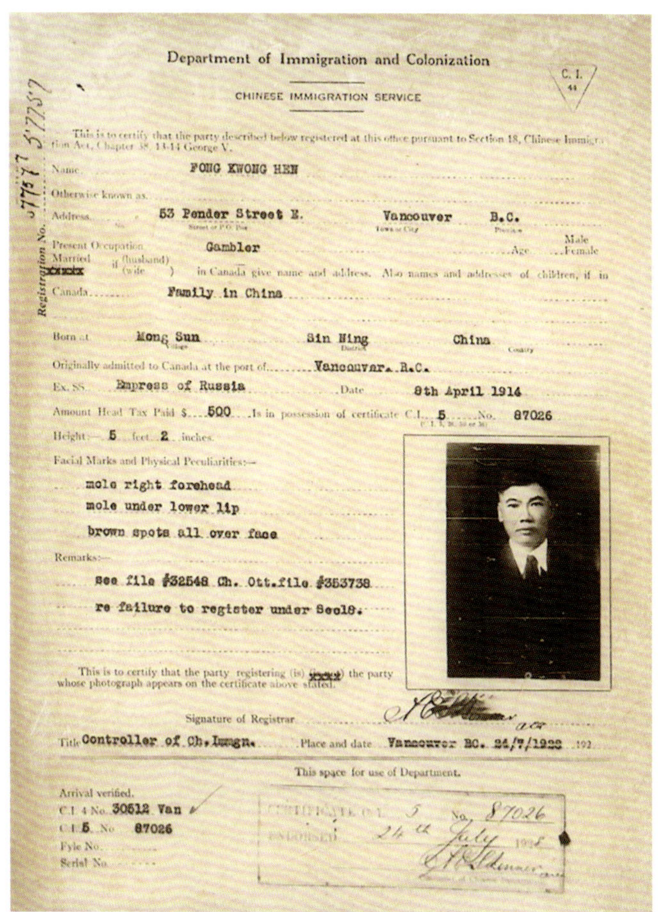

Department of Immigration and Colonization

CHINESE IMMIGRATION SERVICE

C.I. 44

Registration No. 57757 57757

This is to certify that the party described below registered at this office pursuant to Section 18, Chinese Immigration Act, Chapter 38, 13-14 George V.

Name: FONG KWONG HEN

Otherwise known as:

Address: 53 Pender Street E. Vancouver B.C.

Present Occupation: Gambler Age Male/Female

Married if (husband) (wife) in Canada give name and address. Also names and addresses of children, if in Canada: Family in China

Born at: Mong Sun (Village) Sin Ning (District) China (Country)

Originally admitted to Canada at the port of Vancouver, B.C.

Ex. SS: Empress of Russia Date: 8th April 1914

Amount Head Tax Paid $ 500 Is in possession of certificate C.I. 5 No. 87026

Height: 5 feet 2 inches.

Facial Marks and Physical Peculiarities:—
mole right forehead
mole under lower lip
brown spots all over face

Remarks:—
see file #32548 Ch. Ott.file #353738
re failure to register under Sec18.

This is to certify that the party registering (is) (is not) the party whose photograph appears on the certificate above stated.

Signature of Registrar

Title: Controller of Ch. Immgn. Place and date: Vancouver BC. 24/7/1928

This space for use of Department.

Arrival verified.
C.I. 4 No. 30512 Van
C.I. 5 No. 87026
Fyle No.
Serial No.

Certificate C.I. 5 No. 87026
Endorsed 24th July 1928

The C.I.44 form for a gambler who failed to register until 1928
Image: Library and Archives Canada

In contrast, **FONG Kwong Hen** (*c.* 1879–unknown) tried to hide both himself and his gambling. He was a professional gambler whose attempts to keep his activities away from the watchful eyes of the government led him to not register before the mandatory deadline of June 30, 1924. In fact, Kwong Hen did not register until July 1928. It is not clear why he suddenly decided to register or what repercussions he suffered, but his C.I.44 form suggests that additional files were compiled on him. In this one instance, Kwong Hen's gamble to evade the attentions of the government may have cost him dearly.

HIDING ASSETS

The fear of being robbed was something many in Canada had to guard against, especially at a time when people mainly used cash. For Chinese, who often lived precariously, this fear was especially acute. There are stories of bachelor men who died, and hundreds of dollars were later found squirrelled away under their mattress or sewn in their clothing.

WONG Suey Ping (*c.* 1912–1984), also spelled **WONG Thuey Ping**, was the proprietor of a rooming house located at 24 Water Street in Vancouver. It was a rough-and-tumble area at the time.

In 1947, as the Exclusion Act was ending, Ping decided to take a long-awaited trip to China. He had saved a lot of money for his visit – $1,900 – but was worried about getting robbed. So, Ping carefully sewed all the bills into his underwear. Then he headed to the station where he planned take a train to San Francisco, where he would then catch his ship.

However, the cash must have been noticeably bulky as the RCMP searched Ping at the station and discovered the wad of money. He had much more cash than he was allowed to export under currency regulations. Ping was promptly arrested.

The arrest attracted newspaper reporters, who were fascinated by such a novel way to hide large amounts of cash. Ping was dubbed "The Underwear Bandit."

Fortunately for Ping, he was treated rather well by the authorities: he was fined only $250. As well, the Foreign Exchange Control Board received special permission to bring Ping to trial the very next day so that he could still fly to San Francisco in the evening and join the 180 other Chinese due to set sail. Fortunately for Ping, he managed to get on the ship in time.

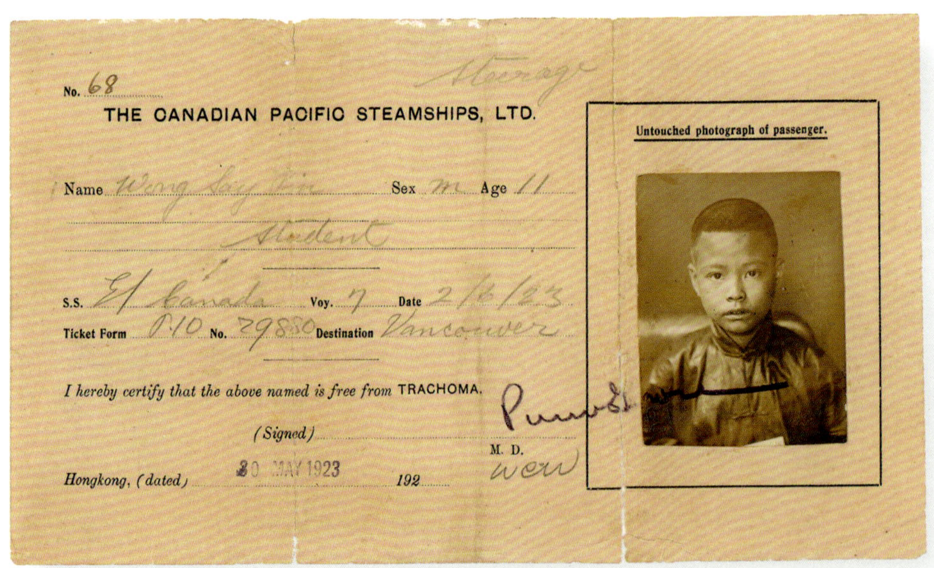

No. 68 Steerage

THE CANADIAN PACIFIC STEAMSHIPS, LTD.

Untouched photograph of passenger.

Name Wong Soy Pin Sex M Age 11

Student

S.S. E/ Canada Voy. 7 Date 2/6/23

Ticket Form P10 No. 29880 Destination Vancouver

I hereby certify that the above named is free from TRACHOMA.

(Signed)

M. D.

Hongkong, (dated) 30 MAY 1923 *192*

Left: Ping in the 1940s ▶

▲ Above: 1923 Steamship ticket from when Ping first arrived in Canada

Images: Randall Mon Cho WONG

CHINESE FINED FOR EVASION
$1900 in Underwear Halts Emigrant
Wong Sue Ping, who was ar-
ested at a railroad station Wed-
esday on his way to China,
on't miss the boat but the
elay cost him a $250 fine pl
lawyer's fee plus plane far
an Francisco.
Ping, 36, rooming-house
rietor, had $1900 cu
itched into his und
orts when RCMP search
the Great Northern dep
o permit to take the mon
Canada.
Magistrate W. W. B. M
n Thursday fined him $
vasion of the currency
egulations.
An official of the Forei
change Control board said special
Ottawa permission was received
have taken the money with permission but went about it "the
wrong way."
The magistrate suspended
nce on a second charge and
Ping to fly to San Francisco
il today.
en Who Are
OING PLACES!
IS Scandals
e of so many
100
B0587544
BANK
OF
CANAD

'Potato Control' Attacked in
Attempt to Capture Business

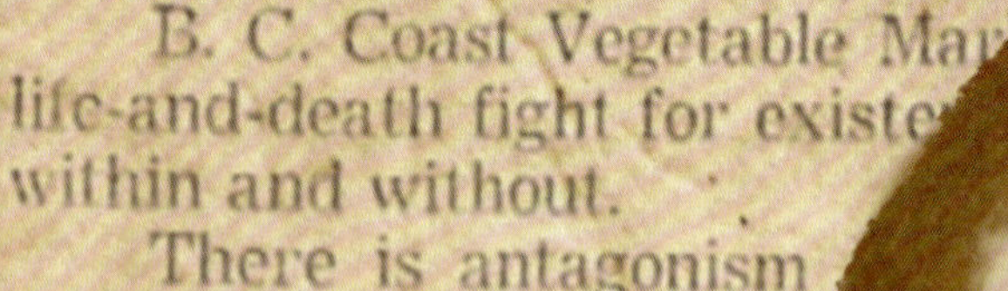
Chinese Sales
Reduced by Change
Few Chinese Growers
Own Their Land

THE POTATO BARON

MAH Bing (1879–1949) was a British Columbia farmer and a powerful and confident businessman. If Bing did not like a situation, he would either challenge it or find creative ways to get around it. He was referred to as "The Potato Baron."

A 1941 *Vancouver Sun* story vividly described Bing's 160-acre farm, the biggest on Lulu Island south of Vancouver: "Thousands of truckloads of vegetables from his prolific acres are sold each year on the Vancouver market. He employs 50 to 100 young Chinese farmers who turn out prodigious crops, one succeeding another in a never-ending succession. The same ground will grow spinach, corn and fall cabbage all in the same season. Mah Bing's workmen can be seen from dawn to dark these days, for activity never ceases on this remarkable farm. Heavy laden trucks move out of his place like a German panzer division strung along the road, cityward, for a mile."

Due to the enormous success of Bing's farm, he frequently faced jealousy, suspicion, and criticism, even when his actions were noble. In 1941, the war was on, and yet there was a glut of potatoes on the market. It looked like thousands of pounds of unsold crops were destined to rot in the fields. Bing decided to do something useful with his excess potatoes: he donated the spuds to the Canadian Army. Instead of being applauded for not letting the food go to waste, Bing was criticized by other farmers and the media and accused of donating the potatoes only because he could not find a local buyer. Yet his generosity had been witnessed years earlier. In the 1930s, when extreme dust storms killed crops across the prairies, Bing donated 4,000 tonnes of his potatoes to prairie families to keep them from starving.

Image: C.I.28, MAH Bing (Richmond, B.C.)

"Instead of being applauded for not letting the food go to waste, Bing was criticized by other farmers and the media and accused of donating the potatoes only because he could not find a local buyer."

THE KING OF THUGS

He was known as "The King of the Thugs," and for several decades, **WONG Jim Goon** (*c.* 1858–1946) lived up to his fearsome reputation. However, the Chinese Exclusion Act led this hardened criminal to change his ways.

Jim Goon's early life in North America remains shrouded in mystery and contradiction. The story passed down is that he first immigrated to San Francisco around 1878 and worked a houseboy in the home of a white lawyer. There, Jim Goon picked up much of his knowledge about the American legal system and developed a mind for law that would serve him in later years.

By 1913, Jim Goon was living in Canada. In Vancouver, he established a protection society for Chinese of the Wong clan. The Wong Wun Sun Society was membership-driven. It served as a squad that would offer protection, settle scores, and influence decisions on behalf of its members.

Over the next few years, Jim Goon's name began appearing in local English and Chinese newspapers stories. Goon was arrested for a shooting; for assault and gambling; for using and selling opium; and even for holding a young white woman a virtual prisoner for the purpose of prostitution.

Yet something changed for Jim Goon as the rumours of a Chinese exclusion law slowly became reality. Unlike his previous endeavours, the former thug changed course and threw his energy into protecting the community in a positive way. In 1923, Jim Goon helped establish a new Wong organization – the Wong Kung Har Tong Benevolent Society – which would provide charity, support, schooling, and legal and banking services to its members.

In his new role, Jim Goon frequently served as an interpreter and a behind-the-scenes legal strategist. He worked alongside white lawyers who had been hired by the Society to take on cases for the Chinese Canadian community. He was the legal mind behind several high profile cases in the 1920s and 1930s.

By the time of his death in 1946, Jim Goon had redeemed himself in the eyes of the Chinese Canadian community. He had become a respected elder. When he died, his funeral took almost a month to organize and involved 80 vehicles in a procession that was more than a mile long.

"In 1923, Jim Goon helped establish a new Wong organization – the Wong Kung Har Tong Benevolent Society – which would provide charity, support, schooling, and legal and banking services to its members."

WONG Jim Goon, c. 1920s ▶
Image: Wongs' Benevolent Association

WO CHINESE ARE SENT TO PRISON

im Goon and Wong Sin
Made Murderous Attack
Chinese "Bouncer."

Wong Yuen alias Jim G
derly Chinese who is repute
ne King of the Thugs in Chin

DEATH FOLLOWS NEW OUTBREAK
TONG CLASH

Falls Dead
Highbinder
ney Sing

city broke out
ast night, when
low by a bul-
der in the local
s time it was a
o was killed. The
ot was fired by a
Sing tong.
red in St. Louis
o'clock. Imme-
was thrown
shots were
ffect. A

COMMITTED FOR TRIAL

Wong Jim Yuen Accused of Procuring Girl for Immoral Purposes.

Before Magistrate Jay in the Police Court this morning the preliminary hearing of the prosecution in the case of Wong Jim Yuen, accused of ing the girl Georgina Mc place. The accused w trial.

The evidence o to the effect t Jim Yuen bro couver. She rooming hou this place i brought Ch moral pu the hous tiously did his to a l

In that that dru na

QUAN Yuen Yen in Victoria, c. late 1930s
Image: Andrea MARU Collection

A LIFE INTERRUPTED

By the time the Exclusion Act was passed, the frequent violent clashes between rival "tongs," or clan societies, in Canadian Chinatowns had subsided. Occasional conflicts remained among Chinese, but rarely would an argument or disagreement lead to violence or death. Even more rare were murders involving a respected leader in the Chinese community.

Louise QUAN (right) with her siblings (right to left) Eva, Eugene, Ernie and Henry, 1946. Missing is Wasson. *Image: Andrea MARU Collection*

QUAN Yuen Yen (*c.* 1897 – 1943) was a fortunate man – he had everything. He owned a Chinese herbal store and a tailor shop in Victoria called Man Yuck Tong. He also co-owned restaurants and real estate and operated successful greenhouses that employed many Chinese. With a wife and six children living with him in Canada, as well as a daughter in China, Yuen Yen was the envy of many Chinese men. The businessman was also a community leader, active in his community, serving on various committees, and raising money for the war effort.

On June 16, 1943, Yuen Yen's life ended unexpectedly. He was bludgeoned to death in his office by a farmer with whom he had some kind of business relationship. Today, no one knows the exact details of the dispute, but Yuen Yen died soon after the attack. The assailant, a man named QUON Yen, fled the scene and later committed suicide. The event stunned the Victoria Chinese community.

For Yuen Yen's wife, Jessie, and their children, the death left a mark that would last for years. For his eldest child in Canada, Louise, who was only 13 at the time, it meant a childhood that became filled with co-parenting responsibilities. Louise now had to help care for her five younger siblings while also going to school and serving as an English interpreter for her mother in business matters. When Jessie died suddenly a few years later, Louise became the de facto mother to the youngest children.

Despite her many duties at home, Louise entered university and obtained a degree in pharmacy. At a time when most women were marrying in their late teens and early 20s, Louise did not marry until her mid-30s. Initially she was reluctant to have children, likely due to the years she spent caring for her siblings. Traumatized by the violence that shaped her life, Louise buried the memory: she never even shared with her husband the story of her father's brutal death.

A BITTER MEMORY

Ming Hung posing in one of his fine suits
Image: Melanie WONG Collection

> *"He described the conditions as terrible and that the Chinese held in that facility were treated like animals."*

WONG Foon Gong (*c.* 1907–1988), also known as **Ming Hung WONG**, accepted the challenges of living in a white-dominated Canada. The only experience for which Ming ever expressed any bitterness was the time he was held in quarantine when he first arrived in Canada in 1921. For two weeks, he was locked down in the immigration detention shed in Vancouver's Coal Harbour, a place also known as "The Pig Pen." He described the conditions as terrible and that the Chinese held in that facility were treated like animals.

When Ming landed in Canada, he had little schooling and spoke only Toishanese. In his early years, he took any work he could find and initially toiled long hours in hand laundries. Later, he found a job as a houseboy in a home in Vancouver's wealthy Shaughnessy neighbourhood. While there, Ming learned the art of dressing well, and throughout his life, he made investments in quality suits.

Ming learned something else in that Shaughnessy house that would serve him well for the rest of his life. He would watch intently as the cooking staff prepared the meals. Over time, Ming became a talented cook himself and could conjure up any kind of Western or Chinese dish without the help of a recipe.

Ming eventually moved on and cooked in a variety of hotels and restaurants in Vancouver, the most famous of which was the Cave Supper Club.

Ming would not marry until the 1960s and only after a friend suggested he find a wife to care for him in his old age. In 1966, he finally married a nurse but by then he was 60 years old.

THE PURE ENGLISH CAMPAIGN

In Moose Jaw, Saskatchewan, the early Chinese were not treated well, according to the stories passed on by **GEE Chan Howe** (*c.* 1895–1974).

Howe had spent three years working on a chicken farm in the southern Saskatchewan town. Despite his poor living and working conditions and being far from his family, Howe felt a sense of belonging since there was a sizable Chinese community in Moose Jaw at the time.

Above: C.I.45, Howe GEE
Below: Postcard of Yellow Grass, Saskatchewan
Image: Don KAYE Collection

Years later, Howe recalled how that good feeling was offset by the way Chinese were treated by the larger white community. Among the memories Howe shared with his family was a period when the town's white citizens began wearing a sign on their breast pocket that read "Pure English." Given the disdain toward Chinese, many men like Howe felt it was a message directed at them: a message that their race was unwelcome in Moose Jaw. In fact, the Pure English campaign, which started in England in 1913, was aimed at preventing the importation of foreign words into the English vocabulary. Certainly, the Chinese community's interpretation of the lapel signs was not far off the mark.

Howe eventually left Moose Jaw and moved to Yellow Grass, Saskatchewan, where he partnered with a cousin to buy the Rex Café. Both men shared the surname GEE. So Howe became known as "Little Gee," a man with a kind heart, and his cousin, being a larger stature, was known as "Big Gee."

Howe would not reunite with his family until the 1950s. His son, **Sam GEE**, would play a role in advocating for head tax redress.

SURVIVING ON THE ROCK

During the almost quarter century that the Exclusion Act was in effect, Newfoundland was the only region that still allowed Chinese to enter, albeit after paying a $300 head tax. It was not an easy place to live.

CHAN Lou (1899–1994), also known as **Tom CHAN**, arrived in St. John's in 1921. He was 22 at the time, and physically capable, but he had a hard time finding work. So, Tom found every opportunity to earn some cash. He became acquainted with some local gamblers and offered to run errands for them in exchange for tips. Tom himself never gambled.

Tom saw another opportunity in the laundry business. He offered his services to a hand laundry for free to prove he was dependable and hard-working. To help drum up business, Tom went from hotel to hotel, asking who needed their clothes laundered. He would haul all the clothes back to the laundry in a bag. He eventually was hired and earned three to five dollars per week.

Despite his meagre wages, Tom regularly sent money back to his wife and children in China and, in 1937, managed to buy some land there and build a family home.

He also saved enough to buy his own convenience store in Newfoundland. However, running the store involved very long hours. Tom barely slept, staying up as late as possible so that his store would be open to customers. He also found creative ways to sell candy. The family recalls that when children lacked the money to buy an entire package of candy, Tom would take the package apart so that the kids could purchase the pieces they could afford. He also learned to bake pies and sold them at the store.

His willingness to embrace new opportunities led Tom into the restaurant business. He bought the Dragon Restaurant in Corner Brook, Newfoundland. From this business, he made his fortune. In 1955, Tom's son, Terry, joined him in Canada, and Tom's wife followed in 1960. After Tom's retirement, Terry carried on the family business.

NEWFOUNDLAND.

...t of St. John's No. 106

14th February 1921

This Certifies that under the provisions of the Chinese ...migration Act Chan Lou a native of Sing Ning in the Province of Canton, China of the age 22 years, and whose title, official rank, profession or occupation is that of a Laundryman who arrived or landed at Port aux Basques or S.S. Kyle on the 31st day of January 1921 vide statement and declaration form No. 106 has paid the fee or duty imposed upon Chinese Immigrants on their arrival in Newfoundland, not being exempt from such payment under the terms of the said Act, and has been registered at Newfoundland under the No. 106 on the day, month and year hereunto affixed.

Above: Tom CHAN in Corner Brook, Nfld., 1939
Below: Terry CHAN (left), Tom's son, outside the Dragon Restaurant, 1956
Image: Terry CHAN Family Collection

BECOMING AN ADVOCATE

During the long period of exclusion and after, **Ko Hong FOO** (1894–1980), or **Charlie FOO**, found himself becoming a political strategist and social activist. At one point, he even was dubbed the "unofficial mayor" of Winnipeg's Chinatown.

Charlie landed in Canada when he was 25 and worked endless hours at his cousin's laundry in Winnipeg. Unhappy with the laundry business and angered by the daily discrimination he encountered, Charlie soon found his true calling when he joined the local Chinese National League and became an activist.

Believing that building bridges between the Chinese and the white communities was key to challenging racism, Charlie helped new Chinese migrants settle into the community and learn English. When the Second World War broke out, Charlie expanded his activism beyond Winnipeg and raised funds for war relief in China.

Charlie also campaigned relentlessly against the Chinese Exclusion Act. Even after Parliament repealed the Act in 1947, he continued to advocate against the remaining restrictions that prevented Chinese in Canada from bringing their relatives over from China. As a representative of the Manitoba Chinese Benevolent Association, he travelled to Ottawa 13 times to lobby for family reunification.

Charlie's advocacy made a difference for the next generation of Chinese Canadians. His legacy has been carried forward by those he helped: from the migrants who settled in Winnipeg to the families he helped reunite to his son-in-law, **Westley WONG**, who became a prominent physics professor at Brandon University.

Charlie FOO (2nd from right) with Winnipeg Mayor Garnet COULTER (3rd from left) in Winnipeg's Chinatown, 1943
Image: Charlie FOO Family Collection

CAFES TO CHINA

Separated from his wife and five children in China, restauranteur **Shack Jang MACK** (1909–2003) went to extreme lengths to prepare for his visits to China.

Shack arrived in Canada at the age of 13. He attended school and apprenticed as a chef. After working for a few years, he saved enough money to open his first restaurant in The Pas, Manitoba.

In 1928, Shack prepared to return to China to find a wife. But he faced a dilemma: what should he do with his restaurant? He couldn't find anyone he trusted to operate his restaurant for the many months he planned to be away. So, he decided to sell his restaurant, the M.C. Cafe.

When he returned to Canada, he opened a new restaurant under a new name. This started a pattern: each time he went back to China, he sold his restaurant before leaving; and when he returned, he would open a new cafe under a different name. By the end of his travels, Shack had opened a string of cafes across Manitoba; he eventually settled in Tisdale, Saskatchewan.

In his various restaurants, Shack would offer the usual fare: Western dishes, such as steaks, burgers, fries, and French toast. As he became established, he began introducing more exotic items to his menu, like chow mein. But he was best known for his delicious cheesecake.

The years spent separated from his family, coupled with the racism that his community endured in Canada, left an indelible mark on him. Much later in life, Shack was determined to right a wrong on behalf of all Chinese Canadians. In 2000, he became one of the chief plaintiffs in a landmark case against the Canadian government, which sought financial redress for the head tax.

Shack Jang MACK as an elderly man
Image: Shack Jang MACK Family

The following year, the courts threw out the class-action lawsuit, arguing that courts could not apply "modern-day constitutional principles to a law that was repealed over 50 years ago."

Canada eventually apologized in 2006 for the head tax and provided compensation to survivors and their spouses. Shack did not live long enough to celebrate. He died in 2003, one of the survivors of exclusion whose efforts and dedication had made the victory possible.

HOME TO WIVES IN CHINA AFTER YEARS IN CANADA

Sixth Party of Chinese Since War Off to Orient With Bags, Sacks

By PIERRE BERTON

The Great Northern station looked like a little bit of old Canton Friday afternoon.

Five hundred Chinese, most of them elderly—their faces creased with lines of labor—waited patiently in the drab, cramped baggage room as a phalanx of customs, immigration and foreign exchange officials inspected their goods and chattels and their tight little wads of American dollars.

After 10, 15, 20 years they were going home at last to the families they left behind.

Many of the older ones will not return. They are too old to work, too sick in many cases to care. Their life in Canada, without a family, has been a lonely one. Thwarted by an eight-year war from making the trip they desired long ago, their only wish now is to get back to the country of their birth.

"DON'T COME BACK"

"I come back later—but old man he don't come back," said Carr Khon, who ran a coffee shop in Lethbridge. He is returning with his aged father to see the wife and child he left behind 15 years before.

"Fifteen years—long time," said Khon. "Don't know what family look like now."

It was an all-male crowd who shuffled through the station in long, weary queues, opening up the shopping bags and gunny-sacks, old suitcases, tin pails, aluminum pots and hat boxes that held their luggage.

When they first came here they weren't allowed to bring their families. That is why no women were returning.

"If the Act wasn't so strict the transportation companies might not have so much business," Frank Mah, the general passenger agent in charge of the draft, pointed out.

Officials checking over the money had their work cut out for them.

One Chinese had 300 one-dollar bills to be counted. Most of the cash was in small denominations.

"If they had large bills—they wanted to change it into small and if they had small bills they wanted to change it into large," Tom Mah, Bank of Montreal clerk, who was helping his uncle with the draft, reported.

All were allowed to take up to $1500 American for the first year and after that, if they continue in China, may take more.

One Chinese turned up with only $2 and another had just $4, but most had their quota of $1500. There was one Manila $100 bill and some Chinese bonds.

NAB LOADED PISTOL

Customs officials confiscated little, but nabbed one fully loaded .38 pistol.

Everybody on the draft comes from the province of Kwong Tung, whose capital is Canton.

This isn't surprising as most Chinese in North or South America comes from the same province.

"The other provinces just don't seem to emigrate," Mr. Mah pointed out. "The Cantonese live near the sea of course. And they were the first ones here. Just like your friends come here. They tell you. The news spreads."

Mr. Mah explained that the Shanghai Chinese all go to the South Seas and Dutch East Indies while people from Western China emigrate to France and Europe.

The Chinese who left yesterday—it's the sixth and biggest draft since war's end—may return if they wish as they are registered mainly as Canadian residents. Those who registered for no return can take all their money with them but can't obtain re-entry.

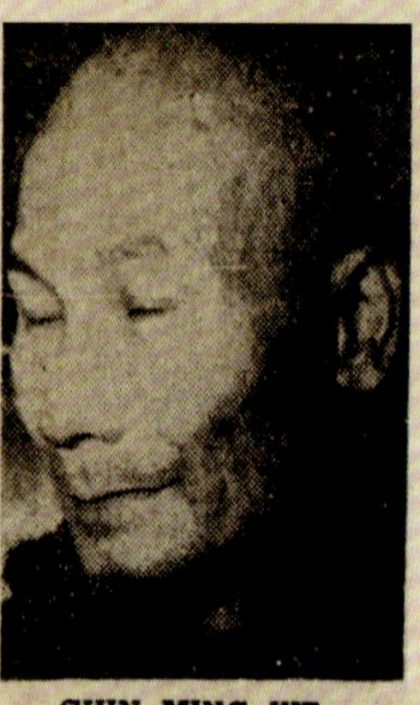

JOHN KUNG KI — CHIN MING KIT — CHIN BUCK MING

GOING HOME AT LAST, these three Chinese are representative of the 500 who le[ft] the Great Northern station yesterday on the first lap of a trip which will take the[m] back to the China they haven't seen since pre-war days. In San Francisco they [will] board the transport General Gordon and sail for Canton. Ki is retired editor of t[he] China Times here. Kit has a heart disease and can no longer make a living in B.[C.] Ming is a former cook who is too old to work.

本埠新聞

民國三十五年十二月六號

◎回國之華僑六百餘

本埠加拿大社六日電・本市訪員是日消息・華人旅居於加拿大者・其中共有六百餘人・于是日離雲埠赴美國三藩市・將於是月九日・乘美國船哥頓號・返回中國・該批中國僑民・因戰事阻滯・以致離開中國之時間・大多數有十年以上之久・故其欲歸故鄉・與家人團聚・據移民局代言人稱・該批歸國華僑・多屬年老者・其中或有百分之四十能復返加國謀生・深信在將來十年內・中國人旅居加拿大之人口・必降低至百分之五十・現時仍有華人入百名購備船位・等候船隻回國・同時仍有數百人正等候購買船票云・

THE EXODUS

For many Chinese in Canada, the long years of separation, longing, worrying, and waiting finally came to an end in 1946. The Second World War was over. Travel between North America and China had been restored. The Exclusion Act had not yet been repealed.

In early December 1946, newspaper stories in both the English and Chinese media reported that hundreds of Chinese men from across the country were making the journey back to China. Some were only going for a visit. Others were going home to live out their final years of life. Three men never made it: they died waiting, with all their worldly possessions packed, their voyage delayed due to a maritime strike in the United States.

> ***"Three men never made it: they died waiting, with all their worldly possessions packed, their voyage delayed due to a maritime strike in the United States."***

Canadian historian and author Pierre Berton was at the train station in Vancouver to witness the exodus. He spoke to some of the travellers and described what he heard: **"Many of the older ones will not return. They are too old to work, too sick in many cases to care. Their life in Canada without a family, has been a lonely one. Thwarted by an eight-year war from making the trip they desired long ago, their only wish now is to get back to the country of their birth."**

The elderly men returning that day were like plum blossoms, the only flower able to survive the harsh cold of winter. Like that winter flower, they had made it through the most miserable of times. Standing in their weary queues, grasping their few belongings, harbouring their memories and hopes, they had endured the long, dark winter of exclusion. They had survived.

Image: Willie CHONG, Vancouver, 194
Willie CHONG Collectio

CHAPTER 4

SOWING THE SEEDS OF CHANGE

DOMINION OF CANADA

IMMIGRATION BRANCH - DEPARTMENT OF THE INTERIOR

姬步隊埠華僑暨華商軍人聯歡會留影

THE SOLDIERS

The start of the Second World War in 1939 would sow the first seeds of change for Chinese in Canada.

Early in the conflict, the war created friction within the community as debates broke out about whether Chinese in Canada should serve. An older generation questioned why the community would sacrifice the lives of its few Canadian-born offspring for a country that treated them with such contempt.

By contrast, many in the younger generation saw the war as an opportunity. If they voluntarily enlisted, they would demonstrate their loyalty to Canada. After the war, they reasoned, there would be no more excuses for denying Chinese Canadians the full rights of citizenship and the right to vote. The fact that most of these young men and women owned a C.I.45 "immigration card," despite having been born in Canada, further galvanized them to head to their local recruitment office.

TESTING OUR DEMOCRATIC SINCERITY

To the Editor:—Not that I, a native born Canadian of Chinese racial origin, am not sharing the war sentiments with the peoples of the British Empire.

Not that my mind is not embroiled with utmost hatred of those tyrannical dictators whose satanic lust for power has plunged the human race into the abyss of of suffering and barbarity.

Not that I would not shed my blood for the defence of this country of Canada, if and when any aggressor should threaten her national freedom and territorial integrity.

Not that I am advocating opposition to the military conscription of Chinese Canadian youths for Home Defence.

But I wish to point out the unfairness which underlies the fact that we are not granted full civic and political rights and privileges in the country of our birth and in which we are to be called upon to defend.

I doubt not the willingness, nay the enthusiasm, of many a Chinese Canadian lad to serve the country at this trying juncture of her national existence; but are they, once in uniforms, to receive equal consideration in military promotions, compensations, pensions, etc., which equality official Canada has consistently denied them in their civic and political life?

LIN YU YOUNG.
3175 Beach Drive.

Image: Chinese Canadian Military Museum

Despite their enthusiasm, most Chinese Canadians who appeared at those recruitment offices in the first two years of the war were shown the back door. The main reason was simple racism: Chinese were viewed as mentally and physically inferior to whites. Some recruitment officers quietly confessed that the fear of Chinese Canadians demanding more rights because of their war service was also a factor in the government's decision to reject them.

However, once Japan entered the war and the conflict became global, the acceptance of Chinese Canadians into the Armed Forces was inevitable. By the time the war ended in the summer of 1945, Chinese Canadians were serving in every branch of the Armed Forces, including Special Operations, and were fighting in every theatre of war. A number stood out for their courage and accomplishments.

Worldwide, more than 60 million people died in that global conflict. At least nine Chinese Canadian soldiers, all of whom had been born in Canada, were among the dead.

Despite all their loyalty and sacrifice, when Chinese Canadian soldiers returned home after the war, they also returned to their status as second-class citizens.

But the seeds of change had been sown. Hardened and emboldened by their experience, these veterans, along with others in the community, started to demand full Canadian citizenship rights and the repeal of the Exclusion Act. If they could fight for their country, certainly that country owed them the rights of citizenship.

BROTHERS IN ARMS

When the Second World War broke out, hundreds of Chinese Canadian families held their breath as their children volunteered for the war effort. Although their sons and daughters could not vote, were barred from practising law, medicine, and engineering, and were forced to sit in the back of theatres, these children of immigrants were nevertheless eager to show their loyalty to Canada.

In some families, more than one child stepped up to join the Armed Forces. In Windsor, both the LEE family and the HONG family saw three brothers sign up for duty. In British Columbia, four KO BONG siblings joined with the daughter, Mary, enlisting first. Meanwhile, all three sons of **JUNG Yick Ching** of Victoria served in the Second World War: Ross, Arthur, and Douglas. One can imagine the mixed feelings their parents might have had knowing that all their children were off to war and possible death.

Ross JUNG (1912–1976) became a medical officer with the rank of captain. He served in North Africa from 1943 until 1945. After the war, Ross joined the U.S. Army Medical Corps in Shanghai. He was on detached service with the Central Intelligence Agency as a physician in classified duties. After the war, he was appointed as one of the physicians to U.S. President John F. Kennedy.

The Air Force became the home for **Arthur JUNG** (1921–1973). After achieving top marks in a pilot training school, Arthur was stationed in England as a pilot with Bomber Command. By the end of the war, he had completed more than 30 nerve-racking missions and was promoted to flight lieutenant. He went on to become a commercial pilot but was killed in 1973 while landing near Edmonton during a blizzard.

The youngest brother, **Douglas JUNG** (1924–2002), was among the first group of Chinese Canadian soldiers to be hand-picked to serve under the Special Operations Executive. Douglas was a member of Operation Oblivion, a covert British mission that sent commandos to operate behind Japanese lines. A parachute training accident prevented him from going on any missions. After the war, Douglas became a lawyer and, in 1957, was the first person of Chinese descent to be elected as a member of Parliament.

> ***“One can imagine the mixed feelings their parents might have had knowing that all their children were off to war and possible death.”***

The JUNG brothers with their parents in the 1930s
Douglas (second from left), Arthur (centre), and Ross (second from right)
Images: Douglas JUNG Family

BEN LEE

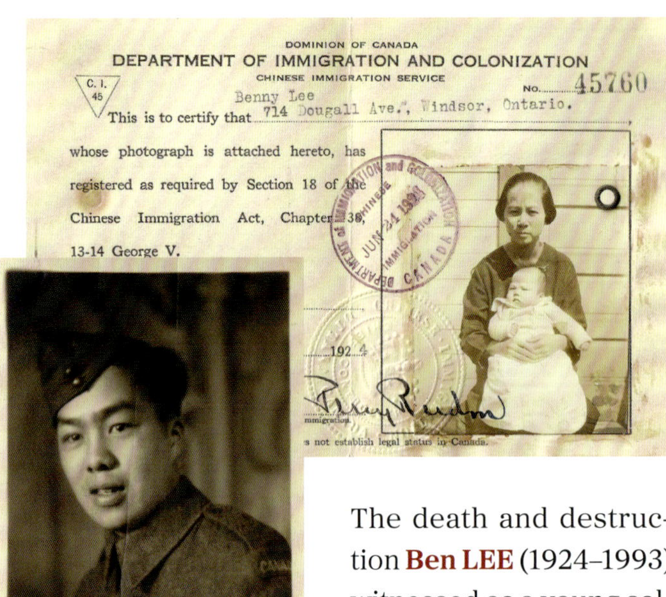

DOMINION OF CANADA
DEPARTMENT OF IMMIGRATION AND COLONIZATION
CHINESE IMMIGRATION SERVICE

C. I. 45 No. 45760

This is to certify that Benny Lee 714 Dougall Ave., Windsor, Ontario.

whose photograph is attached hereto, has registered as required by Section 18 of the Chinese Immigration Act, Chapter 38, 13-14 George V.

192 4

...s not establish legal status in Canada.

The death and destruction **Ben LEE** (1924–1993) witnessed as a young soldier stationed in Europe would haunt him for the rest of his life.

Born in Windsor, Ontario, Ben was one of three brothers who eagerly enlisted and were accepted into military service during the Second World War. Perhaps they were influenced by their father, King LEE, who desired that his children "be good citizens, an honour and credit to the land of my adoption, and the land of their birth."

Ben served five years with the Perth Regiment, 11th Infantry Brigade, 5th Armoured Division and saw action in Italy, France, Belgium, and the Netherlands.

When he came back to civilian life, Ben married, raised a family, and worked long hours in his father's hotel/tavern. Through the years, he seldom spoke about his war experiences.

It was in old age that Ben finally revealed he had been wounded in battle and, on one occasion, he barely escaped when his group was cut off by the enemy.

However, it was only after Ben's death that his wife confessed to their children that the former soldier had suffered from recurring nightmares right until the end of his life.

Ben LEE with his brothers and parents, 1945
(L-R) Ben, Lily, Edward, King, and Peter
Image: Ben LEE Family

NORMAN MON LOW

Norman LOW (1924–1960) did not die on the battlefield, but his time as a soldier during the Second World War shortened his life considerably.

Norman served with a clandestine commando unit called Force 136. He was one of 13 hand-picked Chinese Canadians recruited and trained by British Special Operations and sent to Southeast Asia. Their missions involved parachuting into Japanese-occupied territory and meeting up with local resistance fighters to undertake espionage and sabotage.

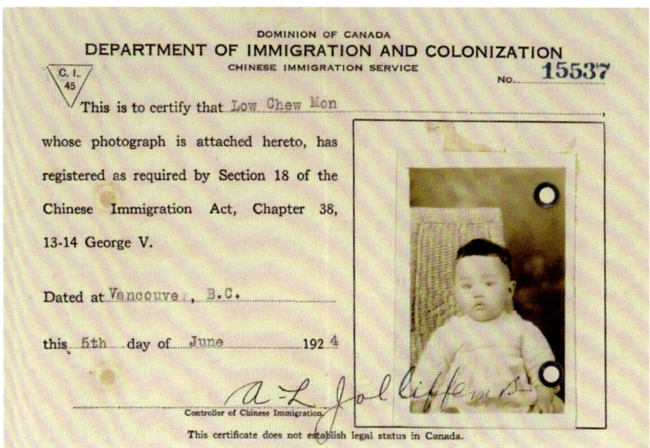

DOMINION OF CANADA
DEPARTMENT OF IMMIGRATION AND COLONIZATION
CHINESE IMMIGRATION SERVICE
C. I. 45
No. 15537

This is to certify that Low Chew Mon whose photograph is attached hereto, has registered as required by Section 18 of the Chinese Immigration Act, Chapter 38, 13-14 George V.

Dated at Vancouver, B.C.

this 5th day of June 1924

A. L. Jolliffe
Controller of Chinese Immigration.

This certificate does not establish legal status in Canada.

September 9, 1946: Norman (right) in a Vancouver hospital bed receiving the news of being awarded the Military Medal. With him is Louie KING, who also served in Borneo. *Image: Vancouver Sun*

Dropped into the hot, humid, insect- and snake-infested jungles of Borneo, Norman was a brave and effective commando. Then he contracted malaria.

When he returned to Canada in February 1946, he was immediately hospitalized with pneumonia and pleurisy arising from his malaria infection. The Vancouver doctors were baffled: how could a Canadian soldier have contracted malaria? Norman was not at liberty to share the details of his deployment as Force 136 soldiers were sworn to secrecy.

In September 1946, Norman and his unit were awarded the Military Medal. A newspaper photograph shows a gaunt-looking Norman receiving the award in his hospital bed.

Norman never fully recovered his health and died in 1960 at the age of 37. He left behind a wife and two children.

KAM LEN DOUGLAS SAM

Serving as an air gunner in bomber command, **Douglas SAM** (1918–1989) survived the downing of his plane over France. He was not captured by the Germans and found himself aided by members of the French Resistance. Rather than return to England, Douglas stayed in France to assist the Resistance movement and help other downed Allied airmen to make it safely out of the country. Using forged identity documents, Douglas posed as a visiting Asian student stuck in France due to the war. He witnessed many atrocities but managed to stay alive. On two occasions he used the high school French he learned in Victoria, B.C., to bluff his way out of Gestapo roundups.

Image: Trevor SAM Collection

DAN CHAN

Tall, smart, and good with languages, **Dan CHAN** (1917–1979) was trained by the Canadian Army to read and speak Japanese. He was rated as one of the best linguists in his class and was assigned to the Canadian Intelligence Corps. Dan's work took him around the world: the U.K., North Africa, Malaysia, and China. By reviewing documents seized from the Japanese, Dan assisted in the war crime investigations on atrocities that took place in Southeast Asia.

Image: Ryan CHAN Collection

MARY KO BONG

A tomboy at heart, **Mary KO BONG** (1917–2011) was the first among her four siblings to enlist. She joined the Canadian Women's Army Corps (W.A.C.) and discovered she had a talent for working with precision machinery and lathes. Among a class of 30 women, almost all white, Mary was one of only five who graduated as an instrument mechanic. She specialized in repairing optical equipment (e.g., binoculars and compasses) and even learned to fabricate replacement parts. Mary felt at home in the W.A.C. and even found time to help entertain the troops with song and dance.

Image: Steve KO Collection

LARRY GEORGE WONG

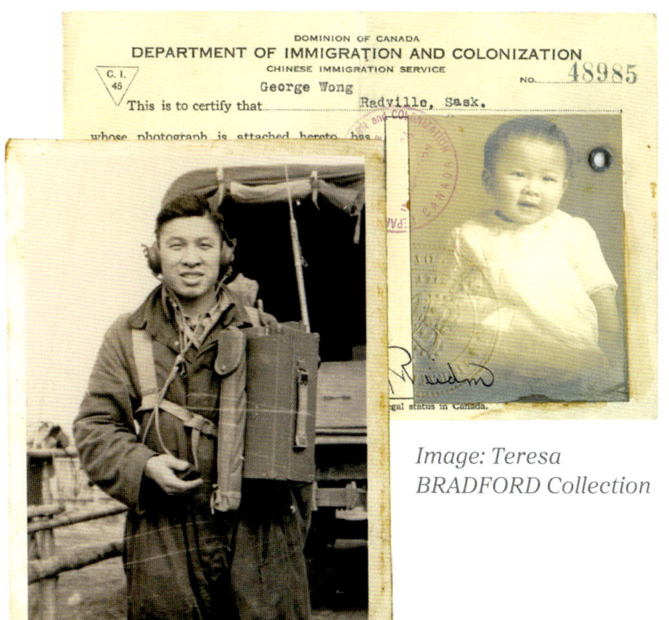

Image: Teresa BRADFORD Collection

Larry WONG (1923–2006) was born in Saskatchewan the year the Exclusion Act became law. By 1942, he had lost both his mother and father and was living in Ocean Falls, B.C., making plywood for P-38 bombers. He held other odd jobs throughout the war until he was conscripted in 1944. At first, Larry was angry at being forced to fight, and possibly die, for a country that treated Chinese as second class. However, once in the Army, his attitude softened. Larry served in the Edmonton Fusiliers before being assigned to Princess Patricia's regiment. In each one, he was the only Chinese serviceman.

PEGGY LEE (NÉE WONG)

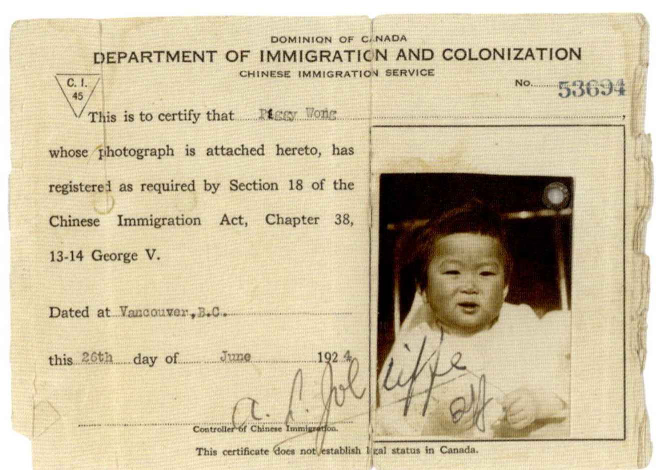
DOMINION OF CANADA
DEPARTMENT OF IMMIGRATION AND COLONIZATION
CHINESE IMMIGRATION SERVICE

C. I. 45

No. 53694

This is to certify that Peggy Wong, whose photograph is attached hereto, has registered as required by Section 18 of the Chinese Immigration Act, Chapter 38, 13-14 George V.

Dated at Vancouver, B.C.

this 26th day of June 1924

Controller of Chinese Immigration.

This certificate does not establish legal status in Canada.

Another young woman who contributed to Canada's war effort, but as a volunteer on the home front, was **Peggy WONG** (1923–2023), later known as **Peggy LEE.**

Born and raised in Prince Rupert, British Columbia, Peggy was one of 11 children.

While still in her teens, Peggy moved to Vancouver to study hair styling, and in 1941, at age 18, she opened her first hair salon. Despite running a busy salon, in 1942, Peggy volunteered to serve on the home front with the St. John Ambulance. Peggy was the youngest member of an all-Chinese platoon of 20 women.

The women had several duties, but one of the most important responsibilities was to patrol each block and ensure residents kept their windows blacked out at night. The darkened windows were a precautionary measure against a possible Japanese invasion: it would make the city harder to spot by any bombing aircraft. Besides enforcing the blackout, Peggy learned how to administer first aid, how to be a stretcher bearer, and how to extinguish small fires.

After the war, Peggy would marry and was among the first of her Chinese friends to wed a white man, something relatively rare in 1951. She would go on to give birth to a son and then a set of triplets, which garnered media attention at the time.

Peggy continued to operate hair salons and did not retire until she was well into her 80s. She also remained active in a lot of business ventures and community work. Peggy was an ardent supporter of the Chinese Canadian Military Museum and its mission to educate new generations on the role these particular soldiers played in securing equal rights for all Chinese. Peggy passed away at the age of 99.

Image: Peggy LEE Family

MARJORIE WONG (NÉE SAM)

1945: Marjorie (centre) and other factory workers celebrate manufacturing the 1,000th tank for the Mosquito bomber.
Images: Marjorie WONG Family

Marjorie SAM (1921–2015), later known as **Marjorie WONG**, served her country by going to work in industry. She helped make the De Havilland Mosquito, a combat aircraft.

Marjorie grew up in her father's cafe in Brantford, Ontario. When still a toddler, she fell in the cafe and wounded her arm and the orbital area of her eye. Her injuries became infected with bovine tuberculosis due to her drinking unpasteurized milk. The bulky bandages protecting her arm are noticeable in her C.I.45 photo.

For treatment, Marjorie's parents sent her to the Children's Wing in the Brantford Sanatorium. She lived there until she was 10, under the care of the head nurse, who taught her English. When Marjorie returned to her family, she had to relearn how to speak Cantonese with her parents.

Despite her injury, Marjorie had a strong right arm thanks to the sanatorium's care. And when the Second World War erupted, she stepped up to do what customarily would have been a man's job: welding.

In 1940, at age 19, Marjorie began training as an aluminum welder, and soon found a job at the De Havilland factory near Toronto. Until the war ended, she welded the fuselage for dozens of Mosquito combat planes. She was the only woman Chinese welder working in the entire factory.

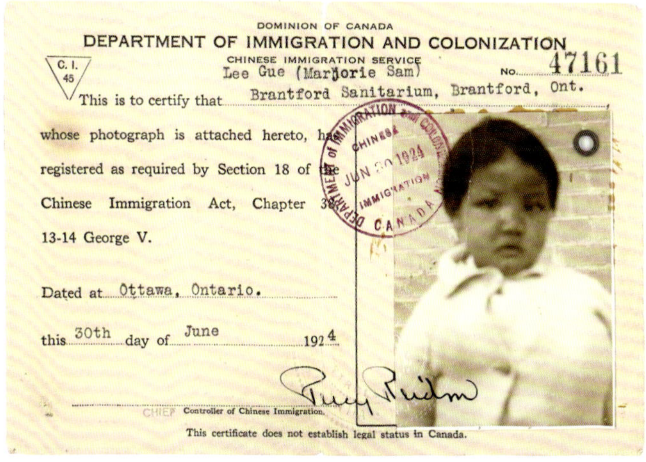

DOMINION OF CANADA
DEPARTMENT OF IMMIGRATION AND COLONIZATION
CHINESE IMMIGRATION SERVICE

C. I. 45

Lee Gue (Marjorie Sam) NO. 47161

This is to certify that Brantford Sanitarium, Brantford, Ont.
whose photograph is attached hereto, has registered as required by Section 18 of the Chinese Immigration Act, Chapter 38, 13-14 George V.

CHINESE IMMIGRATION JUN 30 1924 CANADA

Dated at Ottawa, Ontario.
this 30th day of June 1924

Percy Reid
CHIEF Controller of Chinese Immigration.

This certificate does not establish legal status in Canada.

WILLIAM GUN CHONG

Image: Chinese Canadian Military Museum

Not every Chinese Canadian who served in the war effort did so under the auspices of the Canadian government. A few intrepid souls took their skills to other zones of conflict and served with distinction.

Bill CHONG (1911–2006) worked as a spy and was given the name Agent 50 ("five-oh"), but his assignment was nothing like the spies in a James Bond movie. Bill had been employed as a cook in a wealthy Vancouver home. He was visiting family in Asia in 1941, wrapping up his late father's estate, when the Japanese invaded. Outraged by the atrocities he witnessed, Bill joined the British Army Aid Group and worked as a spy.

Bill disguised himself as a peasant farmer. He travelled everywhere by foot and carried a walking cane with a hidden compartment. Drawing little attention to himself, Bill gathered important information on Japanese activities. He smuggled supplies to medical outputs. He rescued and guided hundreds of downed Allied airmen to safe territory. Bill also escaped death on three occasions.

Bill survived the war and vividly remembered the night he learned the conflict had ended. He recalled, *"I was so happy ... I just sat down on the ground and cried. I don't know why. But I hope I served my country well."*

In 1947, Bill became the only Chinese Canadian to ever be awarded the British Empire Medal for bravery: the highest military honour given by the British government to non-British citizens.

> ***"I just sat down on the ground and cried. I don't know why. But I hope I served my country well."***

ALBERT & CEDRIC MAH

Born in Prince Rupert, B.C., brothers **Albert MAH** (1920–2005) and **Cedric MAH** (1922–2011) already had their pilot's licence when the war broke out. Despite their extensive flying experience, because they were Chinese, they were relegated to training white pilots for the Royal Canadian Air Force. Frustrated, the brothers took their skills to China and volunteered with the China National Aviation Corporation (CNAC).

The brothers were assigned the notoriously dangerous route called The Hump – flying between China and India over and through the Himalayas. With no charts or GPS, no lights, and rapidly changing weather conditions, they flew in unheated and unpressurized Dakotas heavily laden with supplies. Eventually, the brothers were forced to fly at night in order to avoid being attacked by Zeros, the Japanese fighter aircraft.

Although the route was dubbed "the graveyard of the air," by the end of the war, Cedric had completed 337 return missions while older brother Albert had flown a record number 420 return flights.

Albert MAH (above) and Cedric MAH (left) during the war
Images: Chinese Canadian Military Museum

SERVING SOUTH OF THE BORDER

Henry SOONE and brothers **Gerald K.W. LEE** and **Vincent K.K. LEE** were all born in British Columbia during the first years of the Exclusion Act. The three were among a small number of Canadian-born Chinese men who looked to the United States for opportunities to serve in the war effort.

In 1944, Henry decided to enlist in the U.S. Navy and boarded a Greyhound bus to Seattle. Surprisingly, he was accepted with no questions asked. Henry later explained his decision to go to the United States: there were few opportunities for Chinese in the Royal Canadian Navy, and he wanted to avoid military service as a foot soldier in the Canadian Army.

Henry was perhaps the only sailor of Chinese descent on his troop transport ship, the USS *Clinton*. The ship purportedly had a narrow escape from a kamikaze fighter attack in the Pacific during the latter stages of the war.

In 1944, Gerald, 24, also left Canada and enlisted in the U.S. Navy. Like Henry, he served in the Pacific theatre and was assigned to a minesweeper. Gerald was stationed near key battlegrounds such as Okinawa and Iwo Jima. His younger brother, Vincent, also crossed the border and joined the U.S. Army. Vincent served two years and was assigned to combat missions in the Philippines and Japan.

After the war, all three men remained in the United States, became citizens, and raised their families in that country. These former soldiers believed there were more opportunities for Chinese in the United States than in Canada, their country of birth. Henry found a career as an aviation metalsmith at the Alameda Naval Air Station in California. Gerald worked at United Airlines for 32 years as a radio technician. Vincent received a Bachelor of Science degree and worked with Grumman, an aerospace company that helped send the first men to the moon.

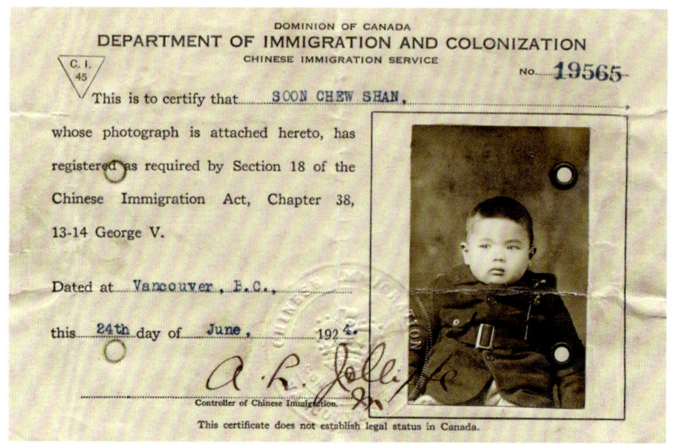

DOMINION OF CANADA
DEPARTMENT OF IMMIGRATION AND COLONIZATION
CHINESE IMMIGRATION SERVICE

C. I. 45 — No. 19565

This is to certify that SOON CHEW SHAN, whose photograph is attached hereto, has registered as required by Section 18 of the Chinese Immigration Act, Chapter 38, 13-14 George V.

Dated at Vancouver, B.C., this 24th day of June, 1924.

A. L. Jolliffe
Controller of Chinese Immigration.

This certificate does not establish legal status in Canada.

DOMINION OF CANADA
DEPARTMENT OF IMMIGRATION AND COLONIZATION
CHINESE IMMIGRATION SERVICE

C. I. 45 — No. 26499

This is to certify that Lee Gerald Kwok Wing, whose photograph is attached hereto, has registered as required by Section 18 of the Chinese Immigration Act, Chapter 38, 13-14 George V.

Dated at Vancouver, B. C., this 26th day of June 1924

A. L. Jolliffe
Controller of Chinese Immigration.

This certificate does not establish legal status in Canada.

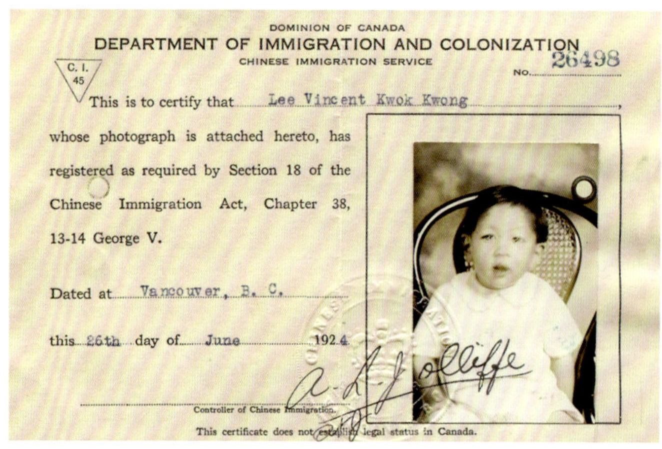

DOMINION OF CANADA
DEPARTMENT OF IMMIGRATION AND COLONIZATION
CHINESE IMMIGRATION SERVICE

C. I. 45 — No. 26498

This is to certify that Lee Vincent Kwok Kwong, whose photograph is attached hereto, has registered as required by Section 18 of the Chinese Immigration Act, Chapter 38, 13-14 George V.

Dated at Vancouver, B. C., this 26th day of June 1924

A. L. Jolliffe
Controller of Chinese Immigration.

This certificate does not establish legal status in Canada.

WE WANT YOU

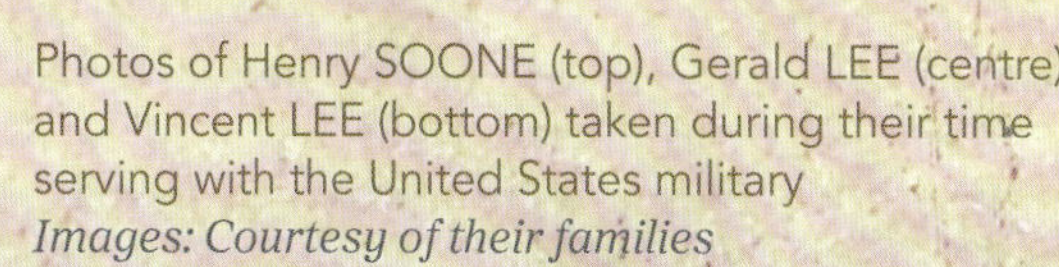

Photos of Henry SOONE (top), Gerald LEE (centre) and Vincent LEE (bottom) taken during their time serving with the United States military
Images: Courtesy of their families

HANK WONG

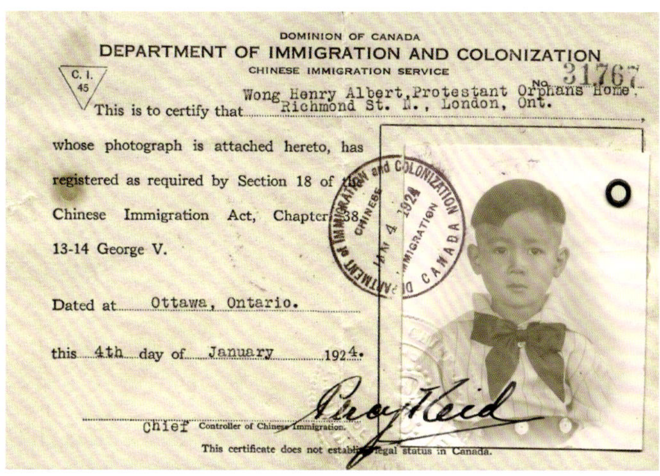

DOMINION OF CANADA
DEPARTMENT OF IMMIGRATION AND COLONIZATION
CHINESE IMMIGRATION SERVICE

C. I. 45 No. 31767

This is to certify that Wong Henry Albert, Protestant Orphans Home, Richmond St. N., London, Ont.,
whose photograph is attached hereto, has registered as required by Section 18 of the Chinese Immigration Act, Chapter 38, 13-14 George V.

Dated at Ottawa, Ontario.

this 4th day of January 1924.

Chief Controller of Chinese Immigration.

This certificate does not establish legal status in Canada.

When the war in the Pacific ended, **Hank WONG** (1919–2019) found himself abandoned in Australia, where he had been stationed. He was forced to beg passing cargo ships to take him home to Canada.

About three years earlier, the Ontario-born soldier had been hand-picked for a special assignment. Hank was one of 13 Chinese Canadian men who were selected to be part of the first all-Chinese commando unit trained to undertake espionage and sabotage operations in Japanese-occupied territory. Known as the Operation Oblivion group, these elite guerrilla-trained fighters were under the command of British Special Operations Executive (now MI6).

Despite their unique contribution to the war effort, Hank's group was not treated the same as other Allied soldiers. When the war was declared over, these men, now based in Australia, simply were told to go home. However, there were no plans to help Hank's group get home. And troopships were prioritizing the transportation of regular American and Canadian soldiers.

Hank eventually found a 25-tonne freighter, the *Kitsilano Park*, that would give his men passage to Canada in exchange for working as deckhands. It was a demeaning end to an otherwise great adventure.

Above: Hank (left) with Eddie CHOW in Australia ▲
◀ Right: Aboard the freighter the *Kitsilano Park*, working as a deckhand to pay for his passage back to Canada after serving in Southeast Asia
Images: Henry A. WONG Collection

TWO DIFFERENT ENDINGS

Two brothers brought their skills to Canada's war effort. Yet their experience of war would end very differently.

Ernie K.W. LOUIE (1918–1971) and his younger brother **Quan J. LOUIE** (1921–1945) were born and raised in Vancouver's Chinatown, the sons of H.Y. LOUIE, a successful and prominent merchant.

Confident and popular, the brothers excelled at both basketball and soccer, and their skills helped the Chinese Students Soccer Team win the 1938–39 Spalding Trophy. Ernie, who was tall, was not afraid of the odd fist fight when playing against a rival white team. Quan, in contrast, was the more studious one, and he enrolled in university when the war began.

Ernie served with Force 136 and was one of the original recruits to that covert unit. He was stationed in Japanese-occupied Malaysia in the dying months of the war and endured harsh conditions with little food and with equipment that constantly broke down. However, it was moving through the dense jungle that was Ernie's worst challenge, according to the book *The Dragon and the Maple Leaf*, by Marjorie Wong.

"They ... set out on what was supposed to be a three-day trip through the jungle. Some of the equipment and kit had to be discarded to lighten their loads. The trip lasted a nightmarish seven days as they tramped 85 miles through swamps and dense jungle. It rained for three full days and their boots disintegrated. They were able to retain only items necessary for their survival because of the lack of carriers."

The Japanese surrendered not long after Ernie arrived in Southeast Asia. That enabled his team to focus on assisting with the Japanese surrender as well as finding and liberating prisoner-of-war camps. Ernie also played a role in arranging for much-needed relief drops of food and medical supplies and keeping the peace between rival guerrilla fighters.

In contrast, younger brother Quan hoped to be a pilot. His training records noted that although he was bright and athletic, the former soccer star became too tense when flying a plane at low altitude. The Air Force decided Quan would become a bomb aimer. In that role, he was positioned in the nose of the aircraft: seated when operating the front gun turret or lying prone on the floor when directing the pilot to the target site just before Quan released the bomb.

When training was over, Quan was assigned to Bomber Command in Europe. On January 16, 1945, his plane crashed near Magdeburg, Germany. Initially, all seven crew members were listed as missing. It would not be until the summer of 1945 that the RCAF could confirm that only two airmen had survived by bailing out before impact. Quan was not one of those men. He would never return home to Vancouver. A prominent family and a community would mourn this tragic loss of life.

Quan LOUIE's bomb aimer half-wing badge denotes his position in the aircrew.
Image: Chinese Canadian Military Museum

Ernie LOUIE, decked out with gear, wears the badge indicating he is a qualified parachutist.
Image: Chinese Canadian Military Museum

J.37185 (R-4)

OTTAWA, Canada, 31 August, 1945

Mr. Mi Hong,
1536 Ottawa Street,
Windsor, Ontario.

Dear Mr. Hong,

Information has now been received through Air Intelligence in the form of a statement made by a French civilian, Andre Galandeau, by our Overseas Headquarters concerning your son, Flying Officer Joseph Hong.

M. Galandeau stated that a lightly armed plane crashed near Sees, Orne. From the wreckage, this was established to be the aircraft of your son and his crew.

Due to the severe nature of the crash, it was not possible to separately identify the five bodies which were buried in the Sees cemetery. As there were six members in this crew, one of the crew is still unaccounted for.

It is the duty of the War Graves Registration Units, which are under the control of the Military authorities, to locate the graves of all personnel known or believed to have crashed and to have been buried in occupied areas. As soon as their report is
ll be passed to you immediately.

I realize that the report will bring little solace
is felt that you would wish to be advised of every
l.

May I again offer you my deepest sympathy.

Yours sincerely,

R.C.A.F. Casualty Officer,
for Chief of the Air Staff

THE GREATEST SACRIFICE

The start of the Second World War in 1939 would sow the first seeds of change for Chinese in Canada. For some Chinese Canadian families, the war would bring unbearable heartache and loss.

We know of at least nine young Canadian-born Chinese men, all in their early twenties and at the beginning of their life's journey, who would never live to celebrate the end of the war.

They would never hold a citizenship certificate or witness the end of exclusion. Nor would they know how much their sacrifice would change the lives of generations of Chinese Canadians who would come after them.

For their immigrant parents, losing a child to a country that had so discriminated against and vilified their community likely made the loss feel even greater and the wound deeper. Added to their pain was the realization that their children's bodies would never be returned to Canada. These grieving mothers and fathers would never have the opportunity or the means to visit their sons' graves in Europe.

> ***"At least nine young Canadian-born Chinese men, all in their early twenties and at the beginning of their life's journey ... would never live to celebrate the end of the war."***

◀ Joseph HONG's plane crashed in France on May 23, 1944. For several months, it was not known if he had survived the crash. It was more than a year before Joseph's parents received confirmation that their son was dead. The HONG family, who lived in Windsor, would suffer a double tragedy in the war. Only four months after Joseph's fatal crash, their younger son, George, was killed in Italy.
Images: Library and Archives Canada

For the families of the dead, like the thousands of others whose sons had perished on the killing fields of Europe, the loss of these young lives left wounds that never healed.

From the Canadian Army, death notices were sent to the families of

Ivan Guy LEE (21) of Montreal
George HONG (21) of Windsor
Diamond QUON (24) of Calgary
Fred HO (23) of Vancouver
Philip TYEE (20) of Pinchi Lake, B.C.

Meanwhile, the Canadian Air Force sent condolence messages to the parents of

Quan J. LOUIE (23) of Vancouver
Joseph HONG (21) of Windsor
Jim Gen LEE (22) of Winnipeg
Peter LIM (23) of Toronto

For the parents of these airmen, the loss was often aggravated by a long, drawn-out process with little information on the fate of their son. The first telegram would simply announce that their son was "missing in action." The words would generate anxiety and endless questions. Did my son survive the crash? Was he hurt? Was he taken a prisoner of war? Was he in hiding?

Most often it was several months or even a year later that the death was finally confirmed and the location of his burial site shared. In the end, to cap heartbreak with the finality of loss, a parcel would arrive containing the last of their son's personal effects: a razor, a keepsake, cufflinks, a photo of a young woman, an unsent postcard ... the last small vestiges of a life cut short.

TWO NEW BATTLES BEGIN

At the end of the Second World War, the Chinese community could proudly look back knowing they had done their part for Canada.

The community had purchased large numbers of Victory Bonds to support the war effort. They had helped build the aircraft and the ships, and helped make the ammunition needed for the battlefront. They had recycled their metals and rubber. They had patrolled neighbourhoods, stood on watch over sea lanes, and been ready in the event of an invasion.

Most importantly, their sons and daughters had served the country with distinction. For a brief period, Chinese Canadians felt accepted, wanted, and valued. For **Alex LOUIE**, who served in the Canadian Army, becoming a soldier was transformational.

> ***"When he put on the soldier's uniform for the first time, he felt like a free man ... [Before that] ... he told me he woke up every day like someone was physically kneeling on his chest, like a crushed person ... who couldn't dream of being free."***
>
> ***Jari OSBORNE, 1999***
> ***daughter of Alex LOUIE***

The successful fight against tyranny and racism on the battlefields of Europe and Asia was both empowering and radicalizing for the Chinese Canadians who served overseas. However, when these soldiers returned to Canada, once again, they returned to being second-class citizens. Nothing had changed at home. Most Chinese Canadians still could not vote. Chinese still remained barred from countless career opportunities and robbed of citizenship rights and having a voice in their own country.

> ***"We were bitter because our country was ready to let us sacrifice our lives but was not ready to give us our rights. We laid our lives on the line without recognition."***
>
> ***Douglas JUNG, 1998***

Consequently, the end of the war was the beginning of two new battles for Chinese Canadians: the fight to obtain equal rights and the fight to repeal the hated Chinese Exclusion Act.

Chinese Canadian soldiers who had been stationed in Britain stop over in Egypt on their way to assignments in Southeast Asia. ▶
Image: Dan CHAN Family

Image: C.I.28, HUEY Chung Duck (Chilliwack, B.C.

CHAPTER 5

FROM THE ASHES OF EXCLUSION

CANADA
CC55
17749
CERTIFICATE OF CANADIAN CITIZENSHIP
CERTIFICAT DE CITOYENNETÉ CANADIENNE
DEPARTMENT OF CITIZENSHIP AND IMMIGRATION
我僑對廢例
當奮鬥到底
洪公
1947

THE FIGHT FOR REPEAL

It took a world war and a nation-wide advocacy campaign to bring an end to the dark exclusion period in Canada. By the time the law was repealed in 1947, it had been in place for 24 years – an entire generation. It had done its damage.

Repealing the repressive legislation required a heroic effort. It involved scores of people from across the country and across the entire spectrum of society: Chinese Canadian Second World War veterans; human rights activists; labour unions; women's groups; and religious and political organizations. Fresh in everyone's mind were the atrocities committed by Nazi Germany and the fact the United States had already repealed their Chinese exclusion law in 1943.

The advocacy campaign in Canada began in earnest in 1946 with the creation of the Committee for the Repeal of the Chinese Immigration Act. Its efforts were led by two lawyers working out of Toronto: **Kew Dock YIP** (葉求鐸), the first Chinese Canadian lawyer, and his close friend Irving HIMMEL, who was of Jewish descent. Their committee strategically launched campaigns in several cities, and soon sympathetic newspapers began devoting extensive coverage to the topic and the meetings. The tide began to turn.

On May 14, 1947, the Exclusion Act was finally laid to rest. However, the ashes of the law, along with the attitudes that gave rise to it, would continue to linger like a noxious shroud. The legislation that repealed the Exclusion Act introduced an onerous and oftentimes impossible obstacle course for any Chinese who wanted to be reunited with their wives and children in Canada.

Yet 1947 became a watershed year for Chinese in Canada. First was the repeal of the hated Exclusion Act. And, earlier in the year, the Canadian Citizenship Act of 1947 finally offered Chinese the opportunity for full citizenship and the right to vote. Despite these victories, exclusion would continue to affect the Chinese community for years and even decades to come.

"The legislation that repealed the Exclusion Act introduced an onerous and oftentimes impossible obstacle course for any Chinese who wanted to be reunited with their wives and children in Canada."

◀ A Canadian citizenship certificate and a *Chinese Times* newspaper article celebrating the repeal of the Exclusion Act are overlaid with a photo of Kew Dock YIP, the lawyer who led the repeal campaign.
Image: Victory Photo, 1945, Toronto, Kew Dock YIP Family Collection

THE FOREVER BACHELORS

DOMINION OF CANADA

IMMIGRATION BRANCH - DEPARTMENT OF THE INTERIOR

THE FOREVER BACHELORS

For hundreds of Chinese men in Canada, exclusion never ended. They became the forever bachelors.

As late as the 1970s, hundreds of elderly Chinese "bachelor" men could be found across Canada, living out their final years of life an ocean away from their families and ancestors. These men never did bring their families to Canada after the 1947 repeal, nor did they return home to China once they were too old to work.

Many of these so-called bachelors had, in fact, been married and had fathered children in China. What most of these men had in common was that they were poor and had spent almost their entire life toiling in low-wage and often seasonal jobs that left them with little by way of savings. They were laundrymen, tailors, cooks, waiters, dishwashers, gardeners, and farmhands. They were also the men who found seasonal employment in fish canneries and on fishing boats, in sawmills and in logging camps. Most had worked hard all their lives, and it showed on their faces.

We learned that some of these men were too ashamed to return to their families as poor and destitute men with little to show for their years in Canada. Others had spent so much of their lives away from China that they now felt like foreigners in their homeland and strangers to their wives and children. Still others had simply resigned themselves to staying and dying in Canada. They had been here so long that it had become a form of home, albeit not always welcoming. These bachelors grew into old men and took their last breaths on Canadian soil.

Sadly, with no descendants to remember these men, their stories have disappeared, gone silent. Yet some of their gestures of kindness or their eccentricities live on in short, postcard-like memories of those who encountered them long ago.

> *"A lot of these men had worked their whole lives, and they never were able to form families. They couldn't get back to China and marry and have kids. And, so, they really had no descendants ... There was really this sense of palpable sadness and loss that they would die alone. Not alone in the sense that they had each other, but that they didn't have a younger generation: they didn't have grandkids who they knew were going to keep a memory of them alive. So, they died alone in this most tragic sense of being forgotten."*
>
> *Dr. Henry YU*
> *Professor of History, University of British Columbia*

Image: C.I.5, YEE Goke Chung (Vancouver, B.C.)

101

LIVING AND DYING

With little money to spare, many Chinese bachelors lived in rooming houses.

Seasonal workers and the most destitute sometimes slept four or more to a cramped room with sparse furnishings – a bed frame made of wood planks, a spittoon, a stool, a single wood stove, and a bare light bulb hanging from the ceiling.

Washrooms and cooking facilities were down the hall and shared. Men squirrelled all their worldly belongings into a single bag or trunk that they kept under their beds.

A step up in lodgings was to have a bed with a curtain or other partition that offered some measure of privacy or a single tiny room with barely enough space for a single bed and a small side table. These lodgings were sometimes in the back of a store or other business, and the shopkeeper was often the landlord.

The cramped and depressing housing conditions led most men to spend their leisure time on the street, at their clan society, in a cafe, or in a gambling den.

Occasionally, Chinese bachelors would pool their money to buy a small house. This was considered the best of all living situations.

Some forever bachelors feared what would happen when they died here in Canada, alone and far from their families. Would anyone bother to bury them? Could they afford to have their bones sent back to China?

In Vancouver's Chinatown, when a bachelor became very sick, Sister **Theresa FUNG** was often called in. If she believed death was imminent, she would call a taxi and take the ailing man to St. Joseph's Oriental Hospital.

In the early 1980s, the then elderly nun shared what happened next with historian Paul YEE. "*A lot of the Chinese were afraid that when they died, no one would bury them. They hid money in their clothes, or rolled it up, sewed it up, and tied it around their waist. So, when someone came in, I made sure to check all his clothes before destroying them ... If there was money, we placed it in our safe. When he died, I would contact his family or county association and say, 'Don't worry, there's money for his burial.'*"

> “***A lot of the Chinese were afraid that when they died, no one would bury them.***”

Image: Vancouver Public Library

REMEMBERING

"There were a lot of elderly gentlemen standing outside the storefronts on Pender Street. I was told that some of the little girls would be on their way to school, and they would pass these old men. And some of the old men would actually look at them. And the girls would say, 'Ew, how come these guys are looking at me?' Well, the reason why those gentlemen were looking at the young girls was ... they didn't have family of their own. So, when they saw these children on the street ... it was a sad reflection on their life. ... What did they miss? Why are they here? ... It makes you wonder ... what did the government do to these men with the Chinese immigration law and the head tax? What the hell did they do to these gentlemen? What did they do to their lives?"

Larry Yung WONG
From C to C: Chinese Canadian Stories of Migration

"I would see these elderly Chinese men looking frail and faded but still respectable: wearing old well-worn suits from the 1940s, or clean work clothes, as they sat on the bench like forgotten men watching a changing world from the fringes. When passing by a group of these elderly Chinese men sitting on a bench, they would stop talking and stare at us children and at our mother as we shopped. I felt empathy seeing these tired, old men ... often sitting or walking alone. Especially after being told that these men could never bring their wives or family to join them, nor could return to their village. I remember the elder's gaze so intently searching, as if looking for any slight semblance of his own daughter or family, in my face ..."

Anna MAH

In the early 1940s, the YOUNG children lived on the top floor of 546 Shanghai Alley in Vancouver.
On the floor below lived several Chinese bachelors, who would dote on the kids.
Image: Lori CHONG Collection

中西衣服
中西藥品

THE UNCLES

Although exclusion left many men without families here in Canada, some found a way to become part of someone else's family.

Those men who developed friendships with a Chinese man who had his children with him in Canada sometimes found a place for themselves in those families: as a weekend visitor, a cook, or a helper in the family business.

A number of these bachelors even took on child-care duties. Perhaps missing their own sons and daughters or longing for the family they never had, these elderly men willingly assumed the role of an occasional babysitter. And, despite having little money to spare, they would dole out small treats to these children, like White Rabbit candy. Sometimes, they would take a child or children to a local bakery or cafe to enjoy Western food or arrange for an outing to a park, theatre, or some other place.

Few of these men were remembered by their real name. Instead, these childminding bachelors were most often referred to simply as "uncle"* by the children they looked after. A few men were elevated to being called "grandfather"** or even "godfather."

Photographs of these doting bachelors are rare. When these images do surface – often discovered in some other family's album – the images frequently capture a tender, caring moment between an elderly man and a young child or children.

Many forever bachelors left warm memories – for someone else's children.

> *"These childminding bachelors were most often referred to simply as 'uncle' by the children they looked after. A few men were elevated to being called 'grandfather' or even 'godfather.'"*

* In Cantonese: "Ah bak" 阿伯, is used for an "uncle figure" older than a child's father; or "Ah suk" 阿叔 for a man the same generation or younger than a child's father.

** Gung Gung 公公 is the term used to denote a maternal grandfather, whereas Yeh-Yeh 爺爺 is the name of a paternal grandfather.

◀ Photo taken in 1938 in front of the Man Yook Tong store in Victoria. Siblings Louise (left) and Wasson QUAN (middle) are with a bachelor uncle they knew simply as Chong and who worked at the Wrigley Greenhouse.
Image: Andrea MARU Collection

SAM GUNG

"Our bachelor uncle was a quiet but well-liked presence in our family. We don't know his real name, his birthdate, nor the date of his death. We simply referred to him as 'Sam Gung,' which literally translates into Third Grandfather ... He never talked about any family in China, and being kids, we never thought to ask him about his family roots.

He lived in a rooming house but visited our multi-generational family home often. He would help out in the backyard vegetable garden. He also helped my cousin build a pigeon coop.

One memory that stands out for me is the time Sam Gung took me to my father's cleaning shop on Powell Street. We were there after hours, just the two of us, and he made me dinner. What made it so special was that he let me put ketchup on my food! Who does that? It was so delicious.

My cousin Edlina shared with me her most vivid memory of Sam Gung. 'One thing I recall was him taking us to buy shoes. I was non-verbal then, so when I didn't like the shoes he picked, I gave him a kick. What a brat! But I did get the red shoes I liked.'

Laura, another cousin, recalled this: 'I remember one time he took me to Chinatown. We walked there on a hot summer day. We went down some stairs and he ordered a grass jelly dessert. It was cubed black grass jelly served with syrup on shaved ice. It was perfect: cool, sweet and so refreshing!' "

Remembered by Diane YAMADA and cousins Edlina and Laura

Sam Gung (back) with Laura (second from left) and Edlina (centre), *c.* 1950, Vancouver
Image: Diane YAMADA Collection

KEW J. YEE

"I was very young, around eight years old. I remember that ***Kew YEE*** *would come visit us at our laundry and sometimes he helped out. He also would have tea in our kitchen with my parents. And he brought Crispy Crunch chocolate bars for all three of us kids. He always had something for all three of us. He was quiet and gentle, a really kind person. He never raised his voice at me, or at any of us.*

We used to visit him at his home too, a rooming house. We would climb the stairs to his floor. I remember seeing all these small room doors. While he and my father visited, I would sit looking towards his door and would notice there were these men walking by. Some would sneak a peek to peer in, and others walked by. I didn't know why these men were all there. I remember feeling they looked kind of sad: there was an encompassing sense of sadness there. I remember that Kew YEE didn't have kids and I never met a wife, but I didn't question that because we shouldn't.

Decades after he died, I discovered Kew YEE was a relative. I learned that he was married and his family in China thought he had abandoned them for another woman in Canada. Yet the sad truth was that he was here, alone, all those years. When he died in 1969, my father paid for his burial and headstone."

Remembered by
Jean YEE

Kew YEE (far right) with Jean YEE (second from right) and her family, Toronto, 1960s
Image: YEE Wai Bun Collection

Image: Christine HAGEMOEN Collection

JEW BARK TANG

"Every Sunday morning, I would call Sizlze at 8:00 a.m. and ask if he would be coming up for lunch with my family. I never asked Mom or Dad. I just called him and asked him to come over. And he would. Sizlze and my Yeh-Yeh (paternal grandfather) would come up for lunch; dressed in their suits and hats ... And every time Sizlze came, he had a package of Wrigley Juicy Fruit gum in his suit pocket that I always helped myself to. He would just smile and laugh as he allowed me to take it from him.

My mother said Sizlze had two children of his own, but we didn't know much about them. I assume his wife raised their children in China as they weren't here in Vancouver.

All I know is that he loved us, and I always called him Gung-Gung (which refers to a maternal grandfather). In fact, I often wondered why I called Sizlze my Gung-Gung. I knew both my dad's father and my mother's father, and neither of them was Sizlze. I figured Sizlze and Yeh-Yeh were good friends and that closeness warranted a title that acknowledged that bond."

Remembered by
Doreen LEE

Gung-Gung Sizlze (centre) with Doreen (second from left), Vancouver, 1972
Image: Doreen LEE Collection

JONG YUN YEE

"We called him Jong Suk, and he worked at our family business, Union Laundry, in Vancouver from about the 1960s to 1980s. He lived in a nearby rooming house but ate most of his meals with our family.

Since Jong Suk was strong and built like a tank, he was tasked with the heavy lifting of the wet and cold work, including pulling dripping wet laundry out of the washer. He would then place this soaking wet laundry into the centrifugal extractor in order to wring the laundry dry. Us kids sometimes called him 'Crazy Jong.' He nicknamed me Gao Doy which, in English, meant 'Puppy.'

Jong Suk at Union Laundry, Vancouver, 1969
Image: Elwin XIE Collection

When I was a small kid, he would manually and very slowly roll me into the inner washing cylinder in order to fetch the coins which had fallen out of people's pant pockets during the wash. Of course, for safety reasons, the electricity to the machine was disengaged first. The coins did not add up to much, but we would split the loot 50/50. It made for a humorous and tender scene."

Remembered by
Elwin XIE

JONG LEW

*"**Jong LEW** was a long-time boarder in our rooming house, which was on Edward Street in Toronto. He worked for many years at the Nanking Restaurant and was also known as Harry LEWIS. He was considered a cousin of my stepfather ... since both their surnames were LEW and they came from the same village.*

Jong LEW was a nice, refined man who had a wife back in China and white girlfriends here in Toronto. As a child, I used to watch him send letters to his wife in China. I was fascinated with how meticulous he was in putting the stamps on the envelope, using a toothpick to make sure the edges of the stamp were secured."

Remembered by
Mavis (CHU) GARLAND

Jong LEW with unidenitfied boy, Toronto, 1940s
Image: Mavis GARLAND Collection

CHIN GEE

"He used to the take me to the Blue Eagle Café. We would sit at the counter and he introduced me to custard pie ... At home I only had rice three times a day. ... There wasn't much in the way of entertainment in those days, so he would take me to the horse races. He never gambled. We just sat on the grass. He enjoyed taking me out, and now I know why. There was no family life for any of these guys: no wives, no kids."

Remembered by
Joe DANG

Joe DANG (left) with Chin GEE, Vancouver, 1940s
Image: Joe DANG Collection

CHUNG CHIN

Jennie JIM recalls **Chung CHIN**, whom she knew as Uncle Mike. *"He used to babysit my brother and I. He would often take us to Bannerman Park and out for ice cream. He also took me out to ride my tricycle. One time he took me to the circus. There was an act with a bear, and I got scared and cried. Uncle Mike consoled me and brought me home. He was ever so gentle with us. He came to Newfoundland on his own and left his family in China. He never had the resources to bring them to Canada, and therefore, sadly, his family were never reunited."*

Gordon JIN, whose father owned Frank's Snack Bar in St. John's, where Uncle Mike once lived and worked, shared this memory: *"I remember Uncle Mike sitting in this chair in our kitchen. He sat where he had a clear view of the snack bar counter so that he could keep a watchful eye on potential shoplifters. I recall ... he knew something about the Horse Stance (used in martial arts)."*

Later in life, Uncle Mike went to live with Bill PING's family. Bill remembers this: *"Uncle Mike came to live with us in our home, which was above our business, the Snow White Laundry. What I remember about him is that he was a quiet man that smiled a lot but didn't speak much English. He was a heavy smoker, and I remember him sitting by the window rolling cigarettes using Vogue cigarette papers. He passed away sitting in a chair in front of the TV in our living room."*

Remembered by
Jennie JIM, Gordon JIN, and Bill PING

Uncle Mike in Frank's Snack Bar, St. John's, c. 1960
Image: William PING Collection

GUM BAK

"Gum Bak was very close to our family and helped with chores for my maternal grandmother," recalls Geoff LOW. *"He regularly mowed and gardened for her. And he babysat her son's three young children and, if needed, took care of my sister and I. On one occasion, he was taking my sister and I on the bus to go to Chinatown. Us kids stepped onto the bus and paid first, but the driver closed the door on him. Gum Bak was so protective that he put his arm in between the closed doors so it wouldn't leave without him. He was yelling in Chinese to get the driver to let him onto the bus as well. This moment was dangerous because he could have badly injured his arm."*

Gerald SOON's early memories are a bit faded but he recognizes the impact this uncle had on his life. *"Gum Bak was someone whom our parents brought into our lives. I was very young, but I recall he would look after us when our parents went away, and we often had dinner with him. I think the fact that we welcomed him into our family instilled in me a desire to care for elders who are alone."*

Remembered by
Geoff LOW and Gerald SOON

Gerald SOON (left) with Gum Bak (centre), Vancouver, 1953
Image: Gerald SOON Collection

SIM SUK

"My parents split up. My mom moved to Seattle. My father rented a house for us five children close to the restaurant he operated in what had been Japantown in Vancouver. Then, in 1953, our dad was arrested for selling narcotics and sentenced to seven years in prison. Us five kids were left to manage on our own.

Luckily, one uncle, whom we called 'Sim Suk,' came and cooked for us every day, so we could always expect one decent meal. The only problem was it was much the same menu each day. Sim Suk would obtain the remains of chickens that were slaughtered in Chinatown and fed us that at every dinner. We never complained openly, but we did wish it was not always skin and bones. After dinner, Sim Suk would play mah-jong with us.

Sim Suk was one of many men who never made it back to their village after 1947. By that time, he was well on in years, so what was the point? His family was dispersed, so he might as well finish his life in Vancouver, which he did. Sim Suk was a good uncle, and eventually we learned to love chicken feet and necks.

We never thought to ask where their families were. We thought that was the way it was. Sadly, we have no photos of Sim Suk."

Remembered by
Winston WING

FOUR MEN

"There were four gentlemen who lived at the back of our house. Most days I would walk down to get coal for our stove, and I would past by these four gentlemen. They all wore long johns. They would be making coffee.

One day they said, 'Hey, come inside.' They had a whole bunch of cats. And they had a wooden stove, that provided heat ... inside the kitchen. And they showed me the bedrooms: just a single bed and very few clothes. These men were doing odd jobs in Chinatown, just to make a living. So that's what they did. They were married bachelors."

Remembered by
Edwin LEE

Image: Two Chinese bachelors, Vancouver, 1940 ▶
Joe DANG Collection

金咸先生百零七歲華誕
壽
蔣中正

LOY GIM SHING

Despite all the hardship and years of separation from family, some Chinese bachelor men were at peace with their plight in life. **LOY Gim Shing** (1850–1957) was one such man.

Known in China for his strength and the "great weights he could lift," Gim Shing (referred to as **LUM Gum Sing** in English) came to Canada in 1885 offering to do any kind of physical labour. He ended up living in Vancouver for more than 70 years, working primarily as a gardener. And although he purportedly had a wife in China, there is no record of him ever having travelled to his homeland for a visit.

During Gim Shing's many decades in Vancouver, he witnessed a lot of events in local and Canadian history. He helped complete the last leg of the CPR tracks into Vancouver. In 1886, he outran the flames of the devastating Vancouver fire that destroyed most of the city. He lived through the 1907 race riots, the Chinese Exclusion Act years, two world wars, and the bleak decade of the Great Depression.

While Gim Shing lived a quiet life in his adopted city, in 1957, he did enjoy a brief moment of fame. A newspaper profiled him as British Columbia's oldest living resident. At the age of 107, Gim Shing was discovered living in a small room at 69 East Pender Street. Despite his advanced age, he went for daily walks and still did his own cooking. The reporter noted that the senior enjoyed smoking and the occasional glass of whisky.

Gim Shing claimed there was no secret to his long life – just that it was important to "be happy." He was one "forever bachelor" who learned to be at peace in a land so often hostile and so far away from home.

LUM GUM SING'S 107 ---and happy all day long

Lum Gun Sing is one of those rare 107-year-olds who doesn't look a day over 106.

Sing, whose motto for his longevity is "be happy," thinks it's a shame people don't want to look their age.

THIS WAS established early in the interview when a reporter commented on his appearance.

"Uh, uh," he replied in a loud voice. "Look my age."

Sing says he will celebrate his 107th birthday on June 6, but isn't planning anything elaborate.

He'll likely follow his usual custom of arising about noon, walking around the block, eating, getting his copy of the Chinese Times and then returning to the reading room of the Sue Yuen Tong, in the heart of Chinatown.

THE DIMINUTIVE (an even five feet) little man is older than the city itself. His first job here was laying the CPR tracks as they came to Vancouver.

He was a spectator at the Great Fire of 1886, but his memory is a little sketchy on this point.

"Lotsa smoke, lotsa fire," is his comment.

Sing's only problem at the moment is deafness. He seems to think others are similarly afflicted.

"You've got good lungs," he was told.

"UH, UH, TALK loud," he admitted.

Sing's social life is naturally confined these days. He lives with 14 other men in the Tong, but looks after himsellf as far as clothing and preparing food is concerned.

DOES HE DRINK?

"Scotch," he says.

"Think it helped you live longer than most people?"

"Uh, uh," he replied. "Happy, all the time be happy. No troubles. Just happy. Live long."

Sing says he's done no heavy work for a number of years. Before that, though, he helped clear what is now Vancouver.

"Trees everywhere then," he says. "Long time ago."

◀ LOY Gim Shing (centre) is honoured with a banner for his 107th birthday in Vancouver's Chinatown in 1957.
Image: Vancouver Public Library

21

A cafe in Vancouver's Chinatown installed a counter with 39 stools. The seating arrangement was designed to accommodate the many Chinese bachelors who still lived in the neighbourhood in the 1970s and 1980s.
Image: Gord McCAW Collection

DOMINION OF CANADA

THE LONG ROAD TO REUNION

THE LONG ROAD TO REUNION

The optimism generated by the end of the Exclusion Act was soon replaced with a harsh, new reality. The attitudes that had given rise to Chinese exclusion had not disappeared in Canada.

Prejudice lingered and shaped how Ottawa drafted the replacement legislation that, in theory, opened the doors for family reunification.

The flawed repeal bill stated that only Chinese who were naturalized Canadians or who had obtained citizenship could apply for their families to join them. This high bar disqualified the vast majority of Chinese living in Canada at the time. In contrast, European migrants had to show only that they had established residency in Canada to apply for the reunion of their families.

In addition, the federal government continued to obsess about the age of Chinese children joining a parent in Canada. Only those under 18 years would be allowed under family reunification and that age had to be proven. The X-ray machine became a powerful verification tool that required the medical system to deem who was eligible to immigrate and who wasn't. Sometimes a wad of cash under the table was what it took to skirt the age restrictions.

It would take some families 10 to 15 and even more years before they found themselves together under one roof. And, once they were together, the long shadow of exclusion manifested itself in new ways.

Fathers were strangers to the children for whom they had sacrificed so much for so long. Some families never bonded. Many men were so old by the time their families arrived in Canada that they died soon after being reunited. Husbands and wives had to get reacquainted after years of absence from one another. Many women, who had become accustomed to making major decisions for the family while in China, now had to learn to defer to their husband's wishes. A number of wives struggled to adapt to the language and customs of a new country.

As revealed in the many stories shared with us, the road to reunify families, separated for decades, was long and twisted.

"The X-ray machine became a powerful verification tool that required the medical system to deem who was eligible to immigrate and who wasn't. Sometimes a wad of cash under the table was what it took to skirt the age restrictions."

Image: C.I.30, Myrtle WONG (London, ON)

I CANNOT SAY FATHER

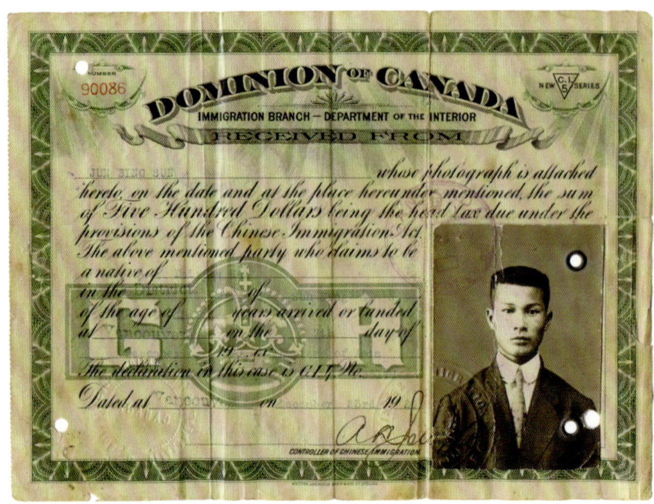

90086

DOMINION OF CANADA

IMMIGRATION BRANCH – DEPARTMENT OF THE INTERIOR

NEW C.I. 5 SERIES

RECEIVED FROM

whose photograph is attached hereto, on the date and at the place hereunder mentioned, the sum of Five Hundred Dollars being the head tax due under the provisions of the Chinese Immigration Act. The above mentioned party who claims to be a native of in the of the age of years arrived or landed at on the day of 19 The declaration in this case is C.I. 7 No.

Dated at on 19

CONTROLLER OF CHINESE IMMIGRATION

JUN Bing Sun (1903–1975) arrived in Canada in 1920 and worked as a cook and later as a laundryman. Despite his meagre wages, he managed to save and made at least five trips back to China. On one those trips he returned to Canada only two days after the birth of his only child, Matthew.

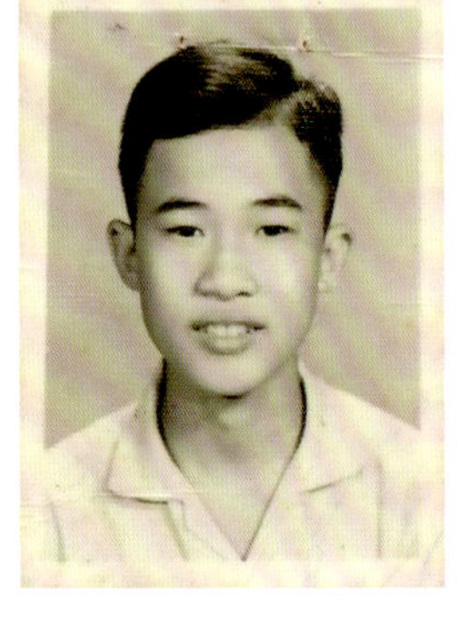

In 1961, his wife and child made their first attempt to reunite in Canada. His son, **Matthew YAN**, only 11 years old at the time, recalled that the application process was gruelling. *"I had to do an interview. I was scared. Being interrogated by an adult is frightening for any child. They were testing me to see if my answers matched my father's memories of our home village."*

He recalls that the questions were very detailed. *"They interrogated me for an hour and asked so many questions. They asked which well did you drink from? How many people lived in the village? How many houses were in the village? Which street did you live on? Which direction did the window in your room face? They asked these sorts of questions and more."*

At the end of the interview, the immigration officer announced that Matthew's answers didn't match his father's. Therefore, Matthew was not the son of Bing Sun. The family's application was rejected. Matthew and his mother were forced to remain in China.

They would wait almost 10 years before applying again to reunite. The second attempt involved not only another interview but also a blood sample taken from Matthew as well as his parents. *"They didn't have DNA testing yet, so instead, they tested my blood type. I was thankful my blood type matched my father's. If I had matched my mother's, they would not have let me immigrate."*

Matthew was now a young man of 21. *"I had never seen my father before. And had never even called him father."* Before they departed for Canada, Matthew's mother gave him some advice. *"When you get to the airport, and see your father, the first thing you should do is call him 'Father' and cement the bond. Otherwise, there won't be another chance."* Matthew agreed. However, *"when I finally got there and saw this old man in front of me, I couldn't say it out loud. I feel really bad that I never ended up calling him 'Dad.' It wasn't that I didn't love him, I just couldn't say it out loud. It's very sad."*

Bing Sun died a mere five years after his family reunited in Canada. In the end, the Exclusion Act, with its years of enforced separation, meant Bing Sun never heard himself addressed as "Father."

JUN Bing Sun (right) with his wife and son, Matthew, in a photo taken upon reuniting in Canada in 1971
Image: Matthew YAN Collection

MEETING A VERY ELDERLY DAD

No. 12496

DOMINION OF CANADA

IMMIGRATION BRANCH – DEPARTMENT OF THE INTERIOR

THIS CERTIFIES THAT

OTTAWA, June 14th 1917

Yee Hing Chang (Yee Leung) of Innisfail, Alta, whose photograph is hereto attached claims to be Yee Hing Chong who arrived at Victoria on the 27th day of April 1908

This certificate is given in exchange for above mentioned and while it is not an admission that the party to whom it is issued was ever legally admitted into Canada

YEE Sing (*c.* 1888–1964), also known as **YUE Hing Chang**, was an aging 60-year-old man when his youngest child, Grace, was born in China in 1948. He would not see her again until 1953 and only after lawyer Douglas JUNG intervened to help secure the little girl's entry into Canada.

Grace fondly remembers the elderly man she knew as her father. *"I was only 4½ when I came to Canada. I viewed my father as my grandfather because he was quite old, white hair, very kindly. ... I thought he was my grandfather. And whenever he took me out, the few times that he did take me out, everybody would ask, 'Is that your grandfather?' "*

Sing had arrived in Canada in 1908. He spent most of his life alone and worked in restaurants to scrape out a living. There were times when money was so tight that Sing used an ironing board as a makeshift bed and cooked watermelon rinds to stay alive.

By the 1930s and 1940s, Sing was doing better. He owned and operated the Dominion Café in Banff, Alberta, and was well known for bringing in fireworks each year to celebrate Victoria Day.

By the time Sing's family joined him in Canada, however, his health was failing. There was much he could not do with his children, and he died when Grace was only in her early teens. But during his slow decline, the elderly father invited into the family a long-time bachelor friend named Happy, who would serve as a surrogate father to Grace. In 1960, Happy gave Grace a Sony radio, making her the first of her peers to own a portable transistor radio. Although worn out and missing a knob, the radio has remained a prized possession for Grace: a treasured memento of a special relationship formed from exclusion.

> ***"By the time Sing's family joined him in Canada, his health was failing."***

LEFT: Grace with her surrogate father, Happy, whom she referred to as "godfather"

BELOW: YEE Sing (far left) with his wife, daughter Grace, and adopted son taken soon after the family was reunited in Canada

Images: Grace BARRINGTON-FOOTE Collection

英記
縫補洗熨衣服
英記
承接洗衣
2
Y. KEE
SUITS

THE GIFT OF REUNION

NUMBER 86703

DOMINION OF CANADA

IMMIGRATION BRANCH – DEPARTMENT OF THE INTERIOR

RECEIVED FROM

whose photograph is attached hereto, on the date and at the place hereunder mentioned, the sum of Five Hundred Dollars being the head tax due under the provisions of the Chinese Immigration Act. The above mentioned party who claims to be a native of in the of of the age of years arrived or landed at on the day of

The destination in this case is C.I.T. No.

Dated at Vancouver on

CONTROLLER OF CHINESE IMMIGRATION

MAH Gim Sing (1898–1983), also known as **MAH Shumon**, is one of five previously unidentified Chinese men who appear in an iconic photograph of early Chinese bachelors in Canada. Taken in 1936 in Vancouver's Chinatown, the photo shows Gim Sing seated between two other men. His hands are crossed. His gaze suggests his mind is elsewhere.

Perhaps his thoughts were with his wife, NG Wah Kim, and two young boys, whom he had visited in China the year before. Gim Sing supported them by working in a butcher shop by day. In the evenings, he played mah-jong and rented a bed in a cramped rooming house that he shared with other married bachelors. At the time of this famous photo, he could not have imagined how long he would have to wait before seeing his family again: the Japanese would invade China, and a world war would engulf Asia.

In 1947, when the war was finally over and the Chinese Exclusion Act repealed, Gim Sing visited China again. He celebrated this long-awaited reunion by bringing his wife, Wah Kim, a pair of beautiful opal earrings. They became her most prized possession.

After the arrival of two more children, Gim Sing's family made their first attempt to join him in Canada. However, when the family was told that one daughter must be left behind in China, Wah Kim refused to leave. So, the family was forced to wait some more.

Finally, in 1958, Gim Sing's wife found a new route by which to enter Canada. The trip would involve crossing the border into Macau. However, once the family was at the border and sensing their desperation, the guards demanded a bribe. Reluctantly, and with immense grief, Wah Kim handed over the only item she had of any value.

The price for this family to be reunited in Canada? The very item that represented their earlier reunion: that pair of precious opal earrings.

"At the time of this famous photo, he could not have imagined how long he would have to wait before seeing his family again: the Japanese would invade China, and a world war would engulf Asia."

◀ MAH Shumon is pictured seated, in the middle, in this 1936 photo. Ellen NG, his daughter, recalls meeting these men in the late 1950s when they would gather at Chin's Meat Shop in Vancouver. Ellen was told to address most of these men as grandfather or uncle. From left to right, Ellen remembers them as: CHIN Quan Lin; Soong Gong; O'Young BAK; MAH Shumon; and Mao Gung. Three of the five men passed away without any family in Vancouver.
Image: Vancouver Public Library

Snow White Steam Laundry, Ltd.

WILLIAM PING
Manager & Director

52-56 Aldershot St.
Phone 3762 - 2144

St. John's, Newfoundland. January 7, 1957 1957

Hon. J.W. Pickersgill,
Minister of Citizenship and Immigration.
Department of Citizenship and Immigration,
Ottawa.

Dear Sir:

I am submitting this letter for your kind consideration. I am a Chinese by birth but I have been a resident of Newfoundland for about 25 years and a Canadian citizen since 1951.

My problem, sir, is this. I am anxious to have my wife, mother and adopted son join me. I have made application to the local immigration authorities but I can't get a visa for my adopted son. So, my wife won't come and leave him behind. After I left China, my wife and mother were very lonely so I advised my wife to adopt a baby, so he is the same to us as a child of our own would be.

Since Confederation, when I learned that we Chinese could have our womenfolk join us, I wrote and told my wife and mother of my intention of having them come to Newfoundland. My wife tells me that since that time my mother cried most of the time. She has had a hard life and I am now in a position to make her few remaining years happy as I am the owner of the Snow White Laundry which provides me with a very comfortable living as it has a value of approximately $100,000. So, you can see that I am, and can well afford to be financially responsible for my family, if you would be kind enough to give the matter of my adopted son's admission for consideration. I am in the position that the happiness of all of us hindge on this matter, as my wife can't leave our son andmy mother, who is getting on in years, can't face the journey alone and leave my wife who has been so good to her through all the years since I left China.

Yours sincerely,

William Ping

TRUTH AND CONSEQUENCES

When the Government of Canada informed **William PING** (1909–1999) of Newfoundland that his son was not eligible to immigrate simply because he was adopted, William knew his dream was dead. The decision meant that all hope was lost that his family would join him in Canada, as his wife refused to leave China without their adopted son.

William had been waiting a long time to reunite his family. He had done everything to prepare. He became a Canadian citizen in 1951. He owned and operated a successful steam laundry business in St. John's. He had considerable assets and some savings. He was an outstanding member of his community. And he had completed all the immigration paperwork with care and honesty.

William PING photographed in St. John's, Newfoundland, *c.* 1940s
Image: William PING Family

Immigration officials would not budge, despite William's last-minute pleas and promises in a 1957 letter. William was now almost 50. It seemed he was doomed to live the rest of his life alone. He had married his first wife in China in 1927 but had been on his own since 1932, the year he arrived in Newfoundland.

William would eventually have a family in Canada. He met a white Newfoundland woman, and they had five children in rapid succession.

William's eldest child, Bill PING, recalled how his father was a quiet man who never spoke about his first wife. *"Perhaps he felt some shame in having a family in both countries,"* he confided. *"In fact,"* Bill adds, *"we didn't know about his first family until 1992, when they got in contact with him. That's when my father found out that his wife and family were still alive. As soon as he found that out, he told us about her and said he had to go back to see them. I know he loved my mom, but I also feel he loved his Chinese wife. Why else would he feel the urge to go back to see her as soon as he found out she was still alive?"*

"He had married his first wife in China in 1927 but had been on his own since 1932, the year he arrived in Newfoundland."

THE SHORT REUNION

Some long-awaited reunions in Canada were tragically brief.

WONG Yuen Gee (1883–1954) had lived on his own in Canada for almost 50 years. He arrived in 1902 and over the decades worked as a cook in Calgary and later in Vancouver in the home of a wealthy businessman and philanthropist. Meanwhile, back in China, he supported a wife and four children.

As soon as he could, Gee applied for and was granted Canadian citizenship. This was in 1950. That same year, Gee made his first application for reunification, requesting that his two younger children be admitted to Canada. Weeks before Christmas, Gee received the letter that his request had been rejected as both children were now over 18 and ineligible for family reunification under the regulations. Weeks later, the government adjusted the age restriction and started to allow children 21 years and younger to come to Canada for reunification. Gee's children were finally admitted.

NUMBER 13475

DOMINION OF CANADA

C.I. 36

IMMIGRATION BRANCH – DEPARTMENT OF THE INTERIOR

THIS CERTIFIES THAT

OTTAWA. April 8th 1918

Wong Gee (Wong Yuen Gee) – of Centre St, Calgary, Alta, whose photograph is hereto attached claims to be Wong Gee who arrived at Victoria on the 7th day of October 1902 who was registered at Ottawa under No 42364 at Victoria under No 23502 and to whom C.I. 5 No 37169 was issued.

This certificate is given in exchange for C.I. 5 above mentioned and while it is not an admission, that the party to whom it is issued, was ever legally admitted into Canada, it may, unless cancelled upon presentation, be used, when registering out under C.I.9.

CHIEF CONTROLLER OF CHINESE IMMIGRATION.

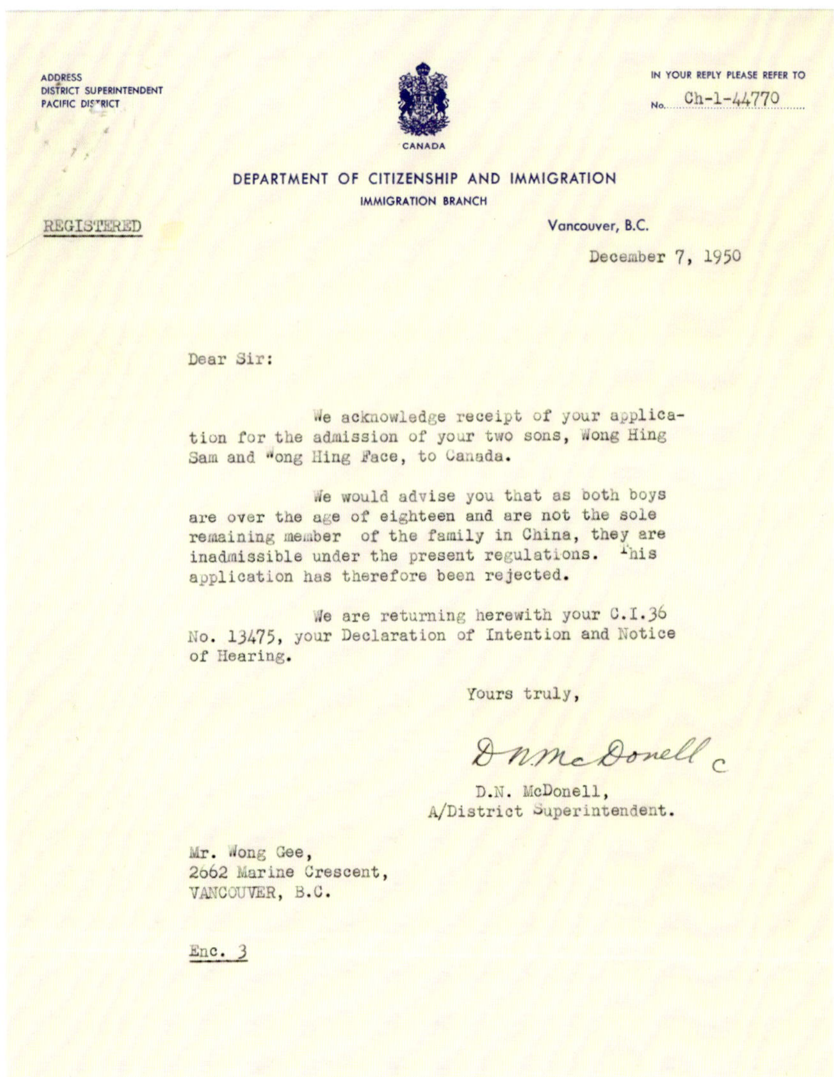

ADDRESS
DISTRICT SUPERINTENDENT
PACIFIC DISTRICT

CANADA

IN YOUR REPLY PLEASE REFER TO
No. Ch-1-44770

DEPARTMENT OF CITIZENSHIP AND IMMIGRATION
IMMIGRATION BRANCH

REGISTERED

Vancouver, B.C.

December 7, 1950

Dear Sir:

We acknowledge receipt of your application for the admission of your two sons, Wong Hing Sam and Wong Hing Face, to Canada.

We would advise you that as both boys are over the age of eighteen and are not the sole remaining member of the family in China, they are inadmissible under the present regulations. This application has therefore been rejected.

We are returning herewith your C.I.36 No. 13475, your Declaration of Intention and Notice of Hearing.

Yours truly,

D N McDonell c

D.N. McDonell,
A/District Superintendent.

Mr. Wong Gee,
2662 Marine Crescent,
VANCOUVER, B.C.

Enc. 3

Gee then applied for his wife, **LOO Shee**, to join him. The process took almost two more years to complete. Shee finally stepped onto Canadian soil in March 1954. Gee had finally achieved his long-awaited dream.

One month later, Gee died.

A REUNION THAT NEVER WAS

MAH Gue Soon (1898–1947) came so close to reuniting with his family. He was close to home ... but he never reached it.

After almost 30 years in Canada, Gue Soon longed to return to his family and retire in China. He was approaching 50, and his body was tired from the long hours working in small-town restaurants in Saskatchewan.

In late 1946, Gue Soon said goodbye to his friends and purchased tickets for the long trip home: a train to Vancouver; an ocean liner from Vancouver to Hong Kong (China); and a river ferry for the last leg of the journey to Guangdong province, where his village was located.

When Gue Soon was within 150 kilometres of his village, his life ended tragically. In the early morning of February 4, 1947, Gue Soon was one of 300 passengers who died when a fire engulfed the river ferry he was on. The ship was laden with cargo, luggage, and sleeping passengers and was berthed at the wharf waiting for its 6:00 a.m. departure time.

Like most who perished in the fire, Gue Soon was trapped deep in the steerage hold of the ship. He had boarded the evening before, lured by the offer of a free place to sleep overnight before the final stage of his journey.

The loss was considered one of the worst shipping disasters in the region's history.

Ironically, the vessel, named the *Sai On*, had been built in 1924, the same year the full force of the Chinese Exclusion Act came into effect.

WATERFRONT HOLOCAUST

SAI ON GUTTED BY FIRE

High Death Toll In Colony's Worst Shipping Disaster

DRAMATIC RESCUE STORIES

A pre-dawn fire yesterday completely gutted the 1,900-ton delta vessel, s.s. Sai On, in one of the worst shipping disasters in Hongkong.

It is believed that at least 140 passengers trapped principally in the steerage holds and the second class decks were burned alive.

Five bodies, including that of a girl of about 10, were later picked out of the water.

Six members of the crew of 110 were reported missing.

Of the 14 passengers who received burns and other injuries and were sent to hospital, one, a girl of about 13, died shortly after admission.

The fire, which s
rapidly that within
was a roaring infer
front and the harb
rose hundreds of feet
brought under control

Damage to the sh
while the damage t
$1,000,000.

> "February 4, 1947, Gue Soon was one of 300 passengers who died when a fire engulfed the river ferry he was on."

YUCHO CHOW STUDIO

THE LEGACY

The stories we collected for this book remind us that the 1923 Exclusion Act cast a long shadow over the Chinese community in Canada decades after the law was repealed.

The trauma of this dark period continued to manifest itself in subtle ways. After years of being targeted by governments, blending in and integrating became a key survival strategy for many Chinese Canadians. Some people referred to themselves as "bananas": yellow on the outside but white on the inside. Silence became the way to bury the tragic memories. Silence ensured those born after exclusion would not be burdened by the scars of the past. Intergenerational silence helped ensure that the humiliation of exclusion would be forgotten within a generation. That, in turn, created the impression that all was now well with the Chinese Canadian community.

Today we know that silence spoke volumes and was one of the legacies of exclusion, as was the impact that exclusion had on many Chinese Canadian families who reunited but struggled with hidden wounds that would never heal.

> ***"Intergenerational silence helped ensure that the humiliation of exclusion would be forgotten within a generation."***

> ***"How can we truly understand the traumatic effects of exclusion and separation on someone's life: on how they grew up, and on how that affects their own children?***
>
> ***What kind of impact does it have when a family is split for decades: when wives are forced to fend for themselves and raise their children alone; when men spend almost their entire life away from their families; and when children never meet their father until late in their life? How can you feel a deep bond or have a familial relationship with someone you have never met?***
>
> ***I think about all those people who weren't able to form trusting, loving relationships with family members after exclusion ended. I believe this shaped family formation in Chinese Canadian communities in the 20th century."***
>
> ***Dr. Henry YU***
> ***Professor of History***
> ***University of British Columbia***

◀ One legacy of exclusion are family photos like this. Although the family appears together, the father and son were photographed in Vancouver, while the mother and child posed in China. The two shots were then combined into one image. These photographs served to bridge the distance: families could be reunited, if only in a photograph.
Image: Ming Wo Collection

Mr. Speaker, I rise today to formally turn the page on an unfortunate period in Canada's past. One during which a group of people — who only sought to build a better life — was repeatedly and deliberately singled out for unjust treatment. I speak, of course, of the head tax was imposed on Chinese immigrants to this country, as well as the o restrictive measures that followed. The Canada we know tod not exist were it not for the efforts of the Chinese labourers who bega to arrive in the mid-nineteenth century. Almost exclusively young men these immigrants made the difficult decision to leave their families behind in order to pursue opportunities in a country halfway around th world they called "gold mountain." Beginning in 1881, over 15,000 o these Chinese pioneers became involved in the most important nation-building enterprise in Canadian history — the construction of th Canadian Pacific Railway. From the shores of the St. Lawrence, across the seemingly endless expanses of shield and prairie, climbing the majestic Rockies, and cutting through the rugged terrain of British Columbia, this transcontinental link was the ribbon of steel that boun our fledgling country together. It was an engineering feat — one for which the back-breaking toil of Chinese labourers was largely responsible — that was instrumental to the settlement of the West an the subsequent development of the Canadian economy. The condition under which these men worked were at best harsh, and at times impossible: tragically, some one thousand Chinese labourers died building the CPR. But in spite of it all, these Chinese immigrants persevered, and in doing so, helped to ensure the future of Canada. But from the moment that the railway was completed, Canada turned its back on these men. Beginning with the Chinese Immigration Act o 1885, a head tax of $50 was imposed on Chinese newcomers in an attempt to deter immigration. Not content with the tax's effect, the government subsequently raised the amount to $100 in 1900, and the to $500 — the equivalent of two years' wages — in 1903. This tax remained in place until 1923, when the government amended the Chinese Immigration Act and effectively banned most Chinese immigrants until 1947. Similar legislation existed in the Dominion of Newfoundland, which also imposed a head tax between 1906 and 194 when Newfoundland joined Confederation. The Government of Canad

THE REDRESS WARRIORS

Many survivors of the long, dark epoch of exclusion could neither forget nor forgive the Canadian government for the suffering, humiliation, and separation imposed over decades by this inhuman legislation. Although the Exclusion Act was repealed in 1947, and the restrictions on family reunification had ended by 1967, there were those who felt that the historical injustice needed to be acknowledged and atoned for.

The official apology by the Government of Canada came in 2006. But it came only after many years of organizing and public pressure exerted by the Chinese Canadian National Council (CCNC), local community groups, and the unyielding efforts of those who had paid the head tax and their descendants.

The campaign for head tax redress, which began in earnest in 1983, involved lobbying politicians, writing postcards and letters to decision makers, conducting countless media interviews, signing petitions, and launching court challenges that ultimately failed. Meanwhile, more than 4,000 elderly surviving head tax payers from across Canada, including their spouses and descendants, registered to be part of the redress campaign.

In the end, it was almost 60 years after the repeal of the Exclusion Act that the Canadian government officially apologized to the Chinese Canadian community and offered financial restitution for the head tax. To the disappointment of many in the community, only the original head tax payers, or the surviving spouses of deceased head tax payers, were to be compensated. By 2006, most survivors were now well into their nineties and many head tax payers had already died, so very few received the $20,000 compensation offered by Ottawa. According to some figures, fewer than 800 people were able to claim the compensation – a small fraction of the 81,000 who had paid the head tax. And of those 800 claimants, it is estimated that only 20 individuals were the original payers.

Sadly, most of those who fought for redress and whose C.I. certificates were submitted to *The Paper Trail* project did not live to celebrate this bittersweet victory. **HUM Wing Goon** (1898–2001); **LEE Foo** (1913–1968); and **Shack Jang MACK** (1909–2003) all passed away before 2006. Only **Charlie QUAN** (1907–2012) from Saskatchewan and **James WING** (1912–2008) from Quebec were alive to hear the official apology from then Prime Minister Stephen HARPER in June 2006. It was Charlie who received the first cheque.

When it came, the government's apology focused heavily on the Chinese head tax; there was little mention of the 1923 Chinese Exclusion Act and the almost quarter century it was in effect. Yet it was the Exclusion Act that caused the most suffering; no amount of money could properly compensate for the human cost it exacted. The wounds it inflicted on the lives of those it touched – which lay hidden beneath the surface of assimilation and normalcy – remain a testament both to the inhumanity of the Act and to the enduring spirit of the community it sought to extinguish from the life of this country.

"Fewer than 800 people were able to claim the compensation – a small fraction of the 81,000 who had paid the head tax. And of those 800 claimants, it is estimated that only 20 individuals were the original payers."

Image: C.I.5, Charlie QUAN; overlaid with excerpts of the 2006 apology speech given by Prime Minister Stephen Harper

Image: C.I.30, WONG Gim Tong (Vancouver, B.C

CHAPTER 6
100 YEARS LATER

苛例何日了

照得自民國十二年七月一日
加政府頒行
華僑移民四十三條苛例

屈指歲月不居
流光如駛
倏忽已十週年

務希各界僑胞
于是日一律休業
同伸紀念
以誌不忘

藉圖
早雪此奇恥大辱
幸甚

爲此合行佈告
仰一體知照

中華會館佈告紀念僑恥
中華民國廿一年六月廿九日

摘自1933年6月30日《大漢公報》

When Will this Cruelty End?

On July 1, 1923 the Canadian government
enacted the Chinese Immigration Act
with 43 cruel sections.

Seemingly a lifetime,
seemingly in no time,
we are now into the tenth year.

We hope all Chinese, from all walks of life,
suspend your work or business on July 1
for collective remembrance.

Only together can we remember
and may one day undo
the burning humiliation and shame.

In solidarity,
Chinese Benevolent Association
June 29, 1933

Printed in *The Chinese Times*, June 30, 1933

苛例何日了

照得自民国十二年七月一日
加政府颁行
华侨移民四十三条苛例

屈指岁月不居
流光如驶
倏忽已十周年

务希各界侨胞
于是日一律休业
同伸纪念
以志不忘

藉图
早雪此奇耻大辱
幸甚

为此合行布告
仰一体知照

中华会馆布告纪念侨耻
中华民国廿一年六月廿九日

摘自1933年6月30日《大汉公报》

HOW WE REMEMBERED

ne hundred years after the Chinese Exclusion Act became law, communities across Canada came together to remember this dark period in our nation's history.

The first commemoration plans began in earnest in 2019 when *The Paper Trail* project invited people from across Canada to scan their family's surviving C.I. certificates. About 800 C.I.s and biographies were collected for inclusion in a major online collection – housed at the University of British Columbia Library, Rare Books and Special Collections – and for display in a national exhibition.

A second important step took place in September 2021 when *The Paper Trail* project approached Library and Archives Canada (LAC) and made a special request. We asked for the public release of all Exclusion Act registration forms in time for the centennial. These personal forms had been held for almost 100 years under privacy legislation. Our request necessitated a block review by LAC and by 2022, almost 56,000 individual records were provided to our research team. These files were a gold mine of rich and revealing information and were made accessible to the public on June 28, 2023.

In fact, by the time calendars flipped to 2023, various events and initiatives were being planned in communities across Canada, ranging from a commemoration in a park in Windsor, Ontario, to a collaborative community project in York Region, Ontario, to an exhibition in Calgary, Alberta, to a live streamed discussion at the University of British Columbia, which explored the backstory to the Exclusion Act. There also were announcements, news releases, media stories, blog posts, podcasts, video documentaries, and art pieces. There was even a small graphic book produced.

In Vancouver, the Chinese Canadian Museum – the first of its kind in this country – cut the ribbon to open its new permanent home in the Wing Sang building, the oldest structure in Chinatown.

Meanwhile, in our nation's capital, a very symbolic series of events were underway in the Senate Chamber: the very place where, 100 years earlier, the exclusion law was given its final blessing.

Unfortunately, our research could not find any photos and only a smattering of newspaper articles on how the Chinese Canadian community marked the passage of the Act on July 1, 1923, or the first Humiliation Day a year later. Despite newspaper descriptions of banners, mourning wreaths, and lapel pins, there is nothing today we can find in any archive. In an effort to avoid repeating this same mistake, we dedicate this chapter to what the community did 100 years later. In the following pages, we highlight some of the commemorative initiatives undertaken. By sharing this visual and textual record, future generations will understand how we marked this historic milestone in Canadian history, and how we honoured those who lived through it.

23
23
JUNE
JUIN
FRIDAY
VENDREDI

THE SENATE COMMEMORATION

In the spring of 1923, a senator from British Columbia stood up in the Upper House in Ottawa and delivered these remarks.

"Out of a population of less than half a million we have 30,000 Chinese. ... They are of no use to us; we will never assimilate them, we will never make Canadians out of them. You might far better introduce men more nearly akin to the race to which we belong. The mind of the Chinaman is absolutely different from the mind of the ordinary white mind. You cannot in any possible way find out just how the Chinese mind works. It is very true that in a way the Chinese are good citizens. They make good domestic servants and faithful workers, but they will never help us to build up a Canada of which we will be proud."

With his sentiments shared by many members of the chamber that day, the Senate voted to pass the government's bill. The Chinese Immigration Act, 1923 – otherwise known as the Chinese Exclusion Act – was now law.

One hundred years later, in February 2023, another British Columbia senator stood up and gave an equally impassioned speech to his colleagues. This time, however, the honourable member was of Chinese descent and had a very different call to action.

June 23, 2023: The day Canada's Senate Chamber would host a national remembrance ceremony.
Image: David LAI

"The ignominy of Chinese exclusion began here in Parliament, and it is here in Parliament that the ignominy should be undone," read Senator Yuen Pau Woo, an independent senator. ***"I feel a special responsibility for remembering the hundredth anniversary, because I'm a senator from the province that was most ardently in favour of Chinese exclusion. Odious speeches in favour of the act were made in this chamber, and they were made by my predecessors – senators representing British Columbia."***

Senator Woo would launch a Senate inquiry and announce a series of initiatives that he would lead along with his colleague Senator Victor Oh of Ontario and the Action Chinese Canadians Together (ACCT) Foundation. Their focus would be not just on the past but also on the present and how citizens and lawmakers needed to remain vigilant to combat racism.

"I hope the inquiry is a reminder of how wrong the Parliament of Canada was 100 years ago and how easy it was to get it so wrong. ... Once it became accepted wisdom that Chinese people were a threat to Canada, passing this and other laws to counter the threat became only too easy. Let's make sure history does not repeat itself."

Over the next eight months, several members of the Upper House responded to Senator Woo's inquiry. Powerful remarks were made by Senators Paula Simons, Mary Jane McCallum, Mobina Jaffer, Victor Oh, Stan Kutcher, Ratna Omidvar, Marie-Françoise Mégie, and Mohamed-Iqbal Ravalia. Other activities would be added to the commemoration initiatives held in Ottawa.

SENATE NATIONAL REMEMBRANCE CEREMONY

On June 23, 2023, the Senate of Canada opened its chamber doors to the Chinese Canadian community. The National Remembrance Ceremony invited several speakers to offer a mix of reflections, apologies, hopes, and declarations for a Canada that learns from its past and is free of racism.

Significantly, the first Indigenous Governor General of Canada, Mary Simon, also spoke and touched on the strong historical bond between Chinese Canadians and Indigenous Canadians. She later officiated at the unveiling of a commemorative plaque that would serve as a permanent reminder of Canada's shameful Chinese Exclusion Act.

The arts also played an important role in the ceremony in the Senate. Lyrics from a forgotten song that was written in 1924 to mark the first Humiliation Day and discovered in the archives of the Wongs' Benevolent Association in Vancouver were played for the first time in a century. The song, set to music by composer Ashley Au, was sung by the National Remembrance Ceremony Choir, conducted by Chin Ki Yeung. Young dancers from the Goh Ballet performed two recitals. And spoken word artist Christopher Tse held the crowd with a powerful delivery of his haunting poem *A Song for the Paper Children.*

William Joe

Christopher Tse

THE EXCLUSION OF
CHINESE IMMIGRANTS, 1923–1947

EXHIBITION IN THE SENATE LOBBY

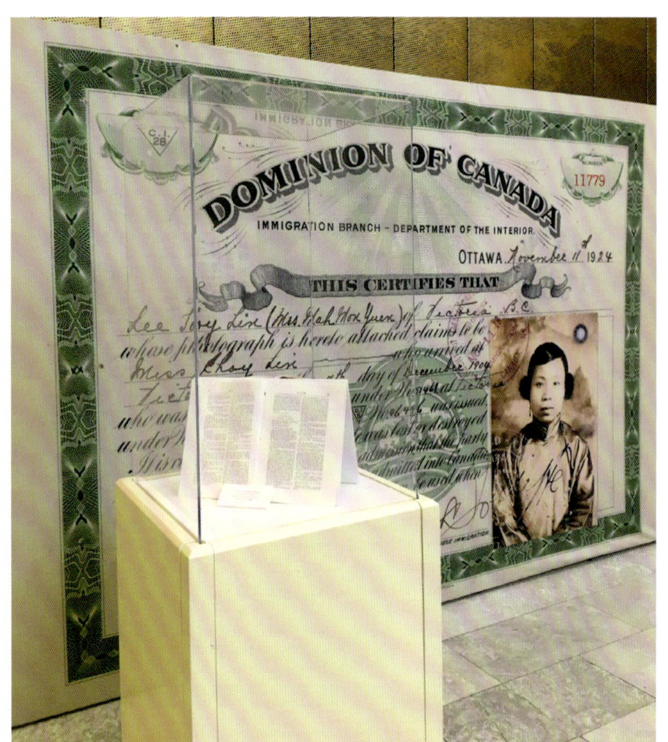

Meanwhile, from June 6 to June 23, 2023, the Senate lobby became the stage for *Exclusion: An Exhibition on the Chinese Immigration Act, 1923.* Curated by Jiaqi Wu, displays featured various C.I. certificates and personal stories, as well as some rarely seen government documents that traced the passage of the Act through Parliament.

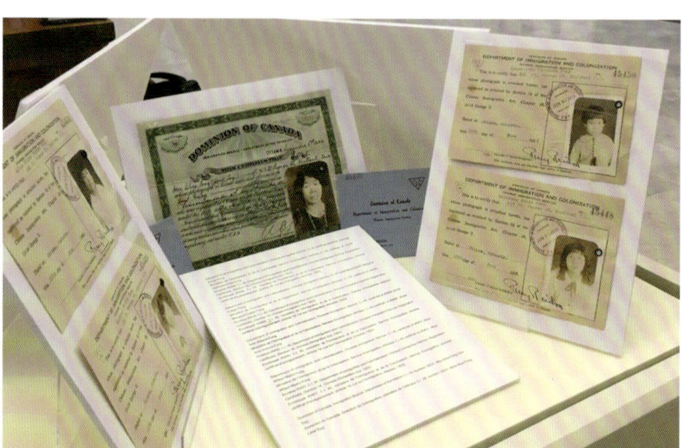

THE RALLY ON PARLIAMENT HILL

Events culminated in a rally on Parliament Hill on June 24, 2023. With almost 4,000 people attending, it was the single largest gathering of Chinese Canadians on the Hill. Besides marking the 100th anniversary of the Act, participants called for a end to anti-Asian racism.

尋影覓跡
1923排華法案
在加拿大移民史冊中，華人歷史有其獨特之處。華人社區經歷了兩重困境，有別於任何其他早期的移民社區：一、系統性的排華政策；二、不計其數的登記文件。
浩如煙海的筆墨紙張、堆積如山的文書檔案、多如牛毛的大小官員，都見證了加拿大華人被監視及被控制的歷史。為嚴密監管、限制、阻嚇並最終排斥華人社區，加拿大政府實施了一系列的政策。各種華人移民表格以及各種用顏色和數字標記的證明文件（此處統稱C.I.）層出不窮。
一浪接一浪的政策在1923年達到頂峰：該年，加拿大聯邦政府通過了《1923華人移民法案》（坊間稱爲《排華法》）。隨後近四分之一個世紀，華人都受制於這前所未有之苛例，整個華人社區處於屈心抑志、孤立無援的境地。
那是加拿大華人所經歷過最灰暗的時代。對不少人而言，那甚至是最絕望的時代。我們講述的故事，正是這段歷史，以及留存至今的蹤影字跡。
THE PAPER TRAIL
1923 Chinese Exclusion Act
In the annals of Canadian migration history, the Chinese hold a unique distinction. Two experiences separate them from all other early migrant communities: exclusion and excessive documentation.
Oceans of ink, reams of paper and armies of bureaucrats were once devoted to the surveillance and control of Chinese in Canada. An ever-expanding and dizzying array of Chinese Immigration forms and colour-coded and numbered certificates (all referred to as C.I.s), were created in an effort to monitor, contain, discourage and ultimately exclude this one community.
This fanatical documentation reached its apex with the passing of the federal 1923 Chinese Immigration Act (known as the Chinese Exclusion Act). The unprecedented and draconian law would lock the Chinese community in a vice grip of repression and isolation for almost a quarter-century.
This is the story of the Chinese community's darkest, and for some most despairing, period in Canada. It is told through the voluminous paper trail it left behind.
寻影觅迹
1923排华法案
在加拿大移民史册中，华人历史有其独特之处。华人社区经历了两重困境，有别于任何其他早期的移民社区：一、系统性的排华政策；二、不计其数的登记文件。
浩如烟海的笔墨纸张、堆积如山的文书档案、多如牛毛的大小官员，都见证了加拿大华人被监视及被控制的历史。为严密监管、限制、阻吓、排挤并最终排斥华人，加拿大政府实施了一系列的政策。各种华人移民表格以及各种用颜色和数字标记的证明文件（此处统称C.I.）层出不穷。
一浪接一浪的政策在1923年达到顶峰：该年，加拿大联邦政府通过了《1923华人移民法案》（坊间称为《排华法》）。随后近四分之一个世纪，华人都受制于这前所未有之苛例，整个华人社区处于屈心抑志、孤立无援的境地。
那是加拿大华人所经历过最灰暗的时代，对不少人而言，那甚至是最绝望的时代。我们讲述的故事，正是这段历史，以及留存至今的踪影字迹。
Victoria Daily Times
MUST BAR ORIENTAL COMPLETELY TO SAVE B.C. FOR WHITE RACE
The Border Cities Star
Chinese "Humiliation Day" on July 1

THE PAPER TRAIL EXHIBITION, VANCOUVER

The Paper Trail exhibition opened on July 1, 2023, at the Chinese Canadian Museum (CCM) in Vancouver on the date that marked the 100th anniversary of the Exclusion Act. The national exhibition showcased the largest collection of C.I. certificates and exclusion period stories ever displayed publicly.

Staged over four galleries (the opening gallery is shown opposite), *The Paper Trail* offered an unflinching look at the exclusion years: it presented haunting stories of loss, despair, and fear as well as powerful examples of courage and perseverance. The exhibition focused on sharing the personal experience of exclusion as revealed through dozens of individual stories, many of which had been lost and were now being told for the first time.

More than 35,000 people visited the exhibition. Many had made the pilgrimage from other parts of Canada and the United States. Some came from as far away as Asia and Europe.

On the following pages we share a few images from the Vancouver exhibition. Thanks to the families and to the following photographers for sharing their images: Larry Chin, William Luk, and Gord McCaw.

bachelors
alley

DOMINION OF CANADA
A WAR ON OPIUM

CHINESE
TIMES

It's Mine!
CANADA
Canadian National Railways
WHITE STAR LINE
CANADA'S CALL TO WOMEN

HON KONG BO LTD.
THE CHINESE TIMES
5 PENDER ST. W. VANCOUVER
BANK OF MONTREAL

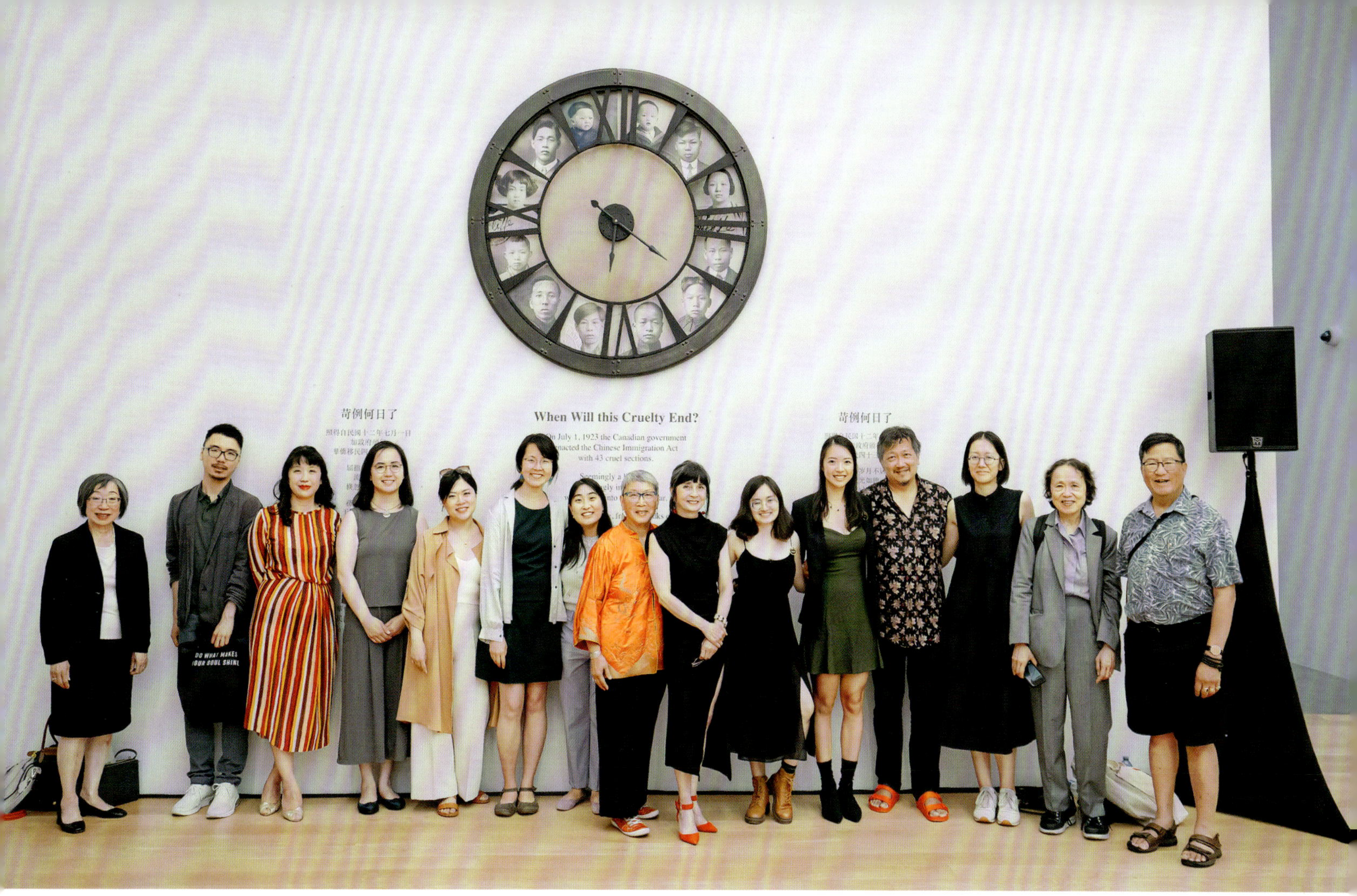

苛例何日了
When Will this Cruelty End?
苛例何日了
CHINESE TIMES

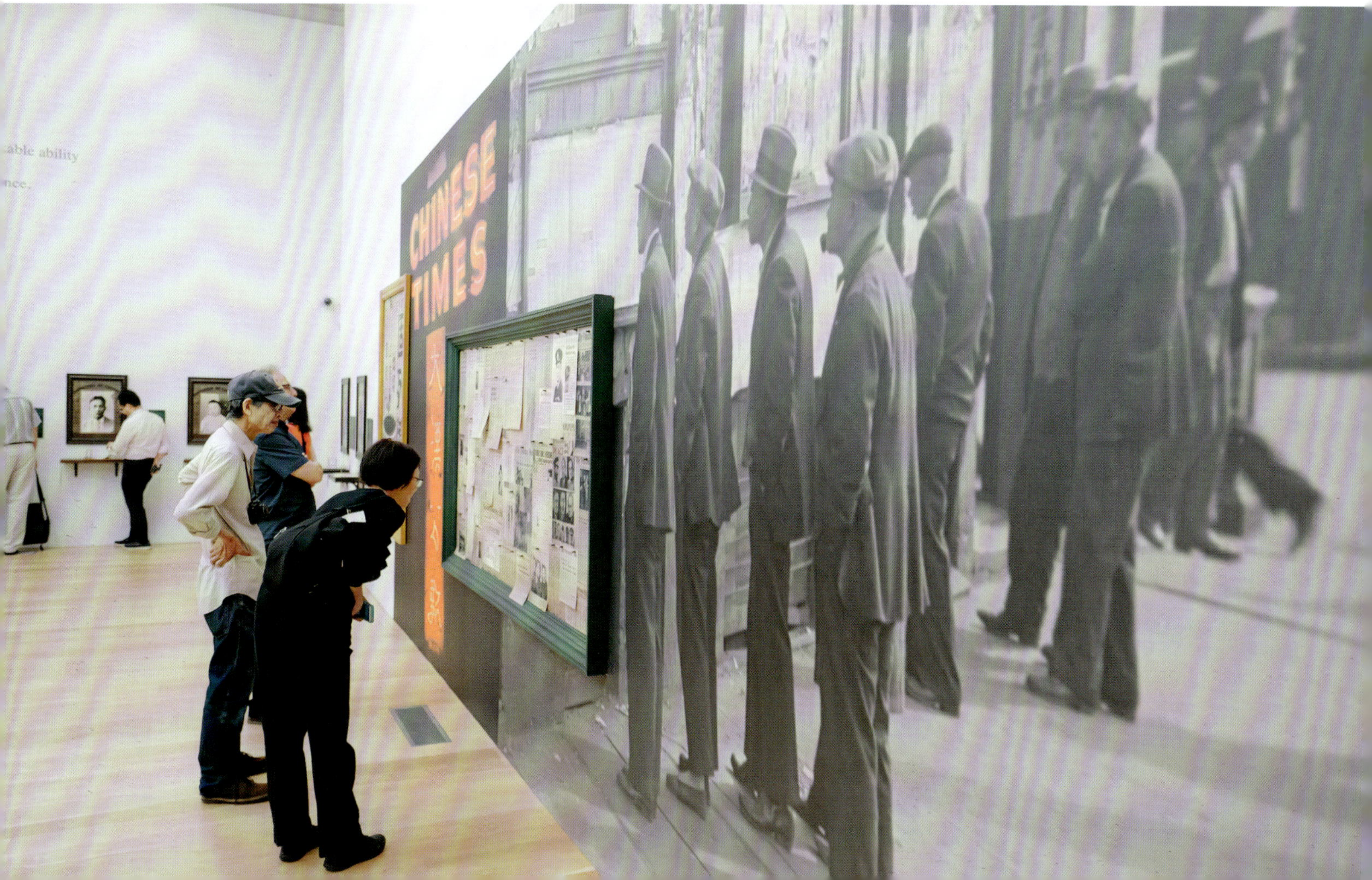

Chong Shee
C.I.S #89813
YEE Quon
1913–1976
When YEE Quon travelled to China for a visit during the exclusion years, he felt out of place and lost.
GIN Wah Yee

DOMINION OF CANADA
C.I.
45
This is to certify that
Ling Fung
c/o George Ling,

DOMINION OF CANADA
DEPARTMENT OF IMMIGRATION AND COLONIZATION
CHINESE IMMIGRATION SERVICE

C.I. 45

No. 19217

This is to certify that JUNG SHU DONG,
whose photograph is attached hereto, has registered as required by Section 18 of the Chinese Immigration Act, Chapter 38, 13-14 George V.

Dated at Vancouver, B.C.,
this 22nd day of June, 1924.

Controller of Chinese Immigration.

This certificate does not establish legal status in Canada.

MONTREAL

The Chinese Canadian Museum and *The Paper Trail* curatorial team worked with various communities across Canada to broaden the understanding of the exclusion story. In Montreal, we worked with the passionate members of the JIA Foundation.

Their team created a micro-exhibition focusing on the C.I. certificates and stories that originated in Montreal. The JIA team also held a scanning day. And finally, in late March 2024, they organized a public talk at Chinatown House, hosted by documentary filmmaker Karen Cho, along with Dr. Simon Wing, whose father was involved in the Head Tax Redress, and *The Paper Trail* curator, Catherine Clement.

Photos by Jessica Chen, Karen Cho, and Parker Mah

TORONTO

In Toronto, CCM and *The Paper Trail* team collaborated with the grassroots community group the Long Time No See Collective (LTNS). This team of artists and activists not only held two community scannings days, but they also brought the exclusion story to the sidewalks of Toronto. LTNS designed three externally mounted micro-exhibitions at Toronto Public Library's Lillian H. Smith Branch, the Scadding Court Community Centre, and the Whippersnapper Gallery.

We also partnered with Toronto Public Library staff, who hosted a capacity crowd for a presentation by curator Catherine Clement and local family historian Jean Yee, whose father survived the exclusion years.

Photos by James Chai, Brenda Joy Lem, Maylynn Quan, Rick Wong, and Ruby Yuen

VICTORIA

The Victoria Chinatown Museum Society worked with CCM and *The Paper Trail* team to help organize two programs to raise awareness of the Chinese Exclusion Act. A special screening was held of *The Paper Trail Highlights Tour*. In June 2024, a new temporary exhibition, *Victoria in the Time of Exclusion*, was opened and examined how exclusion impacted Chinese in Victoria.

Photos by Andrea Maru and Charlayne Thornton-Joe

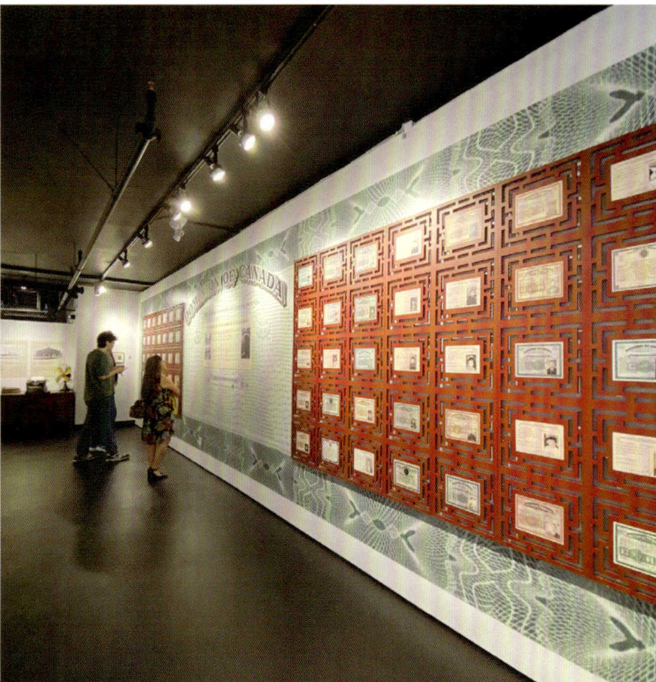

EDMONTON

The small but mighty Mah Society of Edmonton stepped forward to host several community scanning days for *The Paper Trail*. As well, their lead researcher, Connor Mah, located dozens of C.I. certificates buried in the Bruce Peel Special Collections at the University of Alberta and in the Provincial Archives of Alberta.

Finally, the Mah Society organized a public talk in June 2024. The live event screened *The Paper Trail Highlights Tour* video and also hosted a panel discussion entitled "Chinese Societies, A Home Away From Home," featuring Sue Mah, Sarah Wai Yee Ling, and Larry Chin, moderated by Yihua Zhang.

Photos by Sue Mah and Stan Mah

ST. JOHN'S

In St. John's, Newfoundland, the provincial museum, The Rooms, hosted an evening talk and screening of *The Paper Trail Highlights Tour*.

Local community historian Gordon Jin emceed the event, which included celebrated Newfoundland author William Ping, Dr. Melissa Lee (CEO of the Chinese Canadian Museum), and Catherine Clement (*Paper Trail* curator).

Chinese in Newfoundland were a unique group: the region was not part of Canada during the exclusion period. Chinese were allowed to enter Newfoundland but only after paying a $300 head tax. About 380 Chinese migrants paid the head tax to the Newfoundland government.

Photo by Zarin Tasnim

OTTAWA/GATINEAU

The Canadian Museum of History (CMH) in Gatineau, Quebec, sponsored a screening of the *The Paper Trail Highlights Tour* as well as a panel discussion in May 2024.

The panel discussion was emceed by Michelle Liu and included Dr. Melissa Lee of CCM and Catherine Clement, *The Paper Trail* curator. Chinese translation was provided by Darius Wong.

CMH also commissioned and unveiled a striking mural entitled *The Paper Trail Towards the Red Sun*, created by the Canadian artist eepmon (also known as Eric Chan).

Photo provided by Alexis Boyle

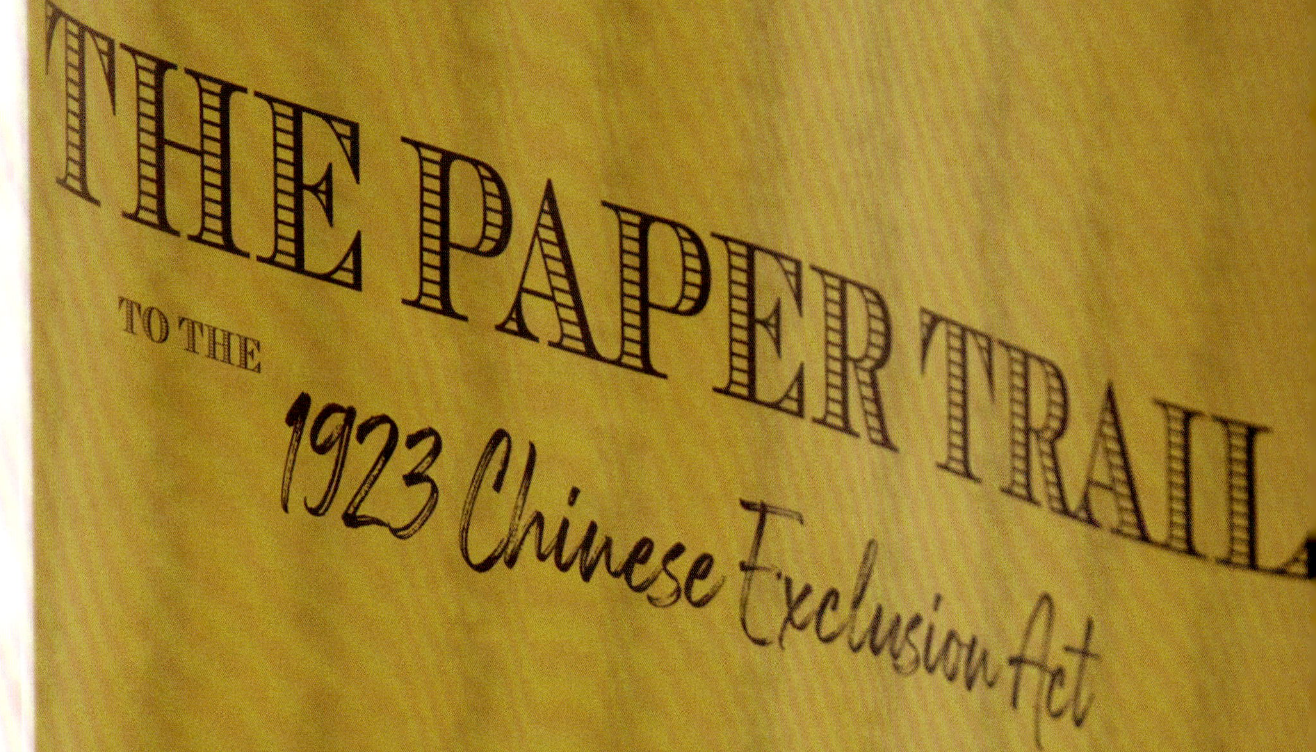

In the annals of Canadian migration history, the Chinese hold a unique distinction. Two experiences separate them from all other early migrant communities: exclusion and excessive documentation.

OTHER WAYS WE MARKED THE CENTENNIAL

The Chinese Canadian Museum along with the *Paper Trail* team organized other initiatives to share the Exclusion Act story with people across Canada. Four instructional online workshops helped people understand and preserve their family's paper trail. As part of *The School Room* podcast series, several interviews were conducted with individuals whose families were affected by exclusion. In-person talks were held on topics ranging from how exclusion influenced artist Don Kwan to how it shaped Elwin Xie's family, who operated a hand laundry business. Museum educators hosted numerous students: from K–12 to post-secondary visitors. And more than 600 guided tours of the *Paper Trail* exhibition were conducted.

THE POETRY OF EXCLUSION

Through earlier research, we learned that on the very first "Humiliation Day" (July 1, 1924), the Bok Young Low Book Shop in Vancouver's Chinatown launched a songwriting contest.

Two months later, the store selected "Never Forget July 1" as the winning song. The lyrics were likely set to traditional Chinese village-style music. Unfortunately, the name of the author has been lost, but the depth of anger and determination still speaks to us from across the decades.

One hundred years later, the Chinese Canadian Museum invited Vancouver singer and songwriter Shon Wong to set the lyrics of the 1924 winning song to a more contemporary sound. With his band, "Son of James," Shon sang his version of the poem on the rootftop of CCM on July 1, 2024.

The Chinese Canadian Museum also launched a poetry contest, inviting Chinese Canadians of different ages to reflect on the impact and meaning of the Chinese Exclusion Act, 101 years later.

We are delighted to share the winning poems from the three age categories: Isabel Hernandez-Cheng (under 18); April Liu (18–64); and Fung Ling Feimo (65 and over).

Photo by Rosalie Gunawan

NEVER FORGET JULY 1

The First of July is just ahead,
Our hearts are filled with mortal dread.
Because of a law which lights a fire
That will sever compatriots caught in its ire.

How can we begin to express the pain
Of 43 clauses that leave us slain.
We will remember, and with all we can muster,
Rid ourselves of this white-led disaster.
We will strive to remove the yoke,
To right the wrongs against our folk.

1924
Original author unknown

(translation by The Honourable Yuen Pau Woo, Senator)

JULY 1, EYES WIDE OPEN

There was something about
Dominion Day. July first, 1923.
But then there was also knowing that I'd
never see them again.

Here are two things that I know:
I. An empty room is so much more when I close my eyes.
It's utterly desperate and pathetic to find myself in the sordidness of this room.
She's there– I can imagine her laughter–
her touch, the way her sharp brown eyes crinkle when she smiles.
Her shadow that's somewhere
in China is in this room also. This wintry room is warm and lit–the sun
can only illuminate half the earth at a time, yet– she can burn her fire for me
from the other ha lf.

And II. An empty room is just an empty room when my eyes are wide open.
I arrived by ship 1919.
Everything we had, gone, to head tax.
Promised my wife, and Mom and Dad, that I'd labour away at the cannery,
earn enough to pay for them too. So that
they could live in this land of feigned freedom, false opportunity, overt exploitation.

Listen, I'll endure it. Bleary, exhausted, muscle-aching, cultural shame, never enough.

Never going to prove myself.

July first. 1923. My suffering has been futile. No chance, no shining beacon,

no saviour and no salvation. I shut my eyes and I can't see them in this room.

This was the beginning of the Chinese Exclusion Act.
This was the end of everything.

Isabel Hernandez-Cheng is a grade 11 student at York House School who is passionate about language arts, fencing, and classical music. Since she was little, she has been an avid fan of all things poetry. Isabel can often be found trying out new coffee shops or at a VSO concert.

A DAUGHTER IN THE SHADOWS
(GUANGZHOU 1938)

We crouch beneath the mulberry tree,
leaves fluttering nervous whispers.
The firebirds' song - a shriek of metal blossoms
bursts through the darkened skyline.

Mother grips my arm, her voice a taut wire,
"Don't look up. Go inside."

We hunch around a sweating flame,
praying for father's letter from Saltwater City,
a place so far, the words are scribbled on tissue
to be cheap and light as air.

"He's alive, but can't send money..." she murmurs,
her bony frame bent across the window
to keep the sky from collapsing in.

Father, a ghost in the photograph,
creased and seared by sun, is speechless
as our world convulsed
as I lost the contours of his face.

Such was our sentence,
enforced by foreign laws that scorned
our "Celestial" features, our family bonds, our right to exist.

The Chinese Exclusion Act would be a slow, interminable burn,
a summary execution of my family – no trial, no last words.

Amid furious streaks of light,
she cut my hair and put me in boy's clothes.
The ancient city smolders under Japanese fire.
I squeeze her hand,
the warmth slipping away,
a mirage in the scorching iron rain.

April Liu is a curator, author, and cultural programmer who is passionate about sharing stories of Chinese Canadian history and heritage. She is currently the Manager of Public Programs and Education at the Chinatown Storytelling Centre in Vancouver, B.C.

YEAR 101

For the "man in the fedora"
for all the "bachelors"
and the families that never were.
No memories nearby
I never knew his name
Nor the people he had to forget
Bade farewell to father, mother, wife?
I never knew his name
Nor the C.I. numbers
and burden he was forced to carry
Calling bingo numbers
    5 – Man alive [1]
    9 – Doctor's orders
    28 – In a state
    36 – Three dozen
    45 – Halfway there
YEAR 101 came too late for the last "bachelor"
Defeated, by time and more
Lose face
Dreams of *gam saan haak* [2]
became *ah baak* [3] instead

Crumpled pieces of C.I. certificates
Matching crumpled dignities
crumpled dreams
Reduced to bingo numbers
No one to tell his story
No one to visit his gravesite
No one to picnic with him come tomb sweeping days
solitary
in a suit and fedora
perched at Chinatown street corners
smoking a cigarette
Head bowed, no gaze
Shadow confined to the brick wall
etched
Never left
muk uk [4] pig pens
Fenced in
Guilt. Guilty of what
Never left
Desolation
Caged on that island, stayed
I never knew his name
For the man in the fedora

[1] Each bingo number is associated with a specific phrase so there is no confusion when the numbers are called in a noisy hall.

[2] *gam saan haak* 金山客 Guest from "Gold Mountain" returning to the village with riches

[3] *ah baak* 阿伯 Older uncle, old-timer

[4] *muk uk* 木屋 Wooden house; detention sheds or holding pens for the Chinese upon arrival

馬鳳齡 Fung Ling Feimo is an arts and culture advocate in the Calgary community. She is an engaged community member of Calgary Chinatown and advised on the Cultural Plan and Area Redevelopment Plan. Recent projects include establishing a community collection at The City of Calgary Archives to preserve Chinese Canadian heritage assets, and research consulting for Heritage Park.

Image: Christine HAGEMOEN Collection

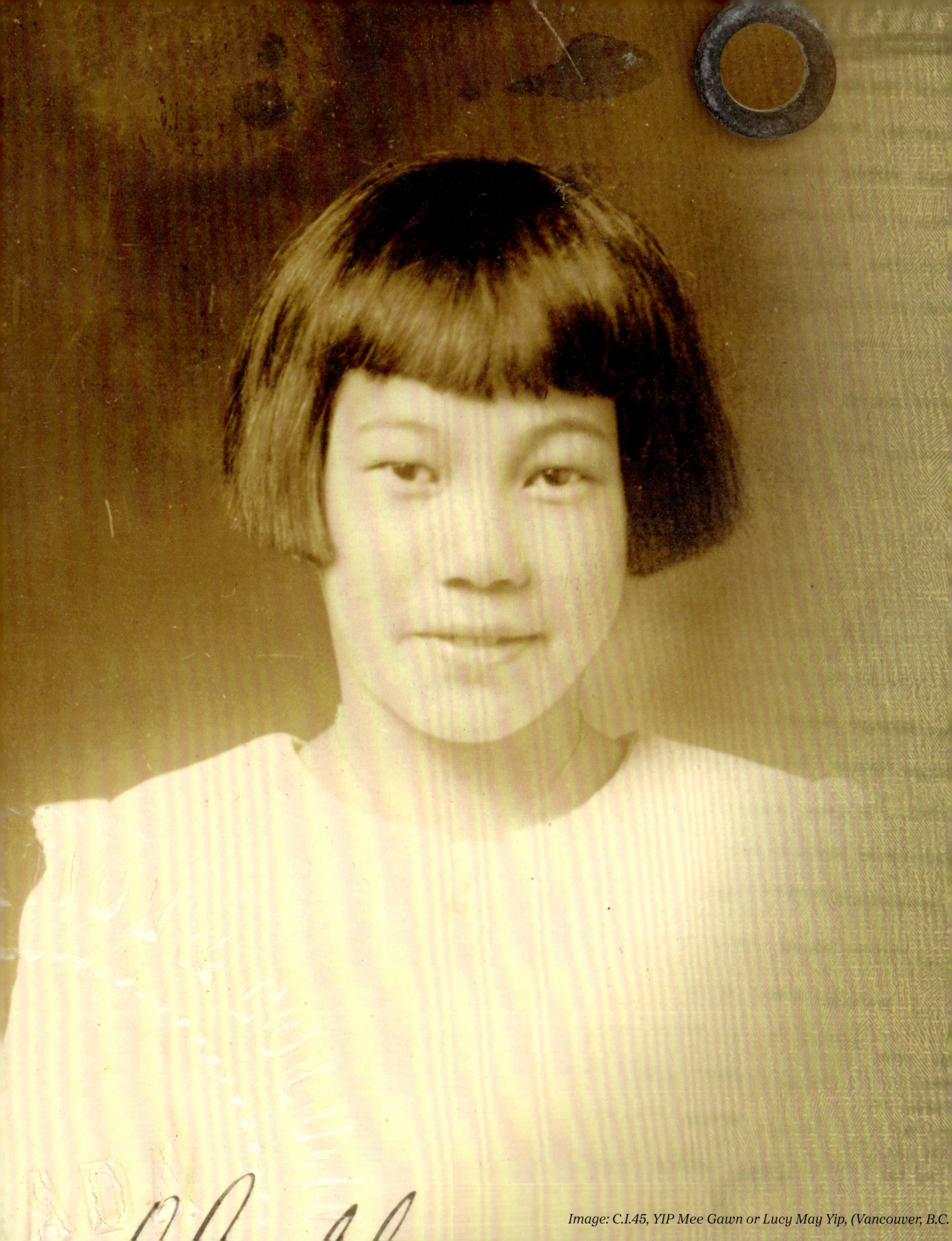

Image: C.I.45, YIP Mee Gawn or Lucy May Yip, (Vancouver, B.C.

LAST WORD

They were silent, but we don't have to be.

Keira Loughran
Director of *Exclusion: Beyond the Silence*
(granddaughter of Jean Lumb)

REMEMBRANCE

Remembrance requires something to remember. But what if we don't know what we should remember? What happens when silence extinguishes memory?

The Paper Trail has taught us that silence speaks volumes. And out of silence can emerge whispers from the past. We need only listen.

Through this 100th anniversary commemoration, we learned how early Chinese Canadians buried the pain and humiliation of the exclusion years by staying silent. The consequence was that within a single generation, memory was lost and a monumental chapter in the history of one community had all but disappeared.

For me, and for hundreds of other descendants of early Chinese Canadians, unearthing these buried voices has been deeply rewarding and emotional, and has fundamentally changed who we are and how we connect to our past. The process of discovery has led us to feel both great empathy for those who went before us and a sense of debt and gratitude to them.

At the same time, we have awakened strong pride in the Chinese Canadian community's ability to endure, to overcome, and ultimately to flourish. For many of us, the project has inspired an interest in uncovering our family history. For others, buried memories have been revived. Understanding has been deepened. Some have recalled the elderly Chinese bachelors they once knew and, for the first time, have reflected on the price some people paid for exclusion. We have come to recognize that for some Chinese men, exclusion was a life sentence.

We have started to appreciate how much exclusion shaped our parents, grandparents, and great-grandparents ... and how it shaped us, the generations born after exclusion. We now realize how the scars were revealed through reprimands and exhortations. Learn to speak perfect English. Keep your head down. Try to blend in. Get a practical education. Leave Chinatown.

We also discovered that the very documents our community once despised can hold new meaning for us today. The silver lining to the government-issued C.I. certificates – part of a comprehensive system of surveillance and control of Chinese – is that today they are the remnants that help us fill the void left by silence. In the absence of having our stories passed on directly, these fragile pieces of paper provide a glimpse and a profile of our past. The mugshot portraits attached to those certificates – photos required only for Chinese people and for prisoners – have left many of us with the only photographic record of some ancestors. Ironically, the paper trail of C.I. certificates has humanized our history – provided faces to names and unlocked stories.

Unfortunately, Canada's past cannot be changed. Only our present and our future can be shaped by the lessons we glean from the mistakes we made as a country and as a community. After all we have learned, we must not go back to being silent. It is now the duty of a new generation to pass on to future generations all that we have discovered and felt ... and remembered.

ACKNOWLEDGEMENTS

This massive, multi-phased project would not have been possible without the support of the Chinese Canadian community. Crowdsourcing, building an online archive, collecting and writing the bios, fabricating and installing the exhibition, programming Canada-wide, and producing this book required countless hours of blood, sweat, and tears from those who shared my vision for this important commemoration.

The people and organizations who helped make this project possible are listed on pages 240–242. However, there are a few individuals who require a special mention.

The small, volunteer-run Chinese Canadian Military Museum was the first organization to support my project idea. They knew my interest in the Chinese Exclusion Act was sparked by my many interviews with Chinese Canadian veterans. Retired B.C. Supreme Court Judge Randall Wong, Teresa Mew, and Steve Ko were my first supporters.

June M. Chow was instrumental in the development of *The Paper Trail Collection*. She took the hundreds of scanned C.I. certificates we handed over and established order and ensured accessibility. She also secured other materials related to the Head Tax Redress applications, and was our point person with Library and Archives Canada. Krisztina Laszlo of UBC Library, Rare Books and Special Collections readily agreed to give the digital collection a permanent home, while Dr. Jennifer Douglas supported June in this work while she completed her Master of Archival Studies degree.

There were many volunteers who took on the scanning of C.I. certificates in different parts of the country. Walter Quan (Victoria) and Gerry Yee (Calgary) deserve special mention as they scanned a disproportionate number of the early certificates and had to do much of that work during the height of COVID restrictions.

Sweden Xiao, our Chinese-language researcher, spent countless hours finding stories buried deep in Chinese newspapers and clan society archives.

Meanwhile, I appreciate those who shared new discoveries with me. Genealogist Linda Yip always was eager to send me whatever new material she came across in her own work, as was family historian Carol F. Lee.

However, the intergenerational silence I encountered while crowdsourcing the C.I. certificates and stories from families made me realize that excavating the buried stories of exclusion would require more resources. The moment I started to feel overwhelmed by the growing scope of this project, Dr. Henry Yu at the University of British Columbia stepped up to help. He assembled a posse of his talented UBC students to work with me on the archive, research, story development, exhibition design, and educational materials. I truly could not have done this national project without Dr. Yu's support and the involvement of his amazing students.

Grace Wong was chair of the new Chinese Canadian Museum (CCM) when I approached her with my proposal in 2022: I had an exhibition in need of a venue; CCM had a new venue in need of a feature exhibition. The stars were aligned. The museum's newly appointed CEO, Dr. Melissa Karmen Lee, offered all the support I needed. She helped underwrite some key design features of the exhibition that my small budget could not accommodate. And Dr. Lee did much more, including dedicating Rosalie Gunawan

Coca-Cola

NOTES

Chapter 2: The Arrival of the Cruelty Act

18 "Must Bar Oriental Completely to Save B.C. for the White Race," *Victoria Daily Times*, November 11, 1922.

20 Image: *c.* 1920–1935, Canadian National Railways, CU12926299, Glenbow Library and Archives.

22 "Chinese Immigrants to Canada to be Registered and Finger Prints Taken," *Edmonton Morning Bulletin*, February 22, 1923.

"Chinese from Coast to Coast Meet to Protest Against Bill," *Toronto Star*, April 30, 1923.

23 "Chinese Lobby in the Senate," *The Province*, May 16, 1923.

25 "An Act respecting Chinese Immigration. Assented to 30th June, 1923." 1923, MG10-C2, Volume number: 8, Library and Archives Canada.

26 Poster: 1923, MG10-C2, Volume number 8, Library and Archives Canada.

27 "R.C.M.P. to Round up Chinese for Registration and Photos," *Regina Leader Post*, August 23, 1923.

"Extra Help to Cope with Heavy Task of Registering Chinese," *Victoria Daily Times*, June 17, 1924.

28 Image: Unknown, *c.* 1920s. "Group photograph of boys and young men on Pender Street," CVA 689-65, City of Vancouver Archives.

29 "Chinese Bitter on Regulation Calling for Registrations," *Victoria Daily Times*, June 14, 1924.

31 Ad for Yucho Chow Studio with reminder of the June 30 deadline for photographs, *The Chinese Times*, June 25, 1924.

"Chinese Crowd to Registration Booth," *The Province*, June 18, 1924.

32 Minister of Immigration and Colonization, *Chinese Immigration Act and Regulations*, 1923, (Ottawa, ON: F.A. Acland, 1923), call no. JV 7285.C5A5.1923, Library of Parliament.

38 "Chinese Protest Immigration Act," *Winnipeg Evening Tribune*, July 2, 1924.

39 "Chinese 'Humiliation Day' on July 1," *The Border Cities Star*, June 14, 1924.

40–41 Map totals based on a memo from Controller to Mr. C.E.S. Smith, October 6, 1943. Immigration Branch, RG76, Volume 223, File 111414, Library and Archives Canada.

42–43 C.I.44 forms and indexes, 1923-1946, Chinese Immigration Records, R1206-294-1-E, RG76-D-2, Library and Archives Canada.

Chapter 3: The Experience of Exclusion

50 Unknown, 1922. "Bow view of first C.P. R.M.S. *Empress of Japan* at sail," 10.14288/1.0217095, Chung Collection, UBC Library Rare Books and Special Collections.

51 Three goodbye notices, *The Chinese Times*, December 28, 1923.

52 "Chinaman Was Tired of Life", *Vancouver Sun*, June 11, 1924.

52 "Chinaman Takes Life," *Toronto Daily Star*, July 24, 1924.

"Chinaman Kills Himself," *Toronto Daily Star*, May 25, 1923.

"Body of Chinaman is Found Hanging in Back of Restaurant," *Calgary Herald*, February 15, 1924.

53 "Ng Lok goes berserk and hangs himself," *The Chinese Times*, February 21, 1924.

"Looking for Wong Kei Fook," *The Chinese Times*, July 1924.

55 Images: Essondale Hospital interior dormitory, S01-SS02-EH.010, City of Coquitlam Archives.

Certification form for Tai Hing Gom, GR-2880-7838, B.C. Archives.

56 "Lethbridge Chinese Gives Away Worldly Goods," *Calgary Herald*, April 4, 1924.

Image: Postcard of downtown Lethbridge, Fourth Avenue South.

58 "Death by Strangulation," *The Province*, July 18, 1924.

59 Coroner's Inquest Report, B.C. Archives.

Image: Georgia Street Bridge, c. 1930, CVA 288-016, City of Vancouver Archives.

60 "Chinese Boys Vainly Sacrifice Themselves to Save Companion," *Victoria Daily Times*, June 12, 1922.

63 "Boy Killed by Chinese Driver," *Vancouver Daily*, November 15, 1921.

Image: Oakalla Jail Cell, CVA 1184-2268, City of Vancouver Archives.

65 "Here's Chinese Fugitive," *Vancouver Sun*, November 12, 1927.

80 Image: Gordon J. Darling, c. 1930. "Royal Hudson Steam Locomotive," (3550498), Library and Archives Canada.

81 Image: Robert A. Bird, n.d. "Main Street, Gleichen, AB," CU169630, Glenbow Library and Archives.

82 "Girl, 14, Sold by Father for $600," *Vancouver Sun*, June 12, 1931.

"Court Frees Bride Bought for $600," *Vancouver Sun*, June 25, 1931.

83 The ratio of 35 adult men to every one adult woman is derived from a memo by the Chief Controller of Chinese Immigration, October 6, 1943, RG76, C-7372, 1290–1291, Library and Archives Canada. The memo tallied the number of Chinese who registered as required by Section 18 of the Chinese Immigration Act, 1923. There were 48,426 adult males who registered but only 1,350 adult females, and 6,204 children under 18 years of age.

92 (clockwise from top left): Front page of *The Chinese Times*, June 30, 1923.

"White Girls in Oriental Cafes Causing Furor," *The Edmonton Bulletin*, January 31, 1924.

"Miss Hellaby Keeps Smile Under Fire," *Vancouver Sun*, March 19, 1935.

"Wednesday at 1:30 pm.," *Vancouver Daily Province*, July 8, 1924.

Article on soup kitchen and the deaths of Chinese men, *The Chinese Times*, January 8, 1935.

"Clergyman Will Not Marry White Girl to Oriental," *The Nugget*, February 13, 1925.

"Witnesses Tell of Janet Smith's Fear of Chinese Servant," *Vancouver Sun*, September 6, 1924.

"Biggest Crash Since 1914 Hits Stock Market," *The Gazette*, October 25, 1925.

93 Image: James Crookall, 1937. "Men Reading Posted Newspapers in Chinatown," CVA 260-758, City of Vancouver Archives.

105 Image: Paul Yee, 1987. "Bill and Jack Wong of Modernize Tailors," 2008-010.1904, City of Vancouver.

108 Chinese Immigration numbers 1906–1949, Immigration Branch, RG 76, Volume 122, File 23625, Part 9, Library and Archives Canada.

112 C.I.9 certificates for Vancouver and Victoria, 1919-1953, Chinese Immigration Records, R1206-170-5-F, RG76-D-2-d-i, Library and Archives Canada.

114 Image: James Crookall, *c.* 1920s. "Men Reading in Chinatown Streets," CVA 260-2170, City of Vancouver Archives.

115 (clockwise from top left): "War Rages in the Pacific," *Brantford Expositor*, December 8, 1941.

Notice from the Chinese Benevolent Association on the 10th anniversary of the Exclusion Act, *The Chinese Times*, June 30, 1933.

"Liner Athenia, Bound for Canada, Torpedoed: Britain and France Now at War with Germany," *The Citizen*, September 4, 1939.

Ad for International Chop Suey Parlor, *The Chinese Times*, October 19, 1923.

"Toronto Tongs Sheath Sword, Chinese Unite Against Japan," *Toronto Daily Star*, February 17, 1938.

Announcement on Arthur Jung in RCAF pilot school, *Victoria Daily Times*, September 18, 1943.

"Case for B.C. Chinese," *The Province*, October 10, 1940.

"Good Canadians ... Three," *The Evening Citizen*, October 11, 1944.

"UBC Soccer Star Missing," *Vancouver Sun*, February 1, 1945.

"Japan to Take Nanking," *Vancouver Sun*, October 14, 1937.

116 Image: 924125059, Adobe Stock.

117 Image: 482497365, Adobe Stock.

121 C.I.44 forms and indexes, 1923-1946, Chinese Immigration Records, R1206-294-1-E, RG76-D-2, Library and Archives Canada.

123 "Chinese Fined for Evasion. $1900 in Underwear Halts Emigrant," *The Province*, September 19, 1947.

124 All clippings are from the news story "Wealthy Chinese in Propaganda War on Market Board. 'Potato Control' Attacked in Attempt to Capture Business," *Vancouver Sun*, July 14, 1941.

125 Image: 169632811, Adobe Stock.

127 "Two Chinese Are Sent to Prison," *The Province*, November 18, 1915.

"Death Follows New Outbreak of Tong Clash," *The San Francisco Call and Post*, March 17, 1913.

"Committed for Trial," *Victoria Daily Times*, March 1, 1917.

136 Pierre Berton, "Home to Wives in China After Years in Canada," *Vancouver Sun*, December 7, 1946.

137 Image: USNS W.H. Gordon, 1950. NH 104839, Naval History and Heritage Command.

Chapter 4: Sowing the Seeds of Change

141 "Testing Our Democratic Sincerity," *Victoria Daily Times*, September 28, 1940.

156 Marjorie Wong, *The Dragon and the Maple Leaf.* Pirie Publishing, 1992/1994.

158 Second World War Service Files – War Dead, 1939 to 1947, RG 24, Volume 27759, Library and Archives Canada.

Chapter 5: From the Ashes of Exclusion

164 (bottom): "Facing the repeal of the law, Chinese Canadians should fight tooth and nail to the end," *The Chinese Times*, May 31, 1947.

168 Image: Stanley Triggs, 1960. "Tung Ah Hotel in Vancouver," 88604D, Vancouver Public Library.

169 Paul Yee, *Saltwater City: An Illustrated History of the Chinese in Vancouver.* Douglas & McIntyre, 2006.

176 Image: Unknown, 1950s, "Elderly Chinese Shopper in Vancouver," Christine Hagemoen Collection.

184 Image: 1957, *The Province* Newspaper Collection, 41643A, Vancouver Public Library.

185 "Lum Gum Sing's 107," *The Province*, March 11, 1957.

194 Image: 1936. Multicultural Canada Collection, 17080, Vancouver Public Library.

196 Letter courtesy of William Ping Family.

198 Letter courtesy of Wendy Leong and family.

199 "Waterfront Holocaust," *South China Morning Post*, February 5, 1947.

Image: C.I.44, Mah Gue Soon.

202 Excerpts from the speech "Address by the Prime Minister on the Chinese Head Tax Redress," Ottawa, June 22, 2006.

Chapter 6: 100 Years Later

206 Image: Larry K. F. Chin.

208 Image: David Lai.

NOTES

Chapter 6: 100 Years Later (continued)

210 Image: David Lai. (from left to right): Mary Ng, Member of Parliament and Minister of Minister of Small Business, Export Promotion, and International Trade; Governor General Mary Simon; Dr. Lloyd Wong, Associate Professor Emeritus, University of Calgary; Teresa Woo Paw, Chair, ACCT Foundation; Raymonde Gagné, Speaker of the Senate of Canada; Dr. Richard Alway, Chair, National Sites and Monuments Board of Canada; and Nadine Spence, Vice President, Indigenous Affairs & Cultural Heritage, Parks Canada.

211 Images: David Lai. (clockwise from top left): Goh Ballet dancers; Senator Victor Oh and Senator Yuen Pau Woo with Governor General Mary Simon; poet Christopher Tse; businessman and philanthropist Brandt Louie; National Remembrance Ceremony Choir; and Senator Woo, with Bill Joe and Raymond Yip.

212 Images: J. Wu.

213 Images: Commission for Marking the 100th Anniversary of the Chinese Exclusion Act.

214 Image: Larry K. F. Chin.

215 Image: Larry K. F. Chin.

216 Images (clockwise from top left): Larry K. F. Chin, Gord McCaw, Larry K. F. Chin, Elwin Xie, and Larry K. F. Chin.

217 Images: William Luk.

218 Images (from top left to right): Catherine Clement, Brenda van Engelen, Wei Wong, Kathleen Lee, Catherine Clement, Larry K. F. Chin, and Larry K. F. Chin.

219 Images (top from left to right): Jennie Jim, William Luk, Ron Chow, Steve Ko, Jean and Sylvia Chong, Elwin Xie, Andrea Maru.

233 Image: Unknown, 1950s. "Silhouetted Chinese man at top of rooming house stairs in Vancouver," Christine Hagemoen Collection.

Last Word

236 Image: Yucho Chow Studio, 1920s. "Wong Mow and unidentified man," Larry Y. Wong Collection.

243 Image: Unknown, c. mid-1940s. Young family with mother in Vancouver's Chinatown, Lori Chong Collection.

247 Image: Chinese Canadian Military Museum.

253 Image: Sabrina Huff.

Wing Lee WONG on a farm in Saskatchewan after the Second World War. Wing was born in China and had paid the $500 head tax, yet he enlisted in the Canadian Army when the war broke out. Wing was picked to be a member of the very first group of Chinese Canadians assigned to Force 136, often referred to as the men of Operation Oblivion. ▶
Image: Chinese Canadian Military Museum

INDEX

H

I

J

K

L

M

INDEX (CONTINUED)

W

X

Y

The HUNE Quon family who returned to China a few years after the Exclusion Act went into effect. When the Japanese began invading parts of China, two of the children were sent back to Canada including HUNE Tan On, also known as Dennis HUNE (far left).
Image: The HUNE family

RESOURCES

Listed are a few key online resources to help you begin to discover your family's paper trail.

The Paper Trail Collection
UBC Library, Rare Books and Special Collections
Online C.I. certificates and stories collected for the centennial project.

https://rbscarchives.library.ubc.ca/paper-trail-collection

Library and Archives Canada
Various Chinese immigration records (e.g., head tax/landing certificates; temporary travel; Exclusion Act registration; passenger lists; census records; and citizenship and naturalization records).

https://recherche-collection-search.bac-lac.gc.ca/eng/home/search

Vancouver Public Library
Chinese Canadian Genealogy
Co-produced by the Vancouver Public Library and Library and Archives Canada, this comprehensive guide explains the nuances of Chinese Canadian genealogy.

https://www.vpl.ca/guide/chinese-canadian-genealogy

University of British Columbia
Chung Collection
Drs. Wallace and Madeline Chung donated their extensive collection of items covering early British Columbia history, immigration, and settlement, particularly of Chinese people, and the Canadian Pacific Railway. Many items are digitized and online.

https://chung.library.ubc.ca/

Past Presence
A website geared to genealogists and family historians, particularly those from the Chinese Canadian community. Lots of information and links to other sources.

https://past-presence.com/

AUTHOR

Catherine Clement is an awarding-winning community historian, author, and curator. Her work focuses on excavating the lesser known and forgotten stories of the Chinese Canadian experience.

Catherine, who is half Chinese, spent part of her childhood in Vancouver's Chinatown. Yet she grew up hearing little about the unique and painful history of the early Chinese community in Canada.

Today she is best known as the creator and curator of a national, award-winning project called *The Paper Trail to the 1923 Chinese Exclusion Act.* Designed to commemorate the 100th anniversary of this dark but largely unknown period in Canadian history, she built a national community archive and curated a landmark exhibition that opened on July 1, 2023, at the Chinese Canadian Museum in Vancouver. The exhibition displayed the largest collection of early Chinese head tax and related identity/surveillance documents ever shown publicly and all gathered from families across Canada.

Earlier, Catherine was recognized for her 10-year search uncovering the hidden works of Yucho Chow, Vancouver's first and most prolific Chinese photographer. After spending years collecting his work – one family at a time, one photo at a time – she curated a retrospective exhibition of Chow's photographs in 2019. Her 2020 book, entitled *Chinatown Through a Wide Lens: The Hidden Photographs of Yucho Chow*, was awarded the prestigious B.C. Lieutenant Governor's Medal for Historical Writing and the 2020 Vancouver Book Award.

Catherine has written articles for *British Columbia History* magazine, *PhotoED* magazine, and history websites. She also has produced short documentary films and curated exhibitions on Chinese Canadian military history.

She is the recipient of numerous historical awards, and in 2021, was awarded an Honorary Doctorate from Simon Fraser University.

Catherine makes her home on the Sunshine Coast of British Columbia.

"I was not really aware of this painful and sad experience growing up since my courses in Canadian history totally ignored this period. And, of course, my father never talked about his past. I just knew it was a very traumatic time for him."

Anne Quan

"I knew your exhibition would be emotional, but I was so moved by your work (including just stewing on how my great-grandfather, and the thousands of men like him, were living in such agony due to the separation from their families ...) that when I exited your exhibit ... I broke down and cried. Hard. I cried so much that one of the museum's volunteers asked if I was OK and then gave me a box of Kleenex."

Winston Ma, descendant of LEE Chuen Oy

The faces featured in this book help us honour those who lived through the Chinese exclusion years.

Endpaper (Back)

(from left to right, top to bottom)

SOO Kee Sum (John), LEONG King, PON Shee, Mary LORE, MAH Hang Foo, WONG Ng Chee (Archie),

Mrs. TOM Lung, Lawrence KWONG, YEN Goon Teong (Tommy), WONG Yen Toy, LOW Yon Hon (Lailey), POON Wing (Frank MAH),

LI Qui Fao, LEE Wa Kang (Harry), YING Tow (Mrs. KWONG), Fred LUM, Won Alexander CUMYOW, Helena WONG